Political Parties and the Winning of Office

Political Parties and the Winning of Office

Joseph A. Schlesinger

Ann Arbor

THE UNIVERSITY OF MICHIGAN PRESS

First paperback edition 1994
Copyright © by the University of Michigan 1991
All rights reserved
Published in the United States of America by
The University of Michigan Press
Manufactured in the United States of America

1998   1997   1996   1995   6   5   4   3

A CIP catalog record for this book is available from the British Library.

Library of Congress Cataloging-in-Publication Data

Schlesinger, Joseph A.
    Political parties and the winning of office / Joseph A.
    Schlesinger.
        p.   cm.
    Includes bibliographical references and index.
    ISBN 0-472-10202-8 (cloth : alk.) — ISBN 0-472-08256-6
(paper : alk.)
    1. Political parties—United States—History.   2. Electioneering—
United States—History.   3. Political culture—United States—
History.   4. Democracy—History.   I. Title.
JK2261.S355   1991
324.273'09—dc20   91-15033
                                                                CIP

For
Mildred, Betsy, and Jacob

Preface

This book represents more than thirty years of thinking, writing, and teaching about political parties in democracies. Throughout that time my objective has always been to develop a coherent theory of parties in democracies that explains why parties behave as they do. I have therefore avoided the normative or prescriptive speculation that is implicit in much of the literature about parties, not because I view existing parties in democracies as ideal, but because I believe understanding must precede reform.

In pursuing a general theory of parties in democracies, I have found it advantageous to use parties in the United States as my starting point. Despite a constitutional structure designed to prevent their emergence, parties developed and flourished in the United States along with the expansion of free popular elections for all significant public offices. Despite waves of reforms aimed at reducing their importance, they have persisted as major aspects of the U.S. political system. Critics, both native and foreign, from Woodrow Wilson to E. E. Schattschneider and James McGregor Burns, from Alexis de Tocqueville and Ostrogorski to Maurice Duverger have found parties in the United States wanting. They have found them lacking both in programs and the discipline required to implement programs. In the view of these critics, parties in the United States have been nothing more than vehicles for seeking and retaining public office. I have no quarrel with these criticisms. At the same time, it seems to me they overlook a simple truth about parties, not only in the United States but in all democracies. Parties are the product of democratic elections and, therefore, destined to be primarily vehicles for allowing individuals ambitious for public office to compete for office effectively.

At the same time, it has been gratifying to see the last decade of the twentieth century begin with the party model developed most clearly in the United States much in vogue in Eastern Europe, birthplace of the disciplined, doctrinal party. This book is, however, by no means an effort to exploit this latest and unexpected resurgence of democracy and its institutions, including the office-seeking party. Such an effort would be premature to say the least. Whether these institutions will take root in the exotic soil of Eastern Europe is not at all certain.

The book is, instead, an attempt to set forth in one place a theory of party organization that has evolved over many years and that is designed to help us understand political parties in democracies as they are, rather than as we would wish them to be. That is why each of the book's chapters is based, in part, on previously published material. It is also why all the previously published material has been extensively revised to produce a cohesive work. Chapter 1, the introductory chapter, is appropriately based on a more recent article entitled, "On the Theory of Party Organization" (*Journal of Politics*, 1984). Chapters 2, 3, and 4 are based on material first published in 1966 in *Ambition and Politics*. Chapter 4 also draws on material that first appeared in "Aging and Opportunities for Elective Office" (written with Mildred Schlesinger), in *Aging: Social Change*, edited by James G. March (1981 © Academic Press). Chapter 5 is based, in part, on "The Structure of Competition in the United States," which appeared in *Behavioral Science* in 1960. It also includes unpublished material on the structure of electoral competition for the presidency. Chapter 6 is a revised version of the article that appeared as "The Primary Goals of Political Parties: A Clarification of Positive Theory," in the *American Political Science Review* in 1975. Chapter 7, inspired by the chapter that appeared in 1965 as "Political Party Organization," in *Handbook of Organizations*, edited by James G. March, has been almost entirely rewritten. Chapter 8, which originally appeared in 1985 in the *American Political Science Review* as "The New American Party," has been revised to follow chapter 7 more effectively. Chapter 9, which demonstrates the theory's use for comparative purposes, first appeared in 1967 as "Political Careers and Party Leadership," in *Political Leadership in Industrial Societies: Studies in Comparative Analysis*, edited by Lewis J. Edinger (copyright © 1967 John Wiley and Sons; reprinted by permission of John Wiley and Sons, Inc. and Wiley-Liss). This essay has been extensively rewritten to take into account my most recent thinking about the application of the theory to parties in democracies other than that of the United States.

I am indebted to Mildred Schlesinger for her editorial assistance in revising and rewriting previously published material to craft a new work. I should also like to thank her for her willingness to apply this theory to the parties of the French Republics.

Contents

Tables

Figures

CHAPTER 1

Introduction: A Theory of Political Parties

Even as the countries of Eastern Europe view political parties in the United States as a model, Americans continue to express concern about their parties' future. This paradox raises the question: how well do we understand parties in democracies? Dissatisfaction with parties in the United States is by no means new. Concern for their survival, on the other hand, reached a near crescendo in the 1970s when academics, journalists, and professional politicians joined in an almost universal chorus to sing of their weakening, decline, and decomposition.[1] The evidence seemed compelling: a declining proportion of citizens willing to identify with any party, the increase in split ticket voting, the severely reduced role of party officials in the nominating process, the growing role of media specialists in electoral campaigns, the growth of political action groups outside the regular party apparatus as a major source of campaign funds, and the difficulties of party leaders in marshalling support for their policies.

Yet even as the "decline of parties" thesis gained ground, it became possible to amass equally as compelling evidence that the parties were stronger than ever. Not since the pre–Civil War era had the two major parties competed over a wider range of constituencies. Indeed, the two major parties were dominating elective offices at all levels of government to a degree unprecedented in the history of the United States. Between 1950 and 1980, only the merest trace of minor party or independent strength was evident in Congress (see fig. 1.1). Two senators accounted for most of that strength, the Independent, Harry Byrd, Jr., of Virginia and the Conservative James Buckley of New York. Moreover, whereas Franklin Roosevelt could describe the Democratic national headquarters of the 1920s as "two ladies occupying one room in a Washington office building" (Key 1964, 322), by the 1980s both

---

1. Journalist David Broder first noticed that the "party was over" (Broder 1971). Burnham (1970) put forth the decomposition thesis. Nie, Verba, and Petrocik (1976) developed the most influential evidence of the decline in party voting. Jack Dennis (1975) charted the decline in public support for the parties. A good statement about the decline is Pomper 1977. Crotty (1984) put together the most complete set of evidence of decline in various contexts. No analysis of any contemporary political problem appears complete without some reference to the difficulties presented by the parties. See, for example, Everson 1982; and Sundquist 1982.

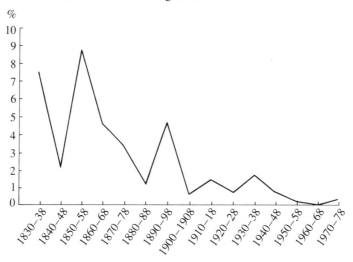

Fig. 1.1. Average percentage of minor party and independent members of Congress (House and Senate), by decade

national parties had sizable staffs that operated continuously. In the 1950s most state parties had no permanent office and unpaid chairs; twenty years later all that had changed.[2] Furthermore, whereas one could find little evidence of any systematic concern by the national apparatus for state and local partisan affairs in the past, by the 1980s both parties were maintaining a close watch on and were actively involved in such critical activities as the recruitment of candidates, campaign strategy, and even in the arcana of state legislative redistricting (see, for example, Ehrenhalt 1983).

If one assesses a party's condition by whether or not it stands for anything, then it would be difficult to find earlier periods when the two major parties were more distinct in program and policy than in the last part of the twentieth century. The presidential choices of Goldwater or Johnson, McGovern or Nixon, and Reagan or Mondale certainly presented the electorate with genuine partisan alternatives. Within Congress, the erosion of the Democratic southern conservative bloc gave partisanship a sharper meaning.

What then are we to make of parties in the United States? What do we make of political parties that do not control their nominations, yet win elections; whose support among the electorate has declined while their electoral record improves; parties whose organizations have supposedly decomposed,

---

2. Compare the findings of Agranoff and Cooke (1964) or of Wiggins and Turk (1970) on state party chairs with those of Huckshorn (1976). Cotter et al. (1980) charted much of the growth in state party apparatus. The growth is discussed in a general context by Huckshorn and Bibby (1982). Evidence of change and renewal also appears in Pomper 1981.

yet whose personnel and payrolls have blossomed; parties that have no control over their members, yet present clear partisan choices to the electorate? We find little help if we look to the literature on parties. Since students of parties have not even been able to agree on what a political party is, they cannot help us discover whether a party is weak or strong, decaying or blossoming. The sole collective effort to state how parties ought to look, the 1950 report of the American Political Science Association's committee on parties, was roundly criticized in its time and is only occasionally revived today.[3] As for the analysis that appears in most textbooks, it gives us what I call the piecemeal approach, a sequence of chapters dealing with what V. O. Key (1964, 163–65) dubbed the "party-in-the-electorate," the "party-in-the-government," and the "party organization." The pieces are treated as though each leads a life of its own; little attention is given to what, if anything, holds them together. Party then is a lot of different things or, in Eldersveld's view (1964), "images."

The piecemeal approach worked, or was not obviously inadequate, as long as party-related matters did not change much or changed gradually. From 1865 until 1960, the Civil War remained the dominant influence upon the competitive relationship between the two parties. The regional pattern set by the war was reinforced after 1896. Even after 1932 it was critical to the understanding of party politics in the United States. As for the reforms of the Progressive era, state and local officeholders had little difficulty in using reforms such as the direct primary to their own advantage. From the close of the Civil War until the 1950s, therefore, parties in the United States did not change markedly. The parties made few structural changes in their procedures. The biggest change came in 1936 when the Democrats dropped their two-thirds rule for the nomination of presidential and vice presidential candidates by the national convention. William Jennings Bryan or Theodore Roosevelt might have found much to marvel at in the United States of 1948, but they would have felt at home in the parties that waged the 1948 presidential campaign.

Then, after a century of stability, changes took place in the later part of the twentieth century that were of great import for political parties. Students of parties, however, were ill equipped to deal with the effects of change on the parties. The opening up of the political process, shifts in voter attitudes, and the technological revolution in communications transformed each part of the sum of what was called party. Yet students of parties, unable to agree on what a party is, had no concept of what holds parties together and, therefore, how they adapt to change. Their attention riveted on the parties' separate parts; they could only interpret change as the parties' weakening and decline.

---

3. Kirkpatrick (1971) reviews the history of the report and its critical reception. See Fiorina 1980 for a call for some return to the notion of responsible parties.

On the other hand, to say that students of parties in the United States have lacked a theory of party is to overstate the case. A theory has lain embedded in most of our writings on parties. We have, however, failed to see it as a whole. Thus the present state of writing about parties in the United States is similar to that described by Charles Lindblom (1957) in his review of Anthony Downs's *An Economic Theory of Democracy*. Lindblom argued that political science, in contrast to his own field of economics, appeared "thin" because political scientists refused to adopt the kind of common approach to a subject that would assure the development of a cumulative theory and findings. Lindblom argued that economists had a guiding framework that, whatever the values or techniques employed, directed their research. Lindblom was not arguing then, and certainly would not now, that economists had developed a solid body of truths. Tied to a common view of market forces, however, economists of all persuasions have been able to develop a much more cumulative discipline than political scientists. We could not, therefore, predict how a political scientist might go about answering the question: "Are parties in the United States declining?" not because political scientists were less competent than economists, but because they did not agree upon the way to approach such a question. Students of voting behavior would answer the question one way, advocates of responsible parties another, and students of party organization, depending on their assumptions, in any of several ways.

Lindblom went on to argue that a basis for a common approach in political science did exist and that Downs had performed the archaeological task of reconstruction. The approach was embedded in the works of writers such as E. E. Schattschneider, Pendleton Herring, David Truman, Robert Dahl, as well as Austin Ranney and Willmoore Kendall. Downs's contribution was to construct a common view from their insights and use it to explain electoral and partisan behavior in democracies. But Lindblom was, I fear, overly sanguine in expecting that Downs's book would lead to the acceptance of a common approach to the study of democratic politics. Whatever influence Downs has had in fostering rational choice theory and the theory of competition among candidates, his work has certainly not been accepted as the common framework for the study of parties.

Nevertheless, Lindblom's point is still valid. There is a general framework for the study of parties in democracies implicit in studies of democratic politics. Indeed, it is one that most students of parties use, at least some of the time, if not consciously in a systematic manner, then as implicit assumptions. It underlies explanations of political phenomena from the two-party system and the oligarchic character of parties, to the impact of the electoral college and reapportionment.

My purpose in this book is both to expose this framework and to use it to elaborate a general theory of parties in democracies. Much of the theory will depend on my knowledge of parties in the United States. But it should also be useful in helping us understand parties in all democracies. In this chapter, my task is to put together a theory of party that allows us to view the political party in a democracy as the sum of its parts, as a complete organization. Herein lies the principal theoretical need in the study of parties. The discordant perceptions of parties in the United States, not to mention of U.S. parties and their counterparts in other democracies, derive from different views of organization. Rational choice theorists, because they have concentrated on candidates' strategies, have ignored the problem of organization for the most part.[4] Students of party organization, because they emphasize the complexities of motivation, see the party defined according to rational choice precepts as a gross simplification (Eldersveld 1964 and 1982; Wilson 1973; Ware 1979). The textbook, or piecemeal approach, on the other hand, treats party organization as though it leads a life of its own, independent of officeholders, candidates, or even campaign specialists.[5] Clearly lacking is a theory that brings these parts together, that recognizes that the unity of the party and its organization are the same, and that, therefore, makes similar assumptions about the motivations and decisions of all of the actors within the party. It is of primary importance to the study of parties to establish what sort of organization a political party is.

The Definition of Party

To theorize about parties as organizations first requires a clear definition of what we mean by a party. Our inability to agree upon such a definition is surely the most telling symptom of our malaise as we approach this subject. Part of the problem arises from methodological conflicts, such as that between advocates of the functional and rational choice approaches. Normative issues about just what a party ought to be also provide grounds for conflict. Nothing I say here can resolve these conflicts. Yet another difficulty arises because

---

4. Rational choice theorists have paid some attention to the sequence of elections with which parties in the United States must deal, as well as to the need for candidates to appeal both to party followers and to the general electorate. See, for example, Coleman 1971; Aranson and Ordeshook 1972; Wittman 1973 and 1983; Aldrich 1980. Much of the difficulty rational choice theorists have had in studying party organization stems from problems with defining the goals of parties. I return to this question in chap. 6.

5. Writers of texts on parties are fully aware that parties operate well beyond the boundaries of their formal apparatus, yet they retain the term and idea of organization for that apparatus. V. O. Key (1964) set the tone. Other texts followed suit, e.g., Gelb and Palley 1975; Henderson 1976; Sorauf 1976; Scott and Hrebenar 1979; Blank 1980; Goodman 1980.

many want to define party to include all the numerous political organizations that call themselves by that name.[6] However useful a theory of party based on such a broad definition would be, the theory I propose to elaborate is less ambitious. It seeks to explain only parties that contest in free democratic elections, and primarily those parties that are able to win elections over time. The reason for this limitation is the assumption that parties that contest in free elections have had to adapt to an environment sufficiently different from that of parties facing no such contest to justify a distinctive theory. Similarly, we cannot assume that parties that have no expectations of winning elections are subject to the same tensions and constraints as parties that do and will, therefore, behave in the same manner. Having limited the theory to parties that contest successfully in free elections, I am prepared to adopt the definition of party posited by Downs in his theory of democracy: a party is "a team seeking to control the governing apparatus by gaining office in a duly constituted election" (Downs 1957, 25).

Implications of the Definition

Let us spell out some of the implications of the Downsian definition for a theory of parties. First, the definition directs us to rational choice explanations of party behavior. In so doing it reflects both the view that politics is goal oriented and the assumption that political actors are rational in the ways they seek to achieve their goals. Thus the definition directs us away from psychological explanations, by which I mean a concern for the sources of these goals or wants. Note also that the definition does not refer to the functions that parties perform for the political system. Consequently, those who prefer psychological or functional explanations of political phenomena will be unsatisfied by this theory. The theory, however, neither denies that parties perform broad political functions nor that they respond to psychological needs. Rather, it asserts implicitly that, if parties do such things, they do them as byproducts of the pursuit of their goal as stated in the definition.

Note, too, that true to rational choice theory, the only elements sharply stated in the Downsian definition are the goal (control of the governing apparatus) and the means of achieving it (winning office in a duly constituted election). The reason is that rational choice theory works best in the context of well-defined structures such as markets or political institutions where individuals can be observed working to satisfy specific wants. In effect, it is not the

---

6. Alternative perceptions of party are explored by William E. Wright (1971). Kay Lawson (1976, 3) defines party broadly to encompass governing groups that seek authorization from the public, regardless of whether they face competitive elections. A similarly wide net is cast by Kenneth Janda in his major survey (1980).

individual (that would lead us to psychological concerns) but the institutions that are defining the individual's goals. The self-evident fact that individuals make overt efforts to achieve these goals gives us some confidence in our assumption that these goals are indeed what they want. Similarly, neither the individual nor the party defines the basic means of attaining the goals; rather, it is the political structure through its "duly constituted elections." Rational choice theory, therefore, is really a revival of the institutional approach to politics and for that reason it is compatible with much of the long tradition of the study of politics (Rohde and Shepsle 1978).

The institutional basis of the Downsian definition also implies that the theory can apply only to parties that seek office through means of democratic elections. Even among parties that do nominate candidates for election in democracies, the theory is applicable only to those parties that have a realistic chance of winning elections over time. For parties that either seek power outside of the electoral arena or use elections for some purpose other than gaining office, the goals and means are unspecified by the democratic institution of elections. Thus, a theory that rests upon an institutional definition of goals and means cannot be applied to these parties. In contrast, the goals and means of parties that do contest elections with some hope of winning can be observed. Simple observation cannot tell what other goals they may have, but this we do know: they are constrained by the institutionally defined goal of winning office and by the institutionally defined mechanism for attaining that goal.

Finally, the Downsian definition gives us only a terse description of parties by referring to them as teams. To be a team implies some degree of deliberate cooperation among two or more individuals to achieve some purpose. Since this is one classic definition of an organization, we conclude that the political party is some kind of organization (Barnard 1938, 4). Yet the character of the organization, how it is arranged, what (if any) lines of authority it has, how disciplined it is, how much division of labor exists, is not part of the Downsian definition of party. These omissions are essential if the definition of party is to be flexible enough to understand changes in the party's form.

The Downsian definition also keeps our view of parties flexible because it sets narrow, yet imprecise, limits for those included within the party. They are narrow because only those who might reasonably be considered part of the team are included; imprecise because just who they are is not defined. The team surely includes the candidates and those who actively work for their election, as well as all officials who join forces under the party label in government. Yet the definition excludes those who are essentially choosers among competing parties, that is, the voters. Between candidates and voters, also, lies a host of interest groups, media experts, and activists of all sorts whose relationship to the party, according to the Downsian definition, remains problematical.

The exclusion of the voter from the party in this definition is a point whose importance must be emphasized. Much of the difficulty political scientists have had in developing a theory of political parties has come from not knowing what to do with the voters. In some measure this difficulty flows from normative conflicts over just what the role of voters should be in a democracy. Proponents of the participatory role see voters as integral to any party formation; thus they will inevitably be dissatisfied by any definition that omits them. For others, such as E. E. Schattschneider (1942), who see competition among parties as the vital aspect of democracy, the voters must be choosers; of necessity they remain outside the parties. We cannot resolve the issue at this point. We should recognize, however, that the Downsian definition reflects the latter perspective.

Beyond the normative issue, the position of the voter in a theory of parties has been clouded by the advent of voter surveys, whose purpose is to link voting and party behavior. Systematic surveys have allowed us to chart with great refinement the sorts of people who vote for each party and to probe their reasons for doing so. The very richness of this data has had considerable impact on the way scholars and journalists view parties. But even politicians have come to fashion their political perspectives on the basis of survey techniques rather than on the basis of their experiences with the parties themselves. Thus it has become common practice to talk of parties as though they were coalitions of voters, as in the phrases, "the New Deal coalition," or the "party coalitions of the 1980s" (Lipset 1978). It is of the greatest importance to recognize, however, that such coalitions are simply constructs in the minds of observers who are only noting that parties draw their support disproportionately from various categories of the population. None of these are coalitions in the proper sense of the word. None represent conscious, explicit agreements by members of these categories to pursue joint action. Indeed, if one examines the principal categories used in surveys, age, sex, income, education, region, union membership, and religion (the exception is race), we find that none of these categories votes in blocs. In surveys of voters in the United States, a 60:40 split, or even narrower divisions, reflects the size of commitment of any of these "blocs" to a particular coalition (Abramson, Aldrich, and Rohde 1990, chap. 5).

More insidious for a theory of parties has been the psychological approach, with its implication that party resides simply in the *minds* of voters. In 1960, V. O. Key, in a review of the ground-breaking *The American Voter* (Campbell et al. 1960), expressed concerns about what he called the "politically relevant in surveys." While Key doubted the relevance to politics of much of the previous survey research, he was more sanguine about the turn reflected in *The American Voter.* Certainly that work stands as a landmark in our understanding of modern politics. Yet it also contained the germ of an idea that has undermined our commonsense notions of a political party, the concept of party identification.

Initially, party identification was useful as one of the basic attitudes that, along with the voters' views toward the candidates and the issues, produced the voting decision. In all of the early literature, including *The American Voter,* there was no hint that voters who paid attention to the candidates or to issues were not also voting for a party. The triad of party, issues, and candidates were simply components of a decision that necessarily was partisan for the simple reason that there is no way one can isolate each component when voters cast their ballots in the real world. More to the point, since it is the parties that nominate the candidates who take stands on issues, the distinction can never be between partisan and nonpartisan factors. It can only be between different aspects of partisan behavior, some of longstanding duration, others of current concern.

Yet as survey after survey has been run through the mills of secondary analysis, each of the three components has taken on a life of its own. To pay attention to a party's candidates or to be concerned with issues has come to imply a lack of concern for party. In an influential book, *The Changing American Voter* (Nie, Verba, and Petrocik 1976), the concept of party is thus reduced to a nonrational sentiment residing in the minds of voters. The authors chart the decline in what they call party voting because the factor of party identification has become less important in voting decisions. Even the person who votes for all of a party's candidates all of the time cannot, by their definition, be a party voter if that decision is based primarily on the voter's judgments of the candidates or of their stands on issues. Thus, party becomes a phenomenon separated from the real world of party behavior.

If we would recapture the reality of party, then, surely we must exclude the voter from its confines. Voters are choosers among parties, not elements of the parties. This is not to say that the reasons for voters' choices are unimportant to our understanding of party behavior. Parties gain a great advantage by having large numbers of voters inclined in their favor. Yet the ultimate test of a party's strength, its electoral performance, rests with its ability to win elections, not with its ability to command the identification of the electorate. In a competitive party system, a weakening of partisan identification simply raises the level of competition among parties: what one party loses others must gain. Indeed the growth of Republican strength in the Old South and that of Democrats in former Republican bastions of the Midwest have depended precisely on this erosion of partisan identification. This seeming paradox, parties growing stronger while they are growing weaker, is a paradox only if we make the error of equating partisan strength with partisan identification, of insisting on seeing the voter as an integral part of the political party.[7]

The Party as Organization

The political party of our definition, then, is a team that seeks to control government by winning elective office. On this team are those who seek and those who hold office in the party's name. Excluded are the voters who are the choosers among parties. Yet the team must encompass many more individuals than office seekers and officeholders as it seeks the voters' support. Such individuals must be recruited and their activities organized. The political party, in other words, must prove itself as an organization.

To understand the identity of party and organization on the basis of the experience of the United States is, however, a complex matter because much of the activity aimed at winning office must take place outside the confines of the formal party apparatus. The United States is unique among democracies in the extent to which it has sought to regulate and define party organization. State laws have created a panoply of party offices encompassing local, county, and state governmental units, most of which have little or no mandate to take part in the nomination of candidates for public elective office, to run the candidates' campaigns, nor, certainly, to direct the performance of successful candidates in government. This is not to say that officials who fill these positions are irrelevant to office seeking or government. Rather, in U.S. politics, their relevance is an open matter to be determined in a multitude of ways.[8] More important, the legal definition of the party apparatus has not prevented the development of an array of efforts aimed at seeking office outside its confines.[9] To equate the party organization with the official apparatus, therefore, is to thrust into the realm of disorganization much, if not most, of the effort put into winning office in the United States. To make this equation is to promote only discrete analyses of such key elements in gaining

---

7. The strength of partisan identification may or may not have much to do with the stability of democratic systems. For a discussion of the conflicting evidence on this issue see Abramson 1983 (82–85).

8. For example, Jewell and Olson (1982, 112–20) examine the various procedures that formal structures use to affect primary nominations. Huckshorn (1976) notes the varied roles played by state party chairs. Mayhew (1986) gives an assessment, state by state, of where formal party officials were most important in the 1960s.

9. Informal coalitions have always existed. Some of the extralegal structures have formalized as clubs, associations, and political action committees. Contemporary financial reporting laws have required many of these structures to give themselves titles and to keep records, whereas they operated more obscurely in the past.

office as the recruitment of candidates, the role of the media in electoral campaigns, and the gathering of money for electoral purposes.

The discrepancy between the formal party apparatus and the partisan efforts designed to win office should not, however, lead us to give up in despair. Certainly it should not lead us to assert that parties lack meaningful organization. Rather it should force us to reexamine our perspectives on party organization itself. In this respect, there is an advantage in looking at party organization in democracies from the perspective of the United States, where the formal structure is so obviously not the real organization. This forces us to break away from the purely descriptive and develop a framework that encompasses the major parties of the polity. In countries such as Great Britain or France, where parties have been free to organize as they see fit, there is a less obvious disjunction between the formal party apparatus and the operative organization and, therefore, a less obvious need for a general framework. At the same time, a theory free to speculate without descriptive restraints can encompass party organizations in all democracies.

In order to perceive much of the diverse partisan activity in the United States as taking place within a discrete organization, we must first be able to recognize the distinctiveness of the party as an organization. While a party shares characteristics with other types of organizations such as political interest groups or voluntary associations that are also involved in politics, it has characteristics that make it very much unlike these groups. Indeed, by the standards of any other kind of organization, a political party may well fall short. Yet just as we would neither judge an interest group by the standards of a business, nor a public bureau in the same way we would an interest group, our assessment of a political party as an organization must rest upon its peculiar characteristics.

The Properties of Party Organization

My model of the political party as an organization utilizes properties that characterize all organizations. Each property reflects a response to the basic questions that all organizations must answer. How does the organization maintain itself? What is the principal work of the organization or what is its principal output? How does the organization compensate its workers or participants? To analyze the party's responses to these questions I have developed three dichotomous variables: (1) maintenance of the organization through market exchange or through nonmarket devices; (2) the primary output of the organization as a collective or private good; and (3) compensation of participants either directly or indirectly. The structural characteristics of the party model depend upon how it combines these variables.

In the following discussion we shall see how each property or answer to the basic questions about organizations creates a force directing the behavior of the organization. We shall look at each variable with respect to the political party, comparing the party with other basic types of organization: the business firm, the public agency or bureau, and the interest group. We shall then examine the consequences for the party of the way in which it answers each question. Once we have defined the effects of each variable, we shall be able to see the combination of properties that define the structure and behavior of political parties. We shall then be able to test the model by looking at the consequences of altering one or more of its assumptions.

Party: A Market-Based Organization

Our first distinction is between organizations that do or do not maintain themselves through market exchange. Market-based organizations trade their output or product with others in a direct, quid pro exchange for money or other essential resources.[10] The business firm is the prime example of such an organization. As long as it sells its product for at least as much as it costs to produce, then the firm can maintain itself. Many organizations, in contrast, are not market based. Thus the salient characteristic of a public agency or bureau is that its maintenance rests on the political budgetary process. Some may, as in the case of a post office or urban mass transit, sell their services in a market, but the willingness of the state to make up their deficits shows that society prefers not to let their services depend on market forces. Another nonmarket-based organization is the political interest group. The group may attract supporters who wish to receive the benefits sought by the group, but it does not trade these policies directly for support. Interest groups may sustain themselves through sidepayments by selling journals, cookies, or calendars, yet no one considers these products to be their primary output.

Is a political party market or nonmarket based? Elections are a type of political market, in which parties offer their candidates and their policies in exchange for the votes needed to gain office. In this market, parties gain what is surely their key resource, control of public office. Just as a business can maintain itself by selling its product at an adequate price, a party able to win office has no difficulty in obtaining all the elements of a viable organization: attractive candidates, willing workers, and financial contributors. And just as the economic market sends clear and unambiguous messages to the business firm concerning the success or failure of its product, the political market evaluates the output of the political party openly, automatically, externally, and with exquisite numerical precision.

---

10. In this analysis I draw heavily on Anthony Downs 1967. Downs's propositions deal with bureaus. Since the political party is the antithesis of the bureau in all respects (except that both produce collective benefits), I have turned Downs's propositions around.

The political and economic markets are not, of course, identical. The most important difference between the two kinds of market lies in the character of what is being traded. Elections create an imbalanced market. Undoubtedly the imbalance of the political market is the reason we have difficulty in recognizing the market character of elections. What the parties receive in the electoral transaction is always very clear. Parties receive votes and the control of office. But these are private benefits or goods that go only to the party and to its candidates. From the voters' standpoint it is seldom clear just what it is that they are getting from the electoral exchange. Parties offer candidates and policies to voters, benefits that go to everyone regardless of the votes cast. True, the officeholder represents a clear payoff for the voter. Yet the president, senator, and mayor become everyone's officeholders, not just the officeholders of those who "paid" for them with their votes. Thus while parties receive private benefits, they offer only collective benefits in exchange. This is in sharp contrast to the economic market in which both sides to a transaction give and receive private or selective goods. The fact that the parties' output consists of collective goods is of major consequence to them as organizations. We shall consider this shortly. At this point we are interested in the consequences for party organization of being market based. For since our concern is with a theory of party organization and not of the voters' behavior, it is the clarity of the electoral market from the party's standpoint that matters.

Consequences of the Market Base: Goals. The major impact of the market on organizations is that market goals dominate their decisions. The reason is simple: the maintenance of the organization is closely tied to success in the market. It is true that a major advance in the theory of organizations has been the recognition of the complexity and, indeed, the ambiguity of organizational goals.[11] Even the business firm has been shown to be less clearly driven by profit maximization than is assumed by market theory. Nevertheless, because businesses operate in a market, they have a well-defined test of their success, a test that reverberates throughout their organization. Whatever goals may compete with market goals, a business cannot escape the need to sell its product to cover its costs. Failing that, the firm collapses and all of the competing goals with it. Similarly, a political party that fails to win elections,

---

11. Cyert and March (1963) have demonstrated the complexities of decisions within business firms. March and Olsen (1976) have developed a "garbage can" model of decision making, particularly for academic bureaucracies. Schwartz (1990) has applied this concept of ambiguity to political party organization. Given the inherent diffuseness of parties compared with businesses or bureaucracies, my own view is that approaching them as ambiguous structures is starting at the wrong end. The central question is, how do parties make decisions and persist, despite their ambiguities and conflicts?

and even more important, holds no prospects of winning elections at any time in the future, also faces collapse.

Besides the life or death quality of the test that the market imposes upon market-based organizations, other qualities of the test reinforce the dominance of market goals. The clarity and automatic nature of the test also give the market's goals precedence over less clearly evaluated goals or objectives. A party's electoral wins as well as its defeats, the size of its electoral victories as well as of its losses, are matters of public record. In this sense, a party is even more controlled by its market than a business, for no amount of creative accounting can alter the size of a party's victory or defeat. No other party goal is subject to as clear a test of achievement: policies are more or less implemented; patronage is more or less satisfactory. If clear and unambiguous marks of achievement dominate those that are less clear, we can see why market goals take precedence in parties.

Finally, market goals dominate in market-based organizations because they are essential to the achievement of other goals. Office, like money, is a neutral or value-free goal that is instrumental. Both can be used for high or low purposes, but they are needed for these purposes. Herein lies the germ of the rationalization that permits politicians to retain their principles and ideals while adjusting to the electoral market. As Alf Landon told the Republican convention of 1976, "The art of winning, of winning elections, comes before the art of governing."[12]

In contrast, organizations that are not market based are much less tightly held to any particular goal. The two examples of nonmarket organizations I have referred to, the bureau and the interest group, are free to shape their goals in such a manner that the organization can always justify its existence. The bottom line for a bureau is its budget, and the bureau's task is one of convincing the political authorities of the value of its actions. This is not as difficult a task as the bureau may make it appear. As the literature on policy analysis clearly indicates, tests of success or failure for the bureau are far from self-evident or automatic (Wolf 1979). In the same sense, an interest group, however well defined its policy goals may be, has substantial leeway in defining its objectives and therefore in sustaining itself. Should the group's objectives actually be achieved, it is clearly capable of redefining them to assure continuity (Sills 1957). The difference between the market- and nonmarket-based organization is evident. A market-based organization can neither define its own goals nor transform them and remain the same kind of organization.

---

12. Statement to the Republican National Convention, reported in *New York Times*, 18 August 1976.

In this respect, it is instructive to observe how the interest group's ability to define its own goals allows it to behave differently from the party in the electoral arena. Electoral interest groups that compile hit lists of members of Congress have proliferated in recent years. Since these groups most often target highly vulnerable incumbents, they can usually go back to their supporters for renewed contributions, claiming a creditable record of wins. In other words, these groups have entered the electoral arena setting their own goals and, therefore, capable of announcing their successful achievement. But this is exactly what the political party cannot do. While the party can allocate its resources to achieve its goals, its success will not be measured by some limited, self-defined goal. The party is tied tightly to the win and loss column provided by the total electoral market. In this sense the market is, to use Lindblom's imagery, a prison. Lindblom (1982) argues that the economic market imprisons all policymakers—business personnel, union leaders, as well as government officials—because all are controlled by the market effects of their actions. In precisely the same sense parties, unlike interest groups, as they nominate candidates and pursue policies, are imprisoned by the electoral consequences of these acts.

Once we accept parties as organizations sustained by the market and dominated by its goals we can understand the rationale for the basic hypothesis in Downs's work. The hypothesis states: "Parties formulate policies in order to win elections rather than win elections in order to formulate policies" (1957, 28). Certainly there are conflicting pressures within parties and even within the hearts and minds of candidates themselves. Yet because the imperatives of the political market do not allow a party to treat all of these pressures equally, neither can a theory of party organization treat them equally. Frequent elections and, today, constant polling provide nearly continuous tests of the appeal of candidates, officeholders, and their policies. A party that does not respond to the electoral market will, by definition, lose to parties that do and over the long run will find itself supplanted by responsive parties.

Consequences of the Market Base: Influence. The market also affects the pattern of influence within market-based organizations. Because the market sends clear and unavoidable signals about performance with respect to its particular goals, individuals or units most responsible for market success can readily be identified. Such individuals gain influence. In a business, people who make successful sales or who are associated with a successful product will rise to power. Similarly for the political party, the winning candidates, or even those who look as though they might win, gain power. Indeed, because the most clearly defined product of the party is its candidate, there is no leeway for argument within the party, as there is in business. Influence within the party will closely follow individual success and failure in the electoral market.[13] Note how this contrasts with nonmarket-based organizations. Lacking the clarity of market-defined goals, interest groups or bureaus must develop their own tests of success and failure. Thus they are relatively free to distribute influence according to such nonmarket criteria as seniority, loyalty, test scores, birth, or friendship, according to the needs of the organization.

Party: A Producer of Collective Goods

Having seen how the party's market base affects the question of maintenance, we turn now to the nature of the party's output and its effect on party organization. With respect to this property of organization, I proposed the distinction between organizations producing private goods and those producing collective goods as their primary output. The private goods–producing organization faces few organizational problems deriving from the nature of its product. For the private goods it produces, it receives a private product (usually money) that can be used as an incentive enabling it to continue the production of private goods. The simplicity with which the private goods–producing organization can make use of its products by no means guarantees its existence. We have already seen its existence is determined by the market. All the same, the simplicity of its output frees the private goods–producing organization from the problems raised for organizations that produce collective goods.

Political parties, along with interest groups and public bureaus, are organizations that produce collective goods. Such organizations have always posed a problem for the theory of organization. Since everyone receives the collective products or benefits, whether or not they have done anything to produce them, we are led to ask why anyone produces these goods. With respect to government agencies, it is not difficult to see the answer. Through the coercion of the taxing power, government agencies can produce enough private benefits to insure the continued production of collective goods. For parties and interest groups that lack such coercive powers, the answer to the dilemma is less obvious. There has always been, to be sure, a straightforward explanation: it makes sense for people with common interests to band together in pursuit of their interests. Yet this explanation has never faced the reality that few with common interests organize in the defense of those interests. Even when such organizations do form, few people who share the interest actually

---

13. It follows from this argument that influence accrues to anyone in the party who is seen as helping the party win elections. Losing candidates who do better than expected or those who run in hopeless situations thus may actually gain strength. Those who either give money or who are good at gathering it, as well as those with desirable skills, can similarly expect to exert influence (Kornberg, Smith, and Clarke 1979, chap. 7). Whatever influence they have, however, derives not from their personal characteristics as such but from the fact that others perceive them to be useful to the party in meeting its market-defined goal of gaining office.

join. Finally, as has been widely observed, even among those who join, still fewer take an active part in pursuing their interest. Much of the literature on political interest groups consists of efforts to resolve such questions.[14] To a great extent the answers are given in nonrational terms; they are rooted in expressions such as apathy, alienation, or a sense of inefficacy. They arise, then, from assumptions incompatible with the rational choice theory of party implicit in our definition.

The theory that does explain the development of different types of organizations within the same rational framework is Mancur Olson's logic of collective action. Olson has demonstrated that, in large groups, "rational self-interested individuals will not act to achieve their common or group interests" (1965, 2). Simply by voiding the apparently straightforward explanation that people join organizations because of their collective purposes, Olson has given us a theory that allows us to apply the same assumptions, perspectives, and logic we commonly apply to private goods–producing organizations to organizations that produce collective benefits.

More important for our purposes, we have a theory of organization inherently compatible with our definition of party. The theoretical gap between party organization and party behavior in competitive elections has been closed. Olson's formulation allows us to observe that, in large groups such as a political party, a single participant's effort to achieve the collective good is far more costly than the increment to the collective good—winning the election or implementing a policy—resulting from the effort. No rational person, therefore, will participate to achieve the collective good. In other words, the efforts of one individual will have such a small impact on the achievement of the party's collective benefits that, no matter how attractive these benefits are to an individual, he or she will not contribute to their achievement. To do so would be to behave irrationally, because the cost of the contribution will inevitably be worth more than its marginal impact on the likelihood of achieving the goal. Since people obviously do contribute to parties, in Olson's theory they must do so in order to gain sidepayments or private benefits they would have not received had they not contributed.

Here we must reiterate an earlier point: rational choice theories work best in well-defined institutional settings where the benefits to be gained are well marked and observable, and where the costs of achieving them are easily calculated. Thus Olson's theory is most predictive for economic groups like trade associations, labor unions, and consumer organizations, where the participants can readily measure costs and benefits in monetary terms (Moe

---

14. The more penetrating analyses of these problems are in Truman 1951 and Schattschneider 1960. A more recent effort to analyze these problems in light of the evidence on the development of a variety of groups is Walker 1983.

1980). When we turn to groups such as parties, in which neither benefits nor costs can readily be measured in the same terms, Olson's theory is not invalidated. It is, however, less likely to be completely predictive because the ability to make cost-benefit calculations is unevenly distributed among potential participants.

In order to behave as Olson predicts, one needs information, first about the costs of participating and second about the marginal effects of one's contribution in producing the collective good.[15] In a later work, Olson (1982, 25–29) notes that information about costs and benefits is itself a collective good and, thus, is not likely to be supplied in optimal amounts. As far as politics is concerned, most of the free information available through education and the media overstates the impact of individuals. For example, by attempting to impart a sense of civic duty, they spread the golden lie, "If only one more voter in every precinct had voted for X, he would have won the election," thereby suppressing the fact that there are thousands of precincts. In effect, the information needed for people in parties to behave rationally (in Olson's terms) is not readily available; for most it must be gained from experience. The theory thus predicts that those who participate in political parties only in order to produce the collective goods will have relatively little information about the costs and benefits. These participants are the inexperienced and the young. With experience and, therefore, information such individuals will drop out unless they find in political activity some form of personal or noncollective satisfaction. The logic of collective action thus predicts a high turnover in party personnel. It is borne out by much of what we know about the fluctuations in partisan participation (Eldersveld 1964; Kornberg, Smith, and Clarke 1970; Verba and Nie 1972).

Olson's logic also removes one of the incentives devised by Clark and Wilson (1961) for participating in the output of an organization. Their distinction among material, solidary, and purposive incentives, along with Wilson's distinction (1962) between amateurs and professionals in politics, have given direction to much of our research on party organization. Purposive incentives are, of course, collective. They are also central to the picture of the amateur in politics, as well as to Wildavsky's picture of political "purists" (1965). While not denying that these incentives do attract many activists, Olson's logic indicates that such incentives, unreinforced by private benefits, have little staying power. Attractive candidates and new issues (collective benefits) will bring in new activists, most of whom will disappear. Those who remain may well do so out of a sense of private satisfaction. But the party cannot rely on such a sense alone. The party, like the bureau and the interest group, must also produce, as a sideproduct, private goods and provide private benefits.

---

15. As Downs recognized, information itself is costly, and influence rests upon an uneven distribution of information (1957, chap. 6).

While the incentive system in a party is thus complex, it is clear enough which individuals receive the private benefits: those with ambitions for office. Their payoffs, substantial and personal, are worth the costs of organization. Thus, office seekers are the party's entrepreneurs, who Salisbury (1969) notes are essential for the development of collective goods–producing organizations. This is not to say that other kinds of private benefits do not exist within parties. These range from the material rewards of patronage to the less tangible reward of involvement in public affairs. Nevertheless, the office seekers are the principal beneficiaries of the private benefits that the party can produce. As was the case with the market base, the party's production of private goods as a sideproduct leaves the office seeker its most influential figure.

The logic of collective action then clarifies the phenomenon of oligarchic control in political parties. In parties, as in any voluntary association, individual sensitivities must be acknowledged to prevent participants from withdrawing. Because parties inherently must pit individuals against each other in struggles over nominations and policies, it is inevitable that many will feel injured. Thus, parties share with other collective goods–producing organizations all of the problems of incentives exacerbated by personal and policy conflicts. Since parties ostensibly attract individuals to produce collective goods, the argument that all who participate in any way should resolve these conflicts and govern these organizations is irresistible. Parties, along with other collective goods–producing organizations in the United States, such as professional associations, trade unions, and interest groups, fall into what Truman dubbed the "democratic mold" (1951, 129–55). Yet the evidence points to a reality in which oligarchs or an "active minority" run the organization. This is precisely what we should expect if the key participants are attracted not by the collective but by the private benefits parties provide. Such key players, mindful of the demands of the electoral market, cannot long tolerate the dominance of those interested only in collective benefits. The adverse effect of their dominance becomes clearer when we recall that parties are market based. If, for example, policies are the principal benefits for most participants, it is likely that they will seek to restrain the party in its electoral maneuvering. That, of course, is precisely the argument of Wilson and Wildavsky. Since, however, the party must retain its flexibility in order to respond to the electoral market, such restraints, as well as the influence of those who impose them, no matter how great their numbers must be short lived.

Party: An Indirect Compensator

The third distinctive property I proposed was the form of compensation used by organizations. I distinguished between organizations that compensate their participants directly and those that do so indirectly. This distinction, too, has considerable consequences for organizations. Note first the distinction is similar to that between voluntary and paid work. I prefer the direct-indirect distinction primarily because much voluntary work for charities, professional associations, chambers of commerce, and interest groups has its indirect financial rewards in one's business or profession.

This distinction defines the degree of control that an organization can have over its work force. Direct compensation permits a degree of rationalization of activity that is denied to the organization that can only compensate its workers indirectly. Direct compensation attracts people who show up on time, who have skills designed for required tasks, and who are indifferent to (and therefore unaffected in their work by) the goals or output of the organization. Indirect compensation, on the other hand, recruits people from the leisure market or flexible occupations whose presence is constantly at risk for the organization because of outside diversions. The indirect-paying organization, therefore, must comply fully with its personnel from the time it asks them to work to the tasks it asks them to perform.

The distinction also establishes the extent to which the work force is itself dependent for its livelihood on the continued maintenance of the organization. Most of the work force of the indirect-paying organization does not count on the organization for its livelihood. Indirectly paid participants, therefore, have less of a stake in the maintenance of an organization than do directly paid workers. Disaffection on the part of these participants, whether due to the ways in which they are treated or to the stands of the organization, poses a serious problem for the maintenance of the indirect-paying organization.

Of the four types of organizations we have mentioned, the business and the bureau pay their work forces directly. Interest groups and political parties, even though they may have some paid staff, depend primarily on people whom they do not pay directly. This is of special significance for political parties. Not only are most of its activists indirectly paid, so too are its most important figures, the candidates and officeholders. The latter, of course, are paid by the state, and the party is important in gaining their paid offices. But the party cannot use their pay to direct the officials' behavior, nor can it deny pay if the officeholders are elected without the party's support. This distinguishes parties from interest groups that pay their leaders and staff. Direct payment of the basic work force is certainly a major factor leading to organizational continuity, even if it requires the transformation of the organization's goals.

The Political Party, a Unique Combination of Properties

We are now in a position to bring together the three variables in our model and look at the political party as a whole. The political party offers collective benefits and compensates its participants indirectly, yet is market based. The peculiar character of the party, as well as its ability to adapt to a changing world, derives from this unique combination of properties. Of course in the real world of politics, pressures always exist that tend to move parties, in one or another aspect, away from this model. But the parties resist these changes. Before examining such aberrations, let us first see where the model takes us in understanding party organization.

When viewed from the standpoint of other organizations, the peculiar combination of properties creates what seem to be fatal weaknesses in parties. Compared with other market-based organizations, the party is seriously deficient in its ability to discipline its participants to meet the ever insistent challenges of the market. Compared with other producers of collective goods, the party is incapable of adjusting its objectives in order to maintain its tenuous supporters. It can neither narrow nor broaden its objectives, obscure its purposes, nor alter its timing to await the propitious moment to act.

For us these weaknesses are obvious because most of our experience is with other types of organizations. We know that, if these organizations were to behave the way parties do, they could not last. In the world of business we recognize the importance of cost accounting, of efficiency experts, of the time clock, and of hierarchic decision making. Those of us who are part of a bureau live with clearly defined structures, procedures, and incentives. In our relationships with professional and voluntary associations, we see how and why they adjust their aims and activities to satisfy and retain their members. Our perception of other organizations is so clear that the deficiencies in parties become glaring. We see waste and inefficiency in the use of resources. We see inactivity where activity is called for on the organizational charts. We see parties time and again angering their supporters, driving many away just when they seem to need them most. Party organization seems incomprehensible.

Because we fail to grasp the character of party organization, whenever parties do appear effective we often seek explanations from nonparty perspectives. Thus the bureaucratic model leads us to explain effective party organization by hidden hierarchies of bosses, machines, and behind-the-scenes operatives stalking the corridors of power. Since such phenomena have been hard to find at the national level, a commonplace of political science has been that parties in the United States have no national organizations, except perhaps for a brief period every four years when a president is nominated. Under the intense gaze of modern journalism and social science, today's parties appear weak and debilitated. We look back nostalgically to a time when these parties must have been better organized and surely better loved by the citizenry. Otherwise, how could they have emerged, prospered, or accomplished anything?

To understand parties, we must recognize that they do not perform and adapt as do businesses, bureaus, or interest groups; nor can they be expected to do so, given their peculiar combination of organizational properties. Parties are perhaps best described as forms of organized trial and error. Thousands of individuals and interests seek to control the party's decisions. They push candidates, frame issues, recruit workers, make alliances, and devise campaigns. Among these competing forces choices are made, choices whose correctness is ultimately determined not by the party but by the electorate. Nevertheless, it is the party organization that assures that the right choices, that is, those that win elections, are adopted and the wrong ones are rejected. The right choices are not preordained, but rest upon the peculiar combination of properties delineated in our model (see fig. 1.2). The market base and the characteristics that derive from it assure successful electoral candidates, and their policies, positions of strength within the party. As well as collective benefits, they receive and control whatever private benefits the party has to bestow. Those who support demonstrably losing candidates and policies find no base in the party from which to exert influence. They may choose to remain and try to persuade the party to pursue the collective benefits they favor, but these benefits will clearly retain little attraction and the individuals who favor them little support.

In organizing through trial and error, a party makes none of the usual distinctions we find important in other organizations. It does not favor old over new faces, professionals over amateurs, the loyal over the disloyal, or even leaders over followers. Trial by elections is a ruthless test. Those who would maintain the appearance of power within a party are thus well advised to follow the old Chicago maxim, "Don't back no losers" (Rakove 1975). Furthermore, such concepts as "effectiveness" and organizational "strength" have no meaning in the party beyond the electoral test.

We can also see from this model why party organization is an inevitable or natural consequence of free democratic elections. Popular elections require voting by many individuals. Those who organize beforehand, that is, settle upon and work for a single candidate for an office, can readily defeat those who do not organize. Thus, if there were no parties, rational office seekers would form them. Since elections loom continuously and organizing is costly, office seekers will maintain the parties over time and give them labels that aid in their continuity and in communication with the electorate.

Aberrations from the Model

The party we have outlined is, of course, a model or ideal type against which we can place the variety of parties in the real world. The model delineates the basic forces that operate within party organization; it is designed, of course, to encompass the complex structure of political parties in the United States. Yet the same forces operate within parties seeking office in any democratic elec-

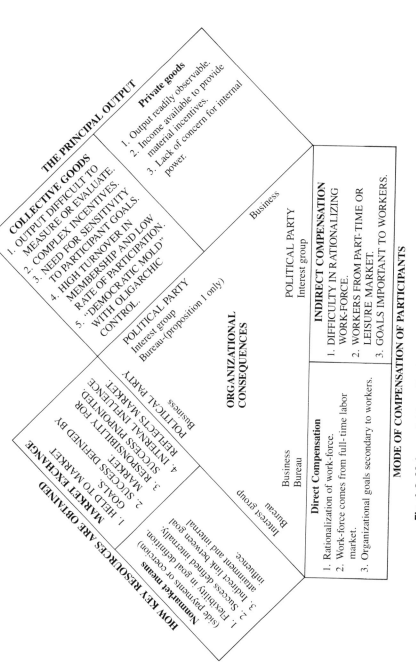

Fig. 1.2. Major variables affecting the organization of political parties

THE PRINCIPAL OUTPUT

COLLECTIVE GOODS
1. OUTPUT DIFFICULT TO MEASURE OR EVALUATE.
2. COMPLEX INCENTIVES.
3. NEED FOR SENSITIVITY TO PARTICIPANT GOALS.
4. HIGH TURNOVER IN MEMBERSHIP AND LOW RATE OF PARTICIPATION.
5. "DEMOCRATIC MOLD" WITH OLIGARCHIC CONTROL.

Private goods
1. Output readily observable.
2. Income available to provide material incentives.
3. Lack of concern for internal power.

Business

POLITICAL PARTY
Interest group

POLITICAL PARTY
Interest group
Bureau (proposition 1 only)

ORGANIZATIONAL CONSEQUENCES

Business
Bureau

POLITICAL PARTY
Interest group

INDIRECT COMPENSATION
1. DIFFICULTY IN RATIONALIZING WORK-FORCE.
2. WORKERS FROM PART-TIME OR LEISURE MARKET.
3. GOALS IMPORTANT TO WORKERS.

Direct Compensation
1. Rationalization of work-force.
2. Work-force comes from full-time labor market.
3. Organizational goals secondary to workers.

Business
Bureau

Interest group

MODE OF COMPENSATION OF PARTICIPANTS

HOW KEY RESOURCES ARE OBTAINED

MARKET EXCHANGE
1. HELD TO MARKET
2. SUCCESS DEFINED BY MARKET.
3. RESPONSIBILITY FOR SUCCESS PINPOINTED.
4. INTERNAL INFLUENCE REFLECTS MARKET.

POLITICAL PARTY

business

Bureau

Interest group

Nonmarket means
(side payments or coercion)
1. Flexibility in goal definition.
2. Success defined internally.
3. Indirect link between goal attainment and internal influence.

toral system. It is not difficult to place U.S. parties within this framework because they have adopted so few of the devices that might pull them away from the specifications of the model. But even parties in the United States are constantly being pulled in some manner to deviate from this model. One way to test the strength of this model, therefore, is to note some of these counter-forces and examine how the parties are constantly being pulled back by the forces implicit in our basic variables. What happens if we alter each of the assumptions in the model?

Party as a Nonmarket-based Organization

If we relax the assumption that parties gain their key resources through market exchange, then, depending on what sort of nonmarket mechanism it uses, we would expect the party to move in the direction of either the interest group or the bureau. If, for example, a party were to emphasize consistency in policy positions over winning elections, it would move away from the test of the electoral market and thus need to develop other means of assuring continuity. In line with Olson's theory, the collective purposes of the group would still be inadequate, by themselves, to maintain the party. It would still need sidepay-ments of a material or solidary kind. Nevertheless, the party would have to be far more concerned in setting its purposes in such a way that it did not repel its participants. Much of the research on parties in the United States during the 1970s implied that they were increasingly dominated by amateurs or purists, that is, activists less concerned with winning elections than with assuring that the parties took the proper position on issues (Abramowitz, McGlennon, and Rapaport 1982; Roback 1980; Soule and McGrath 1975). Should such atti-tudes dominate the decisions of the parties, then certainly we could say that the parties have moved more in the direction of interest groups in the model.

The very flexibility of party organization in the United States, however, gives little leverage to such individuals. The logic of office seeking leads to an approach to organizing parties that is sharply different from that derived from a concern for policy. I shall examine the conflict between the two logics in detail in chapter 6. Here I would simply point out that, in almost every respect, parties in the United States and the laws regulating them follow an office-seeking rather than a policy-seeking logic. The persistent complaints from right-wing conservatives about the ideological failures of the Reagan administration are simple testimony to the parties' ultimate need to subsume such pressures.[16] Indeed, the significant changes in U.S. political rules over the past decades have, if anything, given policy-oriented activists less rather

---

16. Note, for example, "Reagan 'Shift' Upsets Conservatives," *New York Times,* 26 June 1983.

than more control. Thus, the expansion of the direct primary in the presidential nominating process and the channeling of public financial support through candidates have further enhanced the inherent candidate orientation of parties in the United States. Little in the rules restrains candidate, and thus party, maneuverability in the search for votes.

Another way to relax the assumption that parties are market based would be to assure their support through some form of coercion, such as taxation in the manner of a bureau. This is implicit in the public financing of electoral campaigns. To a degree this has, of course, been accomplished in the United States with respect to the presidency and some state governorships. If parties were completely financed by the public budget, then our model would lead us to expect more bureaucratic behavior from them. This would be particularly true if the budgetary allotment were unrelated to the ability of parties to win votes. As far as maintenance is concerned, they would thus be freed from the electoral market. Political parties totally supported by the state and enjoined from gaining additional support, including that of volunteers, would, in the manner of bureaus, be more concerned with assuring continued budgetary support than in contesting elections. They would, in accordance with this model, be far less responsive to the electorate.

Here again, we must note how resistant the U.S. political system has been to such developments. Public financing of electoral campaigns has not gone to the general party apparatus; rather, it has gone to individual candidates. Organizations that revolve around individual candidates are not likely to generate bureaucratic structures.

Party as Producer of Private Goods

If we were to relax the assumption that the primary output of parties consists of collective goods, then they would begin to look more like businesses. They would produce policies designed to help specific individuals and trade these for income. Since parties inevitably produce public policies, their ability to become purely private goods–producing organizations is limited. After all, the national defense cannot readily be distributed privately. Some aspects of it can, however, be distributed privately in the form of defense contracts to specific companies. Such contracts can be traded for campaign contributions. Similarly, ambassadorial appointments can be sold to the highest bidder. Again, the line between private and collective benefits is not always sharp. Thus, a party may urge its legislators to raise the price supports for milk, to take a hypothetical example, in return for campaign contributions from the milk producers' association. Indeed, much of the picture we have of the urban political machine makes it look very businesslike as it trades policies for contributions.

From the party's standpoint, unfortunately, such exchanges are generally perceived as corrupt. A political party that is widely seen as selling policies as private benefits runs the serious danger of losing elections. Charges of bribery, corruption, and unethical behavior historically have been one of the most effective campaign appeals employed by opposition parties. The competitive electoral process is the major constraint against the relaxation of this assumption in the model.

Party as Income Provider

If we relax the assumption of our third variable, that parties pay no one directly, then we move the party closer to either the business or the bureau. In U.S. politics, the picture painted of the classic urban party machine was that of a party that, in effect, employed its workers. While ostensibly they worked for the city, their jobs were entirely at the disposal of the party machine and its boss. Of course the machine also had to control elections. As a political monopoly, therefore, it was not subject to market controls. Thus, the bureaucratic model, rather than that of the business, would seem to be most suitable. The evidence we have of the ways patronage was distributed in Chicago (Wilson 1961) supports this contention.

Today, of course, vast amounts of money are spent by candidates and parties for professional assistance. Does this challenge our assumption? Certainly a large class of professionals who make their living from the electoral process has emerged. According to our model, if this large body of professionals were to become employees of the parties, hired and fired by the parties, promoted and rewarded by them, then a major alteration in party organization would occur. Partisan considerations that are now minor, the need of the parties' paid staffs for status and security and even their attitudes towards policies, would become major concerns. The size of the party's budget and assurance of its continuity and stability would take on a high priority.

When we examine how money for professional services has been expended in U.S. politics, however, we see how resistant party organization has been to the development of dominant professional staffs. In part, the emergence of a staff interest has been prevented because professionals have been hired by individual office seekers. Moreover, where officeholders have had access to assured funding for staff, as in Congress and some state legislatures, the sizable growth in paid staffing has benefited the individual officeholder rather than the party. The parties themselves have preferred to take advantage of the growth of private campaign and polling organizations. These organizations, employing their own staffs, operate nationally or regionally, and contract their services to assorted units of the parties. Floating contract workers do not alter the structure of the parties. Parties, for the most part, continue to operate with personnel who are indirectly compensated. Unpaid work still dominates.

The party organization of our model is thus highly resilient. It resists the inevitable pressures to make it behave more like an interest group, a business, or a bureau. The key to the party's resilience lies in its unique combination of a market base with an output consisting primarily of collective goods. This combination reverses the usual interpretation of how each of these properties affects party behavior. The office-seeking or market force within parties is generally perceived as the one with which the party can compromise; collective goods or policy benefits are usually seen as the doctrinaire and, therefore, uncompromising aspect of party organization. In this model, however, it is the market force, the pressure to win office, that the party organization is unable to resist. The electoral market inexorably tethers the party to this objective. On the other hand, the output of collective goods exerts little effective long-run pressure on the party's behavior because it does not provide the long-run basis for attachment to the party.

As I noted at the outset, this model is embedded in much of our common understanding of how parties operate. Our central assumption is that politicians will respond to their electoral needs and that the organization of parties aids and abets them. This assumption is implicit in the commonsense explanation of the recurrent conflicts in the United States between the presidential and congressional wings of the parties and in the differences in behavior of the Senate and the House. After all, different electoral constituencies will necessarily require different behavior. The model underlies our arguments about the virtues and defects of the electoral college, which assume that presidential candidates and their parties respond principally to the rules of election. Then, too, we express no surprise that such one-time segregationist party leaders as George Wallace and Strom Thurmond were willing to appeal to black voters, after the Voting Rights Act of 1965 altered their electoral market. Similarly, the explanation of the two-party system based on the single-member district derives from the assumption that no one will persist in organizing and working for a party that has no realistic chance of electoral success. When we assert that the major parties undercut minor parties by adopting their popular issues, we again assert the dominance of the office goal and the parties' willingness to adapt their policies to achieve it. These are all mundane examples that assume parties behave precisely as called for in this model.

This model of party organization, then, is central to a more general theory of parties in democracies, based on the assumption that parties are dominated by the drive for public office. This model demonstrates why that assumption is correct. Derived from the general properties of organizations, the model does not spell out the actual structure and content of parties. That is the task of the remaining chapters of the book. We can, however, infer from the model that the structure and content of parties in democracies will reflect primarily what candidates and officeholders see as useful to their election and reelection. In effect, political ambitions and the factors that channel them will determine the structure and behavior of political parties. In succeeding chapters, therefore, I shall expand the theory of parties by examining office seekers' ambitions, the factors that guide them, and the types of parties they produce.

REFERENCES

Abramowitz, Alan, John McGlennon, and Ronald Rapoport. 1982. "Incentives for Activism in the 1980 Presidential Campaign." Paper presented at the annual meeting of the American Political Science Association, Denver.

Abramson, Paul. 1983. *Political Attitudes in America*. San Francisco: W. H. Freeman.

Abramson, Paul, John H. Aldrich, and David W. Rohde. 1990. *Change and Continuity in the 1988 Elections*. Washington, D.C.: Congressional Quarterly Press.

Agranoff, Robert, and Edward F. Cooke. 1964. "Political Profile of State Party Chairmen." Paper presented at the annual meeting of the Midwest Conference of Political Scientists, Madison, Wis.

Aldrich, John H. 1980. "A Dynamic Model of Presidential Nomination Campaigns." *American Political Science Review* 74:651–69.

Aranson, Peter, and Peter Ordeshook. 1972. "Spatial Strategies for Sequential Elections." In *Probability Models of Collective Decision Making*, ed. Richard G. Niemi and Herbert F. Weisberg. Columbus, Ohio: Charles E. Merrill.

Barnard, Chester I. 1938. *The Function of the Executive*. Cambridge, Mass.: Harvard University Press.

Blank, Robert H. 1980. *Political Parties: An Introduction*. Englewood Cliffs, N.J.: Prentice-Hall.

Broder, David. 1971. *The Party's Over*. New York: Harper and Row.

Burnham, Walter D. 1970. *Critical Elections and the Mainsprings of American Politics*. New York: Norton.

Campbell, Angus, Philip E. Converse, Warren R. Miller, and Donald E. Stokes. 1960. *The American Voter*. New York: Wiley.

Clark, Peter B., and James Q. Wilson. 1961. "Incentive Systems: A Theory of Organization." *Administrative Science Quarterly* 6:129–66.

Coleman, James S. 1971. "The Positions of Political Parties in Elections." In *Probability Models of Collective Decision Making*, ed. Richard G. Niemi and Herbert F. Weisberg. Columbus, Ohio: Charles E. Merrill.

Cotter, Cornelius, James Gibson, John Bibby, and Robert J. Huckshorn. 1980. "State Party Organizations and the Thesis of Party Decline." Paper presented at the annual meeting of the American Political Science Association, Washington, D.C.

Crotty, William J. 1984. *American Parties in Decline*. 2d ed. Boston: Little, Brown.

Cyert, Richard, and James G. March. 1963. *A Behavioral Theory of the Firm*. Englewood Cliffs, N.J.: Prentice-Hall.

Dennis, Jack. 1975. "Trends in Public Support for the American Party System." *British Journal of Political Science* 5:187–230.

Downs, Anthony. 1957. *An Economic Theory of Democracy*. New York: Harper and Row.

Downs, Anthony. 1967. *Inside Bureaucracy*. Boston: Little, Brown.

Ehrenhalt, Alan. 1983. "Campaign Committees: Focus of Party Revival." *Congressional Quarterly Weekly Report* 41:1345.

Eldersveld, Samuel J. 1964. *Political Parties: A Behavioral Analysis*. Chicago: Rand McNally.

Eldersveld, Samuel J. 1982. *Political Parties in American Society*. New York: Basic Books.

Everson, David H. 1982. "The Decline of Political Parties." In *The Communication Revolution in American Politics,* ed. Gerald Benjamin. New York: Academy of Political Science.

Fiorina, Morris. 1980. "The Decline of Collective Responsibility in American Politics." *Daedalus* 109:25–45.

Gelb, Joyce, and Marian Lief Palley. 1975. *Tradition and Change in American Party Politics*. New York: Crowell.

Goodman, William. 1980. *The Party System in America*. Englewood Cliffs, N.J.: Prentice-Hall.

Henderson, Gordon. 1976. *An Introduction to Political Parties*. New York: Harper and Row.

Huckshorn, Robert J. 1976. *Party Leadership in the States*. Amherst: University of Massachusetts Press.

Huckshorn, Robert J., and John F. Bibby. 1982. "State Parties in an Era of Political Change." In *The Future of American Political Parties,* ed. Joel Fleishman. Englewood Cliffs, N.J.: Prentice-Hall.

Janda, Kenneth. 1980. *Political Parties: A Cross-National Survey*. New York: Free Press.

Jewell, Malcolm E., and David M. Olson. 1982. *American State Political Parties and Elections*. Rev. ed. Homewood, Ill.: Dorsey.

Key, V. O., Jr. 1960. "The Politically Relevant in Surveys." *Public Opinion Quarterly* 24:54–61.

Key, V. O., Jr. 1964. *Politics, Parties, and Pressure Groups*. 5th ed. New York: Crowell.

Kirkpatrick, Evron M. 1971. "Toward a More Responsible Party System: Political Science, Policy Science, or Pseudo-Science?" *American Political Science Review* 65:965–90.

Kornberg, Allen, Joel Smith, and Harold D. Clarke. 1979. *Semi-Careers in Political Work: The Dilemma of Party Organizations*. Beverly Hills, Calif.: Sage.

Lawson, Kay. 1976. *The Comparative Study of Political Parties*. New York: St. Martin's Press.

Lindblom, Charles E. 1957. "In Praise of Political Science." *World Politics* 9:240–53.

Lindblom, Charles E. 1982. "The Market as Prison." *Journal of Politics* 44:324–36.

Lipset, Seymour M., ed. 1978. *Emerging Coalitions in American Politics*. San Francisco: Institute for Contemporary Studies.

March, James G., and Johan Olsen. 1976. *Ambiguity and Choice in Organization.* Bergen, Norway: Universitetsforlaget.

Mayhew, David R. 1986. *Placing Parties in American Politics.* Princeton: Princeton University Press.

Moe, Terry M. 1980. *The Organization of Interests.* Chicago: University of Chicago Press.

Nie, Norman, Sidney Verba, and John Petrocik. 1976. *The Changing American Voter.* Cambridge, Mass.: Harvard University Press.

Olson, Mancur. 1965. *The Logic of Collective Action.* Cambridge, Mass.: Harvard University Press.

Olson, Mancur. 1982. *The Rise and Decline of Nations.* New Haven: Yale University Press.

Pomper, Gerald M. 1977. "The Decline of Party in American Elections." *Political Science Quarterly* 92:21–41.

Pomper, Gerald M., ed. 1981. *Party Renewal in America.* New York: Praeger.

Rakove, Milton. 1975. *Don't Make No Waves . . . Don't Back No Losers.* Bloomington: Indiana University Press.

Roback, Thomas H. 1980. "Motivation for Activism among Republican Convention Delegates: Continuity and Change, 1972–1976." *Journal of Politics* 42:182–201.

Rohde, David, and Kenneth Shepsle. 1978. "Taking Stock of Congressional Research: The New Institutionalism." Paper presented at the annual meeting of the Midwest Political Science Association, Chicago.

Salisbury, Robert H. 1969. "An Exchange Theory of Interest Groups." *Midwest Journal of Political Science* 13:1–32.

Schattschneider, E. E. 1942. *Party Government.* New York: Rinehart.

Schattschneider, E. E. 1960. *The Semi-Sovereign People.* New York: Holt, Rinehart and Winston.

Schwartz, Mildred A. 1990. *The Party Network: The Robust Organization of Illinois Republicans.* Madison: University of Wisconsin Press.

Scott, Ruth K., and Ronald J. Hrebenar. 1979. *Parties in Crisis.* New York: Wiley.

Sills, David L. 1957. *The Volunteers: Means and Ends in a National Organization.* Glencoe, Ill.: Free Press.

Sorauf, Frank. 1976. *Party Politics in America.* 3d ed. Boston: Little, Brown.

Soule, John W., and Wilma E. McGrath. 1975. "A Comparative Study of Presidential Nominating Conventions: The Democrats of 1968 and 1972." *American Journal of Political Science* 19:501–17.

Sundquist, James L. 1982. "Party Decay and the Capacity to Govern." In *The Future of American Political Parties,* ed. Joel Fleishman. Englewood Cliffs, N.J.: Prentice-Hall.

Truman, David B. 1951. *The Governmental Process.* New York: Knopf.

Verba, Sidney, and Norman Nie. 1972. *Participation in America: Political Democracy and Social Equality.* New York: Harper and Row.

Walker, Jack L. 1983. "The Origins and Maintenance of Interest Groups in America." *American Political Science Review* 77:390–406.

Ware, Alan. 1979. *The Logic of Party Democracy.* New York: St. Martin's Press.

Wiggins, Charles W., and William L. Turk. 1970. "State Party Chairmen: A Profile." *Western Political Quarterly* 23:321–32.

Wildavsky, Aaron. 1965. "The Goldwater Phenomenon: Purists, Politicians, and the Two-Party System." *Review of Politics* 27:386–413.

Wilson, James Q. 1961. "The Economy of Patronage." *Journal of Political Economy* 69:369–80.

Wilson, James Q. 1962. *The Amateur Democrat.* Chicago: University of Chicago Press.

Wilson, James Q. 1973. *Political Organizations.* New York: Basic Books.

Wittman, Donald A. 1973. "Parties as Utility Maximizers." *American Political Science Review* 67:490–98.

Wittman, Donald A. 1983. "Candidate Motivation." *American Political Science Review* 77:142–57.

Wolf, Charles, Jr. 1979. "A Theory of Non-Market Failures." *Public Interest* 55:114–33.

Wright, William E. 1971. "Comparative Party Models: Rational-Efficient and Party Democracy." In *A Comparative Study of Party Organization,* ed. William E. Wright. Columbus, Ohio: Charles E. Merrill.

CHAPTER 2

Political Ambition: The Motive Force of Party Organization

In the preceding chapter I sought to demonstrate why the goal of winning office dominates parties in democracies. I concluded that the drive of individual office seekers was the motive force of party organization. This being the case, an adequate theory of party organization in democracies must derive from a more general theory about the relation between office drives and the behavior of office seekers or an ambition theory of politics. The relevance of political ambition for party organization should be obvious. All other human goals or desires can be achieved elsewhere. Only those desirous of political office find organization on its behalf essential. Only they must organize or join an existing political organization to achieve their goals. For the office driven more than any one else, the creation and maintenance of political organization is worth the effort. At the same time, as rational individuals, office seekers will put forth only as much effort as they believe is essential to realizing their own ambitions. They will only join in creating, shaping, and maintaining political organizations best suited to their purpose.

What guidance will they seek? To state the relationship between political ambition and party organization is to raise important questions about political ambitions that must be answered before we can deal with the nature of party organization in democracies. It is important to consider that ambition for elective office does not run freely throughout democratic citizenries. Political ambition is more than likely to carry with it the connotation of rampant ambition. Yet in democracies, ambition for elective office must be aroused as well as controlled. Running for elective office is more often than not time consuming and costly. Moreover, it exposes individuals to public scrutiny they are unlikely to face in other activities. Elective officeholders also continuously face the risk of having their careers cut short by the voters. But democracies depend for their survival on the existence of individuals willing to take such risks. Democracies, then, must both stimulate and direct political ambitions by their rules and institutions. In the process they stimulate and shape party organization. Thus, before we can discuss party organization, we must both clarify the concept of political ambition and examine the ways in which democracies stimulate and channel it.

Ambition is the heart of politics. Politics thrives on the hope of preferment and the drive for office. Yet in most studies of politicians, ambition for office is taken for granted or ignored.[1] Social scientists who find the psychological insights inspired by Freud or the economic and social insights inspired by Marx useful in explaining political behavior find the ambitious politician an oversimplification. For them, human motives are complex and they are modified by complex social and economic forces. The social scientist's rejection of self-interest as motive is reinforced by and, in turn, reinforces the widely held ethical position that politics ought not to revolve around personal ambitions. The intellectual's preference for political "leaders" motivated by ideology or principle is but a variant of the popular distrust of "politicians" because they are self-interested.

But the popular distrust is rooted in experience that the social scientist is unwise to ignore. In politics, the relation between motive and action is more obvious than in any other social endeavor. The paradox is that it is the simplicity of this relationship that is so often slighted in political analyses. Of all those whose actions are public, politicians leave the clearest tracks between their purpose and their behavior. Ambition sparks all human efforts to do more than subsist. But the place of ambition in the actions of the artist or saint presents us with more complex problems. The artist's desire for immortality on earth and the saint's for immortality in heaven make it unseemly for us to limit our discussion to the drive for immediate personal success. In politics, on the other hand, immediate personal success is so obviously the goal that the social scientist does well to give it primary consideration and surely errs in shunning it. This is true even when principle or doctrine is the declared motive of the politician, as the career of Lenin so well demonstrates. Lenin was no more willing to delay his accession to power for the perfect Marxist revolution than is the office seeker in the United States who polls the voters for policy positions to insure his election. This elementary relation between personal ambition and political action, even in the most doctrinaire political activists, is too often clouded by subtle explanations of political behavior.

In our concern with the complexity of human behavior, we should not forget that democratic political institutions work because they simplify politicians' motives, thereby making politicians' behavior understandable and predictable. Democracies become stable only when they are able to both arouse and control political ambitions. However complex the constitutional statement

---

1. Two studies that show a positive relationship between expectations or ambition and political behavior are MacRae 1958 and Krislov 1959. Namier (1965a and 1965b) has made the best use of political ambition as the focus for historical analysis in his studies of the development of parties in the British parliament.

of governmental powers, its effectiveness depends upon the definition of how individuals are to gain and hold office. In stating the rules of officeholding, a constitution states the outlets for political ambitions and how they are to be realized. If the explicit rules do not reflect the distribution of political influence within the society, they must be flexible enough to allow manipulation until they do. Thus in the United States, political parties rather than constitutional amendment or judicial decision were able to modify the role of the electoral college in the selection of the president, allowing an expanding electorate to have the greater say.

To slight the role of ambition in politics, then, or to treat it as a human failing to be suppressed, is to miss the central function of ambition in democratic polities. Thus in *Federalist Papers,* no. 51, Madison explains how the separation of powers, by allowing ambition to "counteract ambition," will make the proposed constitution effective. At the same time, it is essential to recognize that a democracy unable to kindle ambition for office is as much in danger of breaking down as one unable to restrain ambition. There is, of course, the delicate problem of balance. Politicians' ambitions must not so outrun the possibilities of fulfillment that they refuse to play the game. Students from Aristotle to Crane Brinton have noted that the gap between expectations and achievement is the essential factor in revolution. Nevertheless, within any given polity, political ambition does not run wild. Individuals must have their political ambitions excited as well as restrained. Representative government depends above all upon a supply of individuals with strong office drives. It must provide the refinements of power and status that attract as well as direct men's and women's aspirations. No more irresponsible government is imaginable than one of high-minded individuals unconcerned for their political futures. In democracies, the desire for election, and, more important, for reelection, provides the electorate with a powerful control over public officials.

In calling attention to the importance of ambition for political analysis I do not mean to imply that ambition as the motive for individual political action has been entirely neglected. There has been considerable concern for understanding why individuals have political ambitions. This theme runs throughout the work of Harold Lasswell (see, especially, 1948) and is the dominant question posed by George and George (1956) in their pioneering psychoanalytic biography of Woodrow Wilson. But the answer to the question of why individuals harbor political ambitions does not move us far toward understanding the consequences. Individuals are unlikely to obtain major political offices unless they want them. Their motives in wanting the jobs may run the gamut of human desires. But I would argue that no political system functions well if it relies upon chance to assure that individual motives will work for the public good. We need, therefore, a theory of politics that explicitly accepts the assumption that politicians respond primarily to their office goals, that is, an ambition theory of politics, rather than a theory that explains political ambitions.

More closely related to ambition theory is the work of Anthony Downs, which I referred to in the preceding chapter. The importance of ambition in politics is implicit in the Downsian definition of party I accepted as my starting point. Recall that the definition states a party is "a team seeking to control the governing apparatus by gaining office in a duly constituted election." This implies that the party is, above all, ambitious to govern. All its actions, including the adoption of policies, are seen as directed at achieving this goal.

The Downsian definition of party, however, provides us with a limited view of the role of ambition in politics. Its limitations arise from its assignment of ambition to the party rather than to individuals. Downs, therefore, oversimplifies the democratic process whose most important problems often occur when politicians do not act as teams. Even in Great Britain, where parties come closest to resembling the team model, the formulation of cohesive party policy can falter because of factional conflict arising from conflicting individual ambitions within the two major parties. In the United States, whose parties are rarely viewed as cohesive teams, differences in the parties can easily be traced to the varying relations of their officeholders to government. Governmental control means different things to a president, a congressional committee chairman, a state governor, and a state legislator. Thus, while I by no means wish to understate the importance of Downs's work in calling to our attention the central role of ambition in politics, it is also essential to recognize that it does not help us understand when and why office seekers and officeholders in democracies do or do not act cohesively. Such an understanding is essential to our understanding of party organization.

A more comprehensive view of the relation between ambition and politics must focus on the reasons for which office seekers and officeholders cooperate or not, form parties and party factions to serve their political ends. Parties, factions within parties, and relations between officeholders within the same party at different levels of government derive from strategic differences in individual ambitions and the electoral conditions that satisfy them. These differences also help explain specific overt political acts of a particular partisan officeholder, such as the policy proposals of a governor or the votes of a legislator. In the latter instance, others have tested the hypothesis that a legislator votes in response to the demands of the constituency that elected him. Ambition theory differs in asserting that the constituency to which the legislator is responding is not always the one from which he has been elected. In other words, in seeking to explain or predict a legislator's vote, it is as important to know what constituency the legislator aspires to serve as to know about the constituency he is now serving. The central assumption of ambition theory, therefore, that office seekers engage in political acts and make decisions appropriate to gaining office, requires us carefully to consider varying and alternative ambitions and varying and alternative strategies for their achievement.

We should, of course, acknowledge the problem of isolating political ambition. The politician ambitious for office is an abstraction, and a theory based on a partial view of what moves politicians cannot explain all of their behavior, even the specifically political. Politicians in the real world are no more single-mindedly driven by the desire for office than businessmen are directed solely by the profit motive or doctors by the urge to heal. The abstractions of the businessman and doctor guided by occupational aims are nevertheless useful, if only to discover when, in fact, other values intrude on their behavior. Still, the abstraction of the doctor or businessman does not always present simple answers to the problem of assigning motives. Thus we can never be sure whether the psychiatrist is charging high fees because he or she views it as an essential part of the therapy or because he or she wants the money. As an abstraction, the politician presents even more difficulties than the businessman or doctor in assigning motives, since politicians are always citizens as well as office seekers. The interests of the citizen must always play a part in the decisions of the politician. Thus we would expect the ambitious politician to restrain his or her use of an issue that might gain votes but erode the political system.

The problem of isolating political ambition in the real world is compounded by the partial nature of officeholding in politicians' careers in democracies. For one thing, the income of most public officials does not come solely from the offices they fill. Thus, despite considerable pressure to limit such income, members of Congress can supplement their congressional salaries with honoraria from businesses, trade associations, and unions, as well as with dividends from private investments. For a large share of elective officials in the United States, many state legislators, and most city councillors, an outside occupation is essential since their public office provides only partial support. If we expand the concept of income to include campaign contributions, the question of the office seeker's motive becomes even murkier. When individuals receive all their income from their occupation, it is easier to perceive them as motivated by abstract occupational objectives. But do the members of Congress who receive honoraria, dividends, and campaign contributions from corporations pursue the interests of their constituents or the corporations? Do lawyers who serve in part-time state legislatures represent their clients or their constituents? What ambitions guide the part-time mayor who owns a real estate agency or a mortuary?

Furthermore, not only do most elected officeholders garner their income, in part, from other sources while in office; elective office careers are also sporadic because of the prospect of long periods out of office. An official's current behavior in office, then, may have no relevance at all to his or her aspirations for future political office. Rather, it may bear entirely on his or her aspirations for employment with a major corporation or another interest group. In other words, more than most occupations, elective officeholding is intertwined with other occupations in the economic system. Most officeholders and candidates for office have another occupational base that also stimulates career ambitions.

While the difficulties of isolating ambitions for elective office from other motives should warn us of the pitfalls in a theory of ambitions, they should not close our minds to the utility of such a theory. Of all the motives that can drive politicians, their office drives are the ones the observer can discern with some assurance. Political style may indeed preclude public expressions of office ambitions. Custom may, at the very least, dictate the propriety of expressing reluctance to seek elective office. Nevertheless, a time comes when individuals interested in office must make overt their intentions to run for office. In the United States, they must enter their names in primaries, permit their names to be placed before a convention, or do whatever else is required to place themselves before the voters. Elective offices are not prizes handed out by committees, prizes which the recipients can graciously appear not to have sought. True those who openly try for office do not exhaust the ranks of the ambitious. Nor can the observer say much about the intensity of one individual's ambitions compared with another's. Surely individuals sometimes make overt efforts for an office they do not expect to win and perhaps do not wish to win. Yet it is not difficult to single out such individuals by assessing their chances, thereby making place in a theory of political ambition for mock candidates. The fact remains that the attainment of office is the one observable goal we have in democratic politics. Because democracy itself relies on the observability of office goals, it provides a theoretical base for the understanding of democratic politics.

Since it is impossible to assign specific ambitions to individuals except at the time they overtly seek office, a theory of ambition requires reasonable assumptions about when such ambitions occur. The most reasonable assumption is that ambition for office, like most other ambitions, arises within a specific situation. Ambition for office is, in other words, a response to the possibilities that lie before politicians. Thus, individuals in offices whose previous occupants have gone on to other offices are more likely to aspire to other offices than individuals holding offices whose previous occupants went nowhere. This assumption has the virtue of reinforcing itself, since it is made not only by the ambitious politician but also by the political observer. In the United States, the small band of governors from sizeable and competitive states and the conspicuous members of the Senate who together compose the presidential "hopefuls" are hopeful because the presidential ambitions aroused by their positions are reinforced by the observation of those who follow politics that their ambitions are realistic. Each lesser office has its own band of hopefuls whose hope, to a large extent, rests upon the expectations of the observant public. Such expectations influence politicians because, ultimately, public opinion plays a major role in defining their success or failure. A New York governor who does not win the presidency or at least a presidential nomination has failed in a way his counterparts from Mississippi and South Dakota cannot. Politics is, after all, a game of advancement, and elective politicians succeed only if they advance as far as their situation permits.

Although ambition theory makes assumptions about the circumstances that are likely to arouse ambition for office, it does not assume that office goals are constant in their intensity and direction for the same individual or for other individuals in similar positions. As individuals do or do not advance in their political careers, possibilities change, and if individuals are reasonable, so will their ambitions change. The hopes that lie in the hearts of young men and women running for their first offices are usually kept secret. Some are undoubtedly already thinking about their first presidential inaugural address, while others give no thought to a long-term political career. But as a political career develops, success will encourage ambition and failure will dampen it. The reasonable political aspirations of the thirty-year-old state legislator become unrealistic if they are harbored by his or her seventy-year-old colleague. All those ambitious for office in democracies face the continuous problem of keeping their ambitions and their possibilities constantly aligned. The independent influence of ambition upon opportunity occurs early in the career of democratic politicians. Once politicians move on, both in office and in age, the possibilities modify their ambitions.

One of the most important ways in which ambitions for office vary is in their direction. In the United States, for example, the republic provides a variety of office goals, including the goal of leaving office. Various goals mean that ambitions for office can take a variety of directions. Thus, the principal limitation in the Downsian view of the party as a cohesive team derives from its consideration of only one direction for ambition, the horizontal direction to govern.

Ambition theory, on the other hand, posits three directions that ambitions for office can take. Ambitions can be *discrete*. The office seeker wants a particular office for its specified term and then chooses to withdraw. As a candidate, the pressures are simply those imposed by the immediate objective. If the candidate is an incumbent, he or she is free of all the tensions imposed by office ambitions. In the United States, this type of ambition is not uncommon for many local offices (Prewitt 1970a), for state legislatures (Hain

1974a), and for higher offices as well. Indeed, the Twenty-Second Amendment to the Constitution prescribes this ambition for presidents once they have been reelected.

Ambitions for office can also be *static*. The individual seeks to make a long-term career out of a particular office. In this case, the principal pressures always derive from the same constituency. How widespread such ambitions are we cannot tell, for the possibilities of making a career of one office vary. Nevertheless, it is certainly a clear goal of many U.S. representatives and senators.

Finally, ambitions for office can be *progressive*. The individual aspires to an office more important than the one now held or sought. In this instance, the office seeker is under tension not only from the current constituency but also from that of the office to which he or she aspires. A likely assumption is that in this instance, progressive ambitions or the pressures arising from the office to which the office seeker aspires will dominate. Such pressures will recede only if the chances for the higher office recede.

Ambition theory also assumes that, over a lifetime, the direction of any one office seeker's ambitions may well vary. In the United States, a city councillor may start with discrete ambitions but find politics so exciting that his or her ambitions become static or progressive. Later failure may alter the direction of ambition once again. Many members of Congress retire voluntarily after lengthy terms in office. In their last terms, then, the direction of their ambitions has shifted from static to discrete. Ambition theory, however, is not as much concerned with predicting what the office seeker's ambitions will be over an entire career as with inferring the office seeker's current ambitions and predicting from them his or her political behavior. This does not mean that the office seeker's current ambitions preclude a combination of short-term and long-term goals. Rather, it is a matter of assigning relative weights to each type of ambition. A crucial aspect of ambition theory, therefore, is the means it provides for allowing us to make inferences about the direction of office seekers' ambitions.

At the same time, ambition theory also requires us to isolate the two aspects of a democracy that give direction to individuals' office ambitions: its structure of political opportunities and its structure of electoral competition. Only after we have defined these aspects of a democracy can we hope to understand the party organizations that thrive there.

In a democracy, the structure of political opportunities consists of all the available elective offices as well as the rules and customs that define the opportunities for their achievement. The structure of political opportunities, therefore, allows office seekers to know the number of political opportunities available to them and to discern the routes for office advancement. In a democracy such as the United States, where there are a great many independent elective offices with great disparities in status, bringing order to the political opportunities open to office seekers is by no means an easy task. Nevertheless, it is the task that I shall pursue in the next two chapters. For only by so doing can we infer the direction of political ambitions that is essential to our understanding of party organization. Once having laid out a structure of political opportunities as complex as that of the United States, we should face fewer problems with democracies whose office structures are simpler, such as that of a unitary parliamentary democracy.

Politicians temper their political ambitions not only according to the structure of political opportunities but also according to the structure of electoral competition. The structure of electoral competition directs office seekers' ambitions by defining the chances office seekers have of winning election to the offices set down by the structure of political opportunities. Electoral rules help define the structure of electoral competition. These are the rules that define the office constituency, access to the ballot, the ballot's format, and the criteria for winning elections. Thus they help define the degree of competition for a particular office by facilitating or not the voters' willingness to vote, by facilitating or not the voters' willingness to remain loyal to a partisan label. In chapter 5 I shall discuss more fully the structure of electoral competition and the way in which it guides the ambitions of office seekers.[2]

---

2. Since I published *Ambition and Politics* in 1966, a number of studies have tested and expanded the propositions about the impact of ambition on politics. Some of the propositions have been incorporated into more formal theory by Black 1970 and 1972; and Levine and Hyde 1977. The inception of ambition has been examined by Fishel (1971); Fowler (1979); Carlson and Hyde (1979); Kazee (1980); Fowler and McClure (1989). Applications to historical situations appear in Piereson 1973; and Kernell 1976 and 1977.

The three directions to ambition have also been examined further. Discrete and static ambitions have been studied by Frantzich 1978a and 1978b; Hibbing 1982a, 1982b, 1982c; Brace 1985. Mayhew (1974) sets forth the proposition that most congressional activity derives from static ambitions. Progressive ambitions have been examined by Engstrom 1971; Dutton 1975; Codispoti 1982; Brace 1984. The effects of the three types of ambition on the behavior of officeholders have been studied by Prewitt and Nowlin 1969; Soule 1969; Prewitt 1970a; Frost 1972; Atkinson 1978; Van der Slik and Pernacciaro 1979; Hibbing 1986. Rohde (1979) has related the idea of risk taking to officeholders' political ambitions and devised means for isolating the risk takers among officeholders. This concept has been further explored by Hain, Roeder, and Avalos 1981; and Abramson, Aldrich, and Rohde 1987. The effects of the political life cycle on political ambition have been examined by Hain 1974b; Schlesinger and Schlesinger 1981; and Loomis 1984a.

Many have examined aspects of the structure of political opportunities. Local councils, state legislatures, and state politics have been further explored as aspects of the structure. See Black 1970; Prewitt 1970b; Hain 1974a and 1976; Hain and Piereson 1975; Tobin 1975; Tobin and Keynes 1975; Northrop and Dutton 1978; Keynes, Tobin, and Danziger 1979; Robeck 1982; Squire 1988a and 1988b; Schwartz 1990.

Considerable attention has been paid to Congress as the core unit of the national structure of political opportunities. See Mezey 1970; Bullock 1972; Fishel 1973; Peabody, Ornstein, and

REFERENCES

Abramson, Paul, John H. Aldrich, and David W. Rohde. 1987. "Progressive Ambitions among United States Senators: 1972–1988." *Journal of Politics* 49:3–35.

Atkinson, Michael. 1978. "Policy Interests of Provincial Backbenchers and the Effects of Political Ambition." *Legislative Studies Quarterly* 3:629–45.

Black, Gordon. 1970. "A Theory of Professionalization in Politics." *American Political Science Review* 64:865–78.

Black, Gordon. 1972. "A Theory of Political Ambition: Career Choices and the Role of Structural Incentives." *American Political Science Review* 66:144–59.

Brace, Paul. 1984. "Progressive Ambition in the House: A Probabilistic Approach." *Journal of Politics* 46:556–71.

Brace, Paul. 1985. "A Probabilistic Approach to Retirement from the U.S. Congress." *Legislative Studies Quarterly* 10:107–24.

Budge, Ian, and Dennis Farlie. 1975. "Political Recruitment and Drop-out: Predictive Success of Background Characteristics over Five British Localities." *British Journal of Political Science* 5:33–68.

Bullock, Charles S., III. 1972. "House Careerists: Changing Patterns of Longevity and Attrition." *American Political Science Review* 66:1295–1305.

Bullock, Charles S., III, and P. L. F. Heys. 1972. "Recruitment of Women for Congress: A Research Note." *Western Political Quarterly* 25:416–23.

Bunce, Valerie J. 1980. "The Succession Connection: Policy Cycles and Political Change in the Soviet Union and Eastern Europe." *American Political Science Review* 74:966–90.

Canon, David T. 1990. *Actors, Athletes, and Astronauts: Political Amateurs in the United States Congress.* Chicago: University of Chicago Press.

Carlson, James M., and Mark S. Hyde. 1979. "The Party Activist as Officeseeker." Paper presented at the annual meeting of the American Political Science Association, Washington, D.C.

Ciboski, Kenneth. 1974. "Ambition Theory and Candidate Members of the Soviet Politburo." *Journal of Politics* 36:172–83.

Rohde 1976; Jacobson and Kernell 1981; Salisbury and Shepsle 1981; Loomis 1984b; Canon 1990. Studies of executives as part of the structure of political opportunity have been done by Swinerton 1968; Kirkpatrick 1976; Sabato 1978; Murphy 1980; Cohen 1986.

The expanding role in politics for both women and blacks has led to studies of their special relationship to the structure of political opportunities. See Jennings and Thomas 1968; Bullock and Heys 1972; Kirkpatrick 1974, 1976; Diamond 1977; Sapiro and Farah 1980; Stone 1980; Deber 1982; Sapiro 1982.

Concepts from *Ambition and Politics* have also been applied to countries outside the United States. Among the democracies, see Canada: Clarke and Price 1980; Gibbins 1982; France: Schlesinger and Schlesinger 1990; Greece: Legg 1969; Israel: Pomper 1975; Netherlands: Irwin, Budge, and Farlie 1979; United Kingdom: Budge and Farlie 1975; Macdonald 1987; United Kingdom and West Germany: Frankland 1977. For the Soviet Union and Eastern Europe, see Ciboski 1974; and Bunce 1980; for Japan, see Kuroda 1988.

Beyond politics, Press and VerBurg (1988) have examined ambition and opportunities as the central influences on the careers of journalists.

Clarke, Harold D., and Richard G. Price. 1980. "Freshman MPs' Job Images: The Effects of Incumbency, Ambition, and Position." *Canadian Journal of Political Science* 13:487–510.

Cohen, Jeffrey E. 1986. "On the Tenure of Appointive Political Executives: The American Cabinet, 1952–1984." *American Journal of Political Science* 30:507–16.

Codispoti, Frank. 1982. "American Governors and Progressive Ambition: An Analysis of Opportunities to Run for the Senate." Ph.D. diss., Michigan State University.

Deber, Raisa B. 1982. "'The Fault, Dear Brutus': Women as Congressional Candidates in Pennsylvania." *Journal of Politics* 44:463–79.

Diamond, Irene. 1977. *Sex Roles in the State House.* New Haven: Yale University Press.

Dutton, William. 1975 "The Political Ambitions of Local Legislators: A Comparative Perspective." *Polity* 8:504–22.

Engstrom, Richard L. 1971. "Political Ambitions and the Prosecutorial Office." *Journal of Politics* 33:190–94.

Fishel, Jeff. 1971. "Ambition and the Political Vocation." *Journal of Politics* 33:25–56.

Fishel, Jeff. 1973. *Party and Opposition.* New York: David McKay.

Fowler, Linda L. 1979. "The Electoral Lottery: Decisions to Run for Congress." *Public Choice* 34:399–418.

Fowler, Linda L., and Robert D. McClure. 1989. *Political Ambition: Who Decides to Run for Congress.* New Haven: Yale University Press.

Frankland, E. Gene. 1977. "Parliamentary Career Achievement in Britain and West Germany: A Comparative Analysis." *Legislative Studies Quarterly* 2:137–54.

Frantzich, Stephen E. 1978a. "Opting Out: Retirement from the House of Representatives." *American Politics Quarterly* 6:251–73.

Frantzich, Stephen E. 1978b. "De-recruitment: The Other Side of the Congressional Equation." *Western Political Quarterly* 31:105–26.

Frost, Murray. 1972. "Senatorial Ambition and Legislative Behavior." Ph.D. diss., Michigan State University.

George, Alexander L., and Juliette George. 1956. *Woodrow Wilson and Colonel House: A Personality Study.* New York: Day.

Gibbins, Roger. 1982. *Regionalism: Territorial Politics in Canada and the United States.* Toronto: Butterworths.

Hain, Paul. 1974a. "Political Ambition and Advancement: The Effects of District Size and Partisan Competition." Paper presented at the annual meeting of the Western Political Science Association, Denver.

Hain, Paul. 1974b. "Age, Ambition, and Political Careers." *Western Political Quarterly* 27:265–74.

Hain, Paul L. 1976. "Constituency Characteristics, Political Ambition, and Advancement." *American Politics Quarterly* 4:47–62.

Hain, Paul L., and James E. Piereson. 1975. "Lawyers and Politics Revisited: Structural Advantages of Lawyer-Politicians." *American Journal of Political Science* 19:41–51.

Hain, Paul, Philip G. Roeder, and Manuel Avalos. 1981. "Risk and Progressive Candidacies: An Extension of Rohde's Model." *American Journal of Political Science* 25:188–92.

Hibbing, John R. 1982a. "Voluntary Retirement from the House: The Costs of Congressional Service." *Legislative Studies Quarterly* 7:57–74.

Hibbing, John R. 1982b. "Voluntary Retirement from the U.S. House of Representatives: Who Quits?" *American Journal of Political Science* 26:467–84.

Hibbing, John R. 1982c. "Voluntary Retirements from the House in the Twentieth Century." *Journal of Politics* 44:1020–34.

Hibbing, John R. 1986. "Ambition in the House: Behavioral Consequences of Higher Office Goals among U.S. Representatives." *American Journal of Political Science* 30:651–65.

Irwin, Galen, Ian Budge, and Dennis Farlie. 1979. "Social Background vs. Motivational Determinants of Legislative Careers in the Netherlands." *Legislative Studies Quarterly* 4:447–65.

Jacobson, Gary C., and Samuel Kernell. 1981. *Strategy and Choice in Congressional Elections.* New Haven: Yale University Press.

Jennings, M. Kent, and Norman Thomas. 1968. "Men and Women in Party Elites: Social Roles and Political Resources." *Midwest Journal of Political Science* 12:469–92.

Kazee, Thomas A. 1980. "The Decision to Run for the U.S. Congress: Challengers' Attitudes in the 1970s." *Legislative Studies Quarterly* 5:79–100.

Kernell, Samuel. 1976. "Ambition and Politics: An Exploratory Study of Political Careers of Nineteenth-Century Congressmen." Paper presented at the annual meeting of the American Political Science Association, Chicago.

Kernell, Samuel. 1977. "Toward Understanding Congressional Careers: Ambition, Competition, and Rotation." *American Journal of Political Science* 21:669–93.

Keynes, Edward W., Richard J. Tobin, and Robert Danziger. 1979. "Institutional Effects in Elite Recruitment: The Case of State Nominating Systems." *American Politics Quarterly* 7:283–302.

Kirkpatrick, Jeane. 1974. *Political Woman.* New York: Basic Books.

Kirkpatrick, Jeane. 1976. *The New Presidential Elite: Men and Women in National Politics.* New York: Sage.

Krislov, Samuel. 1959. "Constituency versus Constitutionalism: The Desegregation Issue and Tensions and Aspirations of Southern Attorneys General." *Midwest Journal of Political Science* 3:75–92.

Kuroda, Yasuma. 1988. "Leadership Recruitment Patterns in the Japanese House of Representatives: General Elections 1–30 (1890–1963)." *International Political Science Review* 9:119–30.

Lasswell, Harold. 1948. *Power and Personality.* New York: Norton.

Legg, Keith. 1969. "Political Recruitment and Political Crises: The Case of Greece." *Comparative Political Studies* 1:527–54.

Levine, Martin D., and Mark S. Hyde. 1977. "Incumbency and the Theory of Political Ambitions: A Rational Choice Model." *Journal of Politics* 39:959–83.

Loomis, Burdett. 1984a. "On the Knife's Edge: Public Officials and the Life Cycle." *PS* 17:536–48.

Loomis, Burdett A. 1984b. "Congressional Careers and Party Leadership in the Contemporary House of Representatives." *American Journal of Political Science* 28:180–202.

Macdonald, Stuart Elaine. 1987. "Political Ambition in Britain: A Dynamic Analysis of Parliamentary Careers." Ph.D. diss., University of Michigan.

MacRae, Duncan, Jr. 1958. *Dimensions of Congressional Voting.* Berkeley: University of California Press.

Mayhew, David R. 1974. *Congress: The Electoral Connection.* New Haven: Yale University Press.

Mezey, Michael. 1970. "Ambition Theory and the Office of Congressman." *Journal of Politics* 32:563–79.

Murphy, Russell D. 1980. "Whither the Mayors? A Note on Mayoral Careers." *Journal of Politics* 42:277–90.

Namier, Lewis. 1965a. *Personalities and Powers.* New York: Harper.

Namier, Lewis. 1965b. *The Structure of Politics at the Accession of George III.* 2d ed. London: Macmillan.

Northrop, Alan, and William H. Dutton. 1978. "Municipal Reform and Group Differences." *American Journal of Political Science* 22:691–711.

Peabody, Robert L., Norman J. Ornstein, and David W. Rohde. 1976. "The United States Senate as Presidential Incubator: Many are Called but Few are Chosen." *Political Science Quarterly* 91:237–58.

Piereson, James. 1973. "Career Perspectives and Institutional Change in the United States: The Case of the Federalists and Anti-Federalists." Ph.D. diss., Michigan State University.

Pomper, Gerald M. 1975. "Ambition in Israel: A Comparative Extension of Theory and Data." *Western Political Quarterly* 28:712–32.

Press, Charles, and Kenneth VerBurg. 1988. *American Politicians and Journalists.* Glenview, Ill.: Scott Foresman.

Prewitt, Kenneth. 1970a. "Political Ambitions, Volunteerism, and Electoral Accountability." *American Political Science Review* 64:5–17.

Prewitt, Kenneth. 1970b. *The Recruitment of Political Leaders: A Study of Citizen-Politicians.* Indianapolis: Bobbs-Merrill.

Prewitt, Kenneth, and William Nowlin. 1969. "Political Ambitions and the Behavior of Incumbent Politicians." *Western Political Quarterly* 22:298–308.

Robeck, Bruce W. 1982. "State Legislator Candidacies for the U.S. House: Prospects for Success." *Legislative Studies Quarterly* 7:507–14.

Rohde, David W. 1979. "Risk-Bearing and Progressive Ambition: The Case of Members of the United States House of Representatives." *American Journal of Political Science* 23:1–26.

Sabato, Larry. 1978. *Goodby to Goodtime Charlie: The American Governor Transformed, 1950–1975.* Lexington, Mass.: Lexington Books.

Salisbury, Robert H., and Kenneth Shepsle. 1981. "Congressional Staff Turnover and the Ties-That-Bind." *American Political Science Review* 75:381–96.

Sapiro, Virginia. 1982. "Private Costs of Public Commitments or Public Costs of Private Commitments? Family Roles versus Political Ambition." *American Journal of Political Science* 26:265–79.

Sapiro, Virginia, and Barbara G. Farah. 1980. "New Pride and Old Prejudice: Political Ambition and Role Orientation Among Female Partisan Elites." *Women and Politics* 1:13–36.

Schlesinger, Joseph A., and Mildred Schlesinger. 1981. "Aging and the Opportunities for Elective Office." In *Aging: Social Change*, ed. James G. March. New York: Academic Press.

Schlesinger, Joseph A., and Mildred Schlesinger. 1990. "The Reaffirmation of a Multiparty System in France." *American Political Science Review* 84:1077–1101.

Schwartz, Mildred A. 1990. *The Party Network: The Robust Organization of Illinois Republicans.* Madison: University of Wisconsin Press.

Soule, John W. 1969. "Future Political Ambitions and the Behavior of Incumbent State Legislators." *Midwest Journal of Political Science* 13:439–54.

Squire, Peverill. 1988a. "Career Opportunities and Membership Stability in Legislatures." *Legislative Studies Quarterly* 13:65–82.

Squire, Peverill. 1988b. "Member Career Opportunities and the Internal Organization of Legislatures." *Journal of Politics* 50:726–44.

Stone, Pauline Terrelonge. 1980. "Ambition Theory and the Black Politician." *Western Political Quarterly* 33:94–107.

Swinerton, E. Nelson. 1968. "Ambition and American State Executives." *Midwest Journal of Political Science* 12:538–49.

Tobin, Richard J. 1975. "The Influence of Nominating Systems on the Political Experiences of State Legislators." *Western Political Quarterly* 28:553–66.

Tobin, Richard J., and Edward W. Keynes. 1975. "Institutional Differences in the Recruitment Process: A Four State Study." *American Journal of Political Science* 19:667–82.

Van der Slik, Jack, and Samuel J. Pernacciaro. 1979. "Office Ambitions and Voting Behavior in the U.S. Senate: A Longitudinal Study." *American Politics Quarterly* 7:198–223.

CHAPTER 3

The Structure of Political Opportunities

Concern with the impact of ambition for office on party organization leads to an examination of those factors in a democracy that excite and give direction to political ambition. One set of factors is the structure of political opportunities. The structure derives from the offices elected in democracies and the rules and customs that define the opportunities for attaining these offices. Therefore, the structure can be observed empirically and constructed from data on elective office careers. The structure of political opportunities does not reveal all the opportunities open to the politically ambitious. Certainly we should distinguish between social and political opportunities. Abundant evidence exists, for example, that all citizens do not have an equal chance at public office in the United States. In the United States as elsewhere, political advantage reflects social and economic advantages (Schlesinger 1966, 11–12). Nevertheless a structure of political opportunities independent of the social structure exists. Perhaps, as many assert, only millionaires can become presidents of the United States. Yet only millionaires in strategic political positions can hope to turn the trick. In the game of politics, political as well as social opportunity determines the players.

While the compilation of data on political careers has long been attractive to social scientists, such compilations have yielded few insights about political behavior. A wealth of accumulated data exists on the backgrounds of public officeholders in all democracies. For the United States, we can easily acquire data on the careers of presidents, cabinet members, Supreme Court judges, senators, governors, and state legislators (see Schlesinger 1966, 6, 12–13). Yet despite the industry that has gone into the accumulation of these data, the accumulation has yielded no predictive propositions. This failing is due to the lack of a useful political theory. Theory there is, but it is social or psychological in orientation. In the literature on political careers, therefore, we can find answers to questions about social stratification and social groups, as well as examples of psychopathology. But inferences drawn from the class, group, or personalities of officeholders about their political behavior are faulty. The social, occupational, and personality traits of members of the U.S. Congress are not accurate guides to their voting records. When, for example, Matthews (1960) showed that former U.S. representatives adjusted to the norms and folkways of the Senate more rapidly than governors, his finding was interesting in relation to the Senate as a social, rather than as a political, entity. What he failed to demonstrate was that former governors voted differently from former representatives or that they were barred from eventual positions of leadership in the Senate.

Analyses such as Matthews are wanting because background data have tended to draw political scientists away from their political perspective. Since the data are about officeholders' pasts, political scientists are drawn to the assumption that officeholders are creatures of their past. There is certainly truth in this assumption. It would be absurd to deny that the social composition of legislatures affects their behavior, that the previous experiences of officeholders influence the way in which they go about their business, or that their personalities help determine their reactions to political events. But to seek explanations of political behavior entirely in this manner is to see politics as entirely the product of class, social networks, or personality. It is to test social and psychological, rather than political, theories. Yet social and psychological theories, because they are incapable of explaining or predicting behavior within a limited institutional framework, cannot help us explain such basic political acts as the way a legislator votes.

Ambition theory, on the other hand, gives us a political perspective on data about political careers. Once we accept the central place of ambition in politics, the officeholder's biography becomes a focused story about political ambitions, allowing us to determine the relationship between subsequent political office and earlier political behavior. The biographies of elective officeholders reveal their political ambitions by revealing their overt moves toward gaining public office. Certainly we can say that whatever other political ambitions an individual might harbor, he or she was ambitious for the offices sought publicly. Examining office careers from the perspective of ambition forces us to consider where elective officeholders went as well as where they came from. Thus we realize that when U.S. representatives become senators, the interesting questions do not revolve entirely around the impact of their House experience upon their senatorial behavior. Also of considerable interest is the effect of their ambitions to become senators upon their behavior in the lower house.

When we collect the political biographies of many officeholders in a democracy with ambition theory in mind, we can observe whether there is an overall order to office careers. The collective political biographies of officeholders reveal the relevant rules, customs, and expectations for achieving public office. The perspective of ambition theory allows us to take such mundane data as the tenure and turnover of officeholders, office succession, and the ages of elective officials and construct the "structure of political opportunities." This structure has both size and shape. The size derives from the number of offices and the frequency with which they become available to new personnel (or turnover in office). The shape derives from patterns of movement from office to office.

The Size of the Structure of Political Opportunities

The structure of political opportunities in the United States is very large. It consists of thousands of elective offices at all levels of government. Federalism, bicameral legislatures, and a tradition of electing many executive and judicial officers, as well as special boards and commissions at the state and local levels, provide a plethora of positions to stimulate political ambitions. Short terms of office, restraints on reelection, as well as the ingrained tradition, in the United States, that bans dual officeholding further expand the number of opportunities.

The real, as distinct from the formal, size of the structure of political opportunities, however, is defined by the actual turnover of personnel in office. Both the willingness and the ability of incumbents to gain reelection therefore affect the real size of the structure. In the twentieth century in the United States, legislative office at the federal level, and increasingly at the state level, has had a low turnover in personnel. Thus, regardless of the legal terms of office, the opportunities for these offices have been relatively low. In contrast, executive posts characteristically have had a high turnover, whether mandated by law or not; the opportunities for these offices have been relatively more numerous.

The size of the structure of opportunities is also related to the ratio between offices and population. During the nineteenth century, as the United States expanded and its population grew, the tendency was to increase the number of elective offices in various ways. In the twentieth century, the number of elective officials stabilized or in some instances declined, lowering per capita opportunities. Thus in 1910, when the House of Representatives reached and fixed its present size of 435 members, each member represented, on average, a little over 200,000 people; by 1990, each member represented over 560,000 people. By different means, the number of opportunities for the key offices of governor and state legislator has also been reduced. This has been accomplished by the post–World War II practice of extending governors' terms to four years, as well as the terms of some state legislative positions.

Measuring the Size of the Structure
of Political Opportunities

In measuring the size of the structure of political opportunities, we must first calculate the opportunities for particular offices, then an aggregate figure for a number of key offices in a state or in the nation at large. We can readily measure the opportunities for any single office by measuring the rate of change in its personnel. In trying to take the real measure of opportunity for a particular office, however, we run into a time problem. When office seekers contemplate their chances of becoming governor, senator, or president, they assess their chances within a specific time period, the span of their own political life. But political time runs by two calendars: the normal chronology of months and years and the electoral calendar that measures time in two-, four-, and six-year office terms. Is political time, then, the same in a state where the term of office for governor is four years, as it is where the term is only two years? To the extent that the passage of time derives from the regular occurrence of events, political time passes twice as quickly in states with biennial elections, thereby enhancing the perception of opportunity. Moreover, expressions such as *three-term governor* and *six-term congressman* convey a sense of opportunity independent of the length of the office term. The perception of opportunity is related as much to the number of times officeholders can be reelected as it is to the number of years they can spend in office. Thus, the perception of opportunity for office emerges from a combination of chronological and electoral time.

Opportunities for a particular office are also affected by prevalent attitudes about its proper tenure. Throughout most of the history of the United States, the office of governor has been one of very high turnover. Because the term of office for governors has been increasing over the years, their tenure has also increased. But the actual number of years governors spend in office has not increased at the same rate as the length of their terms. Thus, the governors of Massachusetts had a one-year term until 1920, and the typical governor could expect to be elected to three terms. With the adoption of a two-year term, the typical governor could expect to be reelected only once, as in most states with two-year terms. The adoption of a four-year term increased real tenure for the governor but did not double it.

The Opportunity Rate

To measure the opportunities for a particular office we must take into account both electoral and chronological time. We can measure electoral time in terms of the frequency with which people are elected to a particular office or the frequency of personnel change according to the electoral timetable. This is the *personnel turnover rate*. When offices have the same terms, their rates are comparable. Where the terms of office differ, we need a common denominator. The personnel turnover rate must be translated into chronological time. By multiplying the personnel turnover rate by the number of elections in a

TABLE 3.1. Opportunities to Become a Governor, Senator, or U.S. Representative in the United States, 1914–58

Office	No. of Offices	A No. of Elections (1914–58)	B No. of Personnel Changes (1914–58)	C Personnel Turnover Rate (B/A)	D No. of Elections in 12 years	E Opportunity Rate (C × D)
Governor	48	822	548	.667	204	136.07
U.S. Senate	96	819	399[a]	.487	192	93.50
U.S. House	435	9,509[b]	2,228	.234	2,610	610.74

Source: Schlesinger 1966, 40.

[a]Personnel changes among senators were determined according to each senatorial seat in a state.

[b]The reapportionment of congressional seats every 10 years—ignored in 1920—makes impossible the tracing of turnover continuously for all congressional seats. Where it was possible, a seat was traced through a reapportionment, but where the district lines were seriously reordered, the count of electoral turnover started over with the new apportionment. Therefore, the figure stated above does not include all congressional elections between 1914 and 1958.

given time period we obtain the *rate of opportunities,* or the frequency with which a new person wins an office in the given time period.[1]

I have measured the opportunity rates for the offices of governor, senator, and U.S. representatives for 1914 through 1958 (see table 3.1). I have chosen twelve years as the time period since it is the lowest common multiple of two, four, and six, the standard office terms in the United States. Twelve years is also a sufficiently long period, given the rapid turnover of elected officials in the United States, to warrant being called a political generation. Since most of the elective offices are in the states and localities, my initial measurement of the structure of political opportunities rests on measures of the states. These in turn feed into the national structure, dependent upon the presidency and vice presidency in measurable ways.

What were the relative chances of becoming a governor, senator, or U.S.

---

1. The formula for calculating the political opportunity rate is as follows. For any office

political opportunity rate = personnel turnover rate × potential turnover in 12 years

or

$$\frac{\text{no. of elections with change in personnel, 1914–58}}{\text{no. of elections, 1914–58}} \times \text{no. of elections in 12 years}$$

or

the average real turnover in personnel × constitutional maximum turnover.

representative during these years? The personnel turnover rates (table 3.1, col. C) show that the turnover rate for governors was about three times that for representatives. In other words, two-thirds of the elections for governors placed a new person in office, while that was true for less than one-quarter of the elections for representatives. Senators ranged somewhere in between, with a turnover rate of close to 50 percent (.487). Translated into chances per twelve-year generation, the opportunity rates (table 3.1, col. E) show that, based on the 1914–58 experience, there were 610.7 chances of becoming one of 435 congressmen and 93.5 chances of becoming one of 96 senators. Although there were twice as many senators as governors, the real chances of becoming a governor were greater, 136.07 in a twelve-year generation.

The Size of the Opportunity Structure and Political Ambitions

We should expect varied opportunity rates to excite and direct political ambitions in different ways. The high rate for governors, an inherently desirable office, could be expected to stimulate ambition among a relatively broad range of individuals frequently. At the same time, since the high rate meant the office could not be held for long, aspirants for the governorship would also have to think of where they would go next. Thus, the opportunity rate for the governorship could be expected to foster progressive ambitions. On the other hand, we would expect the low opportunity rate for members of Congress to reduce the number of aspirants. At the same time, the low rate meant aspirants could project a long-term career, and the opportunity rate could be expected to foster static ambitions.

To the extent that political ambitions are generalized, however, frustration in one direction may well lead to the transfer of energies to other more accessible outlets. It is, therefore, useful to combine the opportunity rates for many offices to determine how good opportunities are in general for the politically ambitious, or, in other words, to take the size of the national structure of political opportunities. Since all elective offices in the United States, except for the presidency and vice presidency, emerge from the individual states, we must combine their rates for higher offices. Senators and representatives, governors, and a variety of other state elective officials constitute the higher reaches of each state's structure of political opportunities. Certainly the offices are not interchangeable; many who would run for governor or senator would never run for state auditor or secretary of state. The reverse situation is, however, highly unlikely. Since the direction of ambition is upward, the combination of these offices in all probability reflects the sense of what is available to those in the lower reaches of the structure, state legislators, local officials, and district attorneys.

Based on the experience from 1914 through 1958, I have listed the combined opportunity rates for eight offices in each state in table 3.2. The offices are U.S. senator and representative and the statewide elective offices of governor, lieutenant governor, attorney general, secretary of state, treasurer, and auditor. The figures reflect variations from state to state in the number of federal representatives and statewide elective offices, as well as differences in the length of term for statewide office. Large states, because they had more representatives, had larger opportunity structures in general. On the other hand, when I adjusted for population, the chances of becoming someone of political importance were significantly greater in small states (see table 3.3). A political hopeful in Delaware had about twenty times as much chance of winning an important political office as an office seeker in the large states of New York and California. Note, however, that in neither case were the rankings simply a reflection of the size of a state's population. They were also greatly affected by variations in personnel turnover rates. In sum, in the first six decades of the twentieth century, about 1,273 new individuals filled one of the eight significant offices in the control of the states' electorates in every twelve-year generation.

In the later part of the twentieth century, the structure of political opportunities in the United States has undoubtedly decreased in size. We know that, since the 1960s, the low rate of turnover in the House of Representatives has declined still further. The same has been true for many state legislatures. Furthermore, most of the states have adopted a four-year term for statewide offices. Indeed, given the growth in population, per capita chances for elective office have been considerably fewer during this period. How the structure's size in the twentieth century compares with other time periods requires further research. Further research is also needed to discover how the size of the structure of political opportunities in the United States compares with that of other democracies, although I make some comparisons in chapter 9.

The Shape of the Structure of Political Opportunities

Superficial observations might well lead us to view the structure of political opportunities in the United States as shapeless. In addition to its great size, almost all offices are elected independently. Few elections are linked like that for the presidency and vice presidency, although in recent decades the states have tended to link the elections of governors and lieutenant governors. Furthermore, as far as formal requirements are concerned, one can enter elective politics at any level, at any stage in one's career. There are few prerequisites for office other than age and residency requirements. In particular, there are no office prerequisites. Moreover, while many individuals work their way up, advancing from one office to another, more than a few achieve high office

TABLE 3.2. General Opportunity Rates by State, 1914–58

| | Number of Chances to Achieve Major Office during a Twelve-Year Political Generation | | |
| | Constitutional | | Real (based on personnel turnovers) |
	Minimum	Maximum	
Pennsylvania	12	199	69.05
New York	—	268	66.89
Ohio	—	175	58.42
Illinois	6	172	58.10
Michigan	—	148	45.42
California	—	199	44.35
Indiana	15	97	39.30
Missouri	6	88	35.32
Colorado	12	64	32.90
Texas	—	160	32.17
Kentucky	18	70	31.61
New Mexico	18	52	30.28
Wisconsin	—	94	29.98
Connecticut	—	52	29.41
Massachusetts	2	124	28.95
Alabama	18	76	27.60
Oklahoma	12	58	27.04
Minnesota	—	91	26.71
Delaware	3	34	26.66
Iowa	—	88	26.30
New Jersey	1.5	91	26.27
Nebraska	3	64	25.91
West Virginia	3	55	25.61
South Dakota	3	52	24.69
Kansas	—	76	23.79
North Carolina	6	94	23.22
Louisiana	6	70	23.00
Arkansas	—	70	21.53
Arizona	6	46	19.99
North Dakota	3	52	19.89
Mississippi	12	58	19.83
Virginia	3	74	17.86
Idaho	6	35	17.79
Vermont	—	46	17.36
Maryland	1.5	52	17.29
Rhode Island	—	46	17.16
Utah	6	31	16.51
Montana	3	34	16.33
Washington	—	64	16.15
Georgia	3	76	15.73
Florida	3	64	15.28

TABLE 3.2—*Continued*

	Number of Chances to Achieve Major Office during a Twelve-Year Political Generation		
	Constitutional		Real (based on personnel turnovers)
	Minimum	Maximum	
Tennessee	3	64	15.14
South Carolina	3	55	14.13
Wyoming	3	25	13.75
Oregon	3.5	40	12.80
Nevada	—	25	11.48
New Hampshire	—	22	9.21
Maine	—	28	9.11

Source: Schlesinger 1966, 50.

without prior officeholding experience. Thus, the politically ambitious, when calculating their chances, can never know with certainty all of the sources from which competitors may come. New faces are always gaining prominence; political generations are short. Access to elective office, then, often appears wide open.

On the other hand, close examination of the structure of political opportunities reveals order or shape. It soon becomes clear that not all citizens or even all officeholders have access to all the offices for which they are legally eligible. Access is limited because (1) offices differ in their desirability and, therefore, in their costs; (2) offices differ in the risks imposed for advancement; and (3) offices differ in their relationships with one another, some having a more obvious relationship.

Differences in the desirability of offices impose limitations and, therefore, clarify the structure of political opportunities. Differences in desirability derive from differences in (*a*) powers; (*b*) pay and other perquisites; (*c*) size of constituency; (*d*) length of term; (*e*) tenure potential; and (*f*) potential for advancement. The more attractive an office on some or all of these counts, the greater the number of individuals interested in seeking the office. At the same time, the larger the number of individuals seeking the office, the higher its costs. Higher costs will, however, limit the number of individuals who can realistically aspire to the office. Those most likely to be able to pay the costs, to attract the necessary funds, endorsements, and other electoral assistance, are individuals who have already demonstrated their electoral skills. Since voters are also more likely to recognize candidates who have already held office, these candidates are further advantaged.

On the other hand, movement from one office to another can involve risks. The risks will also limit movement from one office to another, thereby

TABLE 3.3. General Opportunity Rates by State, Adjusted for Population in 1950

	Maximum Chances	Real Chances
Delaware	10.69	8.38
Nevada	15.62	7.17
Wyoming	8.61	4.73
Vermont	12.18	4.60
New Mexico	7.63	4.45
South Dakota	7.97	3.78
North Dakota	8.39	3.21
Idaho	5.95	3.02
Montana	5.75	2.76
Arizona	6.14	2.67
Colorado	4.83	2.48
Utah	4.50	2.40
Rhode Island	5.81	2.17
Nebraska	4.83	1.95
New Hampshire	4.13	1.73
Connecticut	2.59	1.47
West Virginia	2.74	1.27
Kansas	3.99	1.25
Oklahoma	2.60	1.21
Arkansas	3.67	1.13
Kentucky	2.38	1.07
Iowa	3.36	1.00
Maine	3.06	1.00
Indiana	2.47	1.00
Mississippi	2.66	0.91
Minnesota	3.05	0.90
Alabama	2.48	0.90
Missouri	2.23	0.89
Wisconsin	2.74	0.87
Louisiana	2.61	0.86
Oregon	2.63	0.84
Maryland	2.22	0.74
Ohio	2.20	0.74
Michigan	2.32	0.71
Washington	2.69	0.68
South Carolina	2.60	0.67
Illinois	1.97	0.67
Tennessee	1.94	0.66
Pennsylvania	1.90	0.66
Massachusetts	2.64	0.62
North Carolina	2.31	0.57
Florida	2.31	0.55
Virginia	2.23	0.54
New Jersey	1.88	0.54

TABLE 3.3—*Continued*

	Maximum Chances	Real Chances
Georgia	2.20	0.46
New York	1.81	0.45
Texas	2.07	0.42
California	1.88	0.42

Source: Schlesinger 1966, 51.

Note: These are expressed by figures that represent the number of chances per 100,000 population to achieve a major political office during a single political generation (twelve years).

further clarifying the structure of political opportunities. Among the differential risks, those imposed by electoral timing and the loss of a valued current position are most important. Officeholders whose terms coincide with that of another desired office normally must give up the chance at reelection to seek advancement. This is the major constraint that has kept U.S. representatives from running for the Senate.

The risk imposed by identical electoral timing is compounded if the loss of a valued current position is involved. The risk appears greatest to legislators in leadership posts or in line for such posts and may well constrain them from seeking another office. Of course, the risk exists only for legislators whose party is in the majority or can aspire to majority status in the near future. If, on the other hand, one's party appears to be in the permanent minority, as has been the case for the Republicans in the House of Representatives since 1954, the risks attached to giving up a House seat to run for the Senate are considerably less. The risks are further reduced if one can count on a presidential appointment in the event one fails to win a Senate seat. Hence the unusually high number of Republican representatives who were willing to run against Democratic Senate incumbents in 1990.

In contrast, movement is greatly facilitated when office seekers need not absorb the risks imposed by identical electoral timing. The widespread tendency after World War II to give governors four-year terms renewable at the presidential midterm reduced the career risks for sitting governors, making them more amenable to seeking the presidency. Senators, because of the six-year term, have always been in a good position to seek the presidency. Only in alternate elections must they seek reelection during a presidential year. Of the twenty sitting senators who were nominated for the presidency or vice presidency from 1900 through 1988, sixteen were in the happy state of facing no risk of losing office. Of the four whose reelection bids coincided with a presidential or vice presidential nomination, one was Lyndon Johnson in 1960. The Texas legislature resolved his problem by permitting him to run for both offices at the same time. In 1988 another Texas senator, Lloyd Bentsen, was able to take advantage of the "Johnson law" and also run for reelection to the Senate and the vice presidency simultaneously. The only two senators who faced the risk of losing office were Warren Harding in 1920 and Barry Goldwater in 1964. Harding's risks proved minimal; Goldwater lost his Senate seat, only to regain it in a subsequent election.

Finally, offices differ in their relationships with one another. Obvious or manifest relationships encourage focused movement from office to office, thereby helping to shape the structure of political opportunities. Manifest relationships derive from (a) shared or similar electorates; (b) similarity of functions or titles; or (c) shared political arenas.

When two offices have the same or similar electorates it is logical to expect movement from one to the other. Governors have to pass the same statewide electoral test as senators. For that reason alone we should expect governors to try to become senators. Similarly, the fewer a state's number of congressional districts, the more closely the constituencies of representatives will resemble that of governors and senators. Thus, we would expect the greatest movement from the House of Representatives to the offices of governor and senator in small states.

Similarity of functions or even of titles can induce movement from one office to another. The legislative function requires similar skills and talents whether exercised in the state or federal legislature. Thus, we should expect movement along the lines of function, from the lower house to the upper house within the same legislature, as well as from lesser to higher legislatures. There are also offices that carry titles implying, even if they do not require, functions similar to those of the executives they follow in rank. The most obvious are the offices of vice president and lieutenant governor. These offices, too, arouse expectations of movement.

The holders of different offices can carry out at least some of their functions within the same political arena. The most obvious example is that of executives and legislators. Governors and state legislators, the president and Congress spend much of their time dealing with each other. It is therefore inevitable that some legislators, especially those in leadership positions, will see themselves as likely candidates for promotion to top executive offices, and that political observers will concur.

The manifest relationship requires no extensive analysis. It states what the politically knowledgeable expect. When it fails to materialize, the failed relationship becomes a clue to alterations in the structure of political opportunities. Thus, early in the Republic, the vice president emerged as manifestly in line for promotion. Three of the vice presidents from 1797 through 1836 won election to the presidency in their own right. We are alerted to a change in the structure after 1836 because no sitting vice president between Martin Van Buren in 1836 and Richard Nixon in 1960 attained even a major party nomination for president. With Nixon's nomination we are alerted to another change in the structure of political opportunities. Since 1960, every vice president has been an active and serious candidate for promotion. Similarly, the broad decline during the first part of the twentieth century of state legislative experience in governors' and senators' careers and its resurgence since the 1960s call our attention to changes in the opportunity structure.

Plotting the Shape of the Structure of Political Opportunities

The national opportunity structure has two foci, the presidency and the Congress. Each house of Congress has also developed its own internal opportunity structure, which is important in defining the national structure. On the other hand, both national foci are dependent upon the states. Opportunities for congressional office are defined within the states; the ability to advance within the Congress depends on reelection within the states' constituencies. Advancement to the presidency more likely than not also begins in the states. During the period from 1900 through 1958, over two-thirds of the nominees for president and vice president came from a major statewide elective office; over half had, as their last office, the office of governor or senator. If we consider the presidency as a complex of offices that includes the many officials in the national executive and judicial branches appointed by the president, we find these officials, too, arrive in some manner from the states.

The Index of Advantage

To assess the states' role in shaping the national structure of political opportunities, we can measure their relative contributions to the presidential complex by means of an index of advantage. The index is the ratio of a state's share of officials in the presidential complex, as compared with its share of presidential electors. In the period 1900 through 1958, 238 individuals who were presidential or vice presidential nominees, cabinet appointees, or justices of the Supreme Court comprised the presidential complex. Table 3.4 ranks the states according to their index of advantage within this complex. The table shows that thirteen states enjoyed an advantage. The advantaged states provided 62 percent of the presidential complex, although they represented only 32 percent of the electoral college. At the other end of the scale, twelve states made no contribution to the presidential complex, although they represented almost 12 percent of the electoral college. The most heavily advantaged state was Massachusetts, which contributed more than two-and-a-half times the number of officials to the presidential complex than its presidential electors. New York was close behind.

The states' contributions to the presidential office complex during the first six decades of the twentieth century reflect, in large part, the structure of electoral competition for the presidency. In subsequent chapters I shall discuss the structure of electoral competition more fully. Here I will note that large, advantaged states such as New York and Ohio were also electorally competi-

TABLE 3.4.   Positions of the States in the Presidential Complex, 1900–1958

		Percentage of the Electoral College (A)	Percentage of the National Leadership Group (B)	Index of Advantage (B/A)
Mass. N.Y.	Mo. Iowa	15.81	38.23	Heavily Advantaged (2.23–2.51)[a]
Ohio N.M. Utah Neb. Tenn.	Ind. Colo. W.Va. Kan.	16.07	23.10	Moderately Advantaged (1.07–1.78)
Ill. Va. Pa. Ky. N.J. S.C. Mich. Md. Vt.	Wyo. Ore. Tex. Calif. Minn. Conn. R.I. Wash.	44.05	34.88	Moderately Disadvantaged (0.50–0.99)
Ala. Wis. N.C. Ariz. Del.	Ark. Okla. Ga. Miss. Mont.	12.25	3.79	Heavily Disadvantaged (0.19–0.41)
Fla. Idaho La. Me.	Nev. N.H. N.D. S.D.	11.83	0.00	Completely Disadvantaged (0.00)

Source: Schlesinger 1966, 24.
[a]The range of indices of advantage for individual states in the category.

tive for the presidency, while small, disadvantaged states such as Maine or Mississippi were not. Similarly, the border states, Missouri, Tennessee, and West Virginia, undoubtedly gained advantage in the presidential complex because they were more competitive for the presidency than their neighbors comprising the one-party South. Another block of advantaged states ranging westward and south from Iowa to include Kansas, Nebraska, Utah, Colorado, and New Mexico were also competitive for the presidency. This block had a near monopoly on the two cabinet posts identified with their regions, the secretaries of agriculture and interior. But even nonregional cabinet posts, the secretaries of war (and later defense), treasury, and commerce, as well as the position of Supreme Court justice and presidential and vice presidential nominations, went to individuals from these states.

It is possible, of course, that the index of advantage tells us nothing about the political contribution of the states to the national structure of political opportunities. If we accept the conclusions about a national elite put forth by such writers as Hunter (1959) and Mills (1956), then the index instead reflects the distribution of economic power and social influence within the nation. If Hunter and Mills are correct, then the geographical sources of the members of the elite are less an index of the states' political strength or importance than an index of the strength or importance of commercial and industrial centers. New York and Massachusetts contributed disproportionately to the presidential complex, then, not because of their politics, but because New York City and Boston were two of the principal financial and commercial centers of the nation.

While the index does not allow us to test the power center thesis directly, we can isolate the relevance of state politics in the careers of national officeholders. Individuals who reach the top ranks of national politics either have or have not held some kind of state office. If they have, we can assume that state politics is more relevant to their advancement than if they have not. Thus, Dwight Eisenhower advanced to the presidency from New York without having held elective office there. We therefore assume that his advancement was less a tribute to New York politics than were the two presidential nominations of New York Governor Thomas Dewey. Similarly the cabinet appointments of automobile executives Charles Wilson and Robert McNamara were less a sign of the importance of Michigan in the national political structure than the appointment of former Michigan Governor Frank Murphy to the Supreme Court.

When we examine the careers of the 238 national officeholders who comprised the presidential complex during the period 1900 to 1958, we find considerable support for the importance of state politics in their public office careers. While eighty-one or one-third of the officeholders did not hold prior public office in their home states, the remaining two-thirds of the presidential complex did (see table 3.5). These eighty-one support the proposition that there was a national elite independent of the states' political structures. Their concentration in states with large metropolitan centers (see table 3.6) further supports the notion that their advance was not due to local political strength. Over half came from New York, Illinois, Ohio, and Pennsylvania. The large majority of the complex who held prior state office is, however, strong testimony to the important contribution of the states' structures of political opportunities to the national structure.

If we recalculate the states' indices of advantage in the presidential complex, leaving out the eighty-one officials who had not held state office, the states' standings in the complex improve. Six additional states were advan-

TABLE 3.5.   Last Office of Members of the Presidential Complex, 1900–1958

Last Office	Presidential and Vice Presidential Candidates		Cabinet Members		Supreme Court Justices	
	Rep.	Dem.	Rep.	Dem.	Rep.	Dem.
Major elective						
President or vice president	9.1%	4.5%	—%	1.45%	5.0%	—%
U.S. senator	22.7	27.2	2.2	4.35	—	20.0
U.S. representative	4.5	4.5	3.3	8.70	—	—
Governor or other state office	31.8	31.8	4.4	4.35	10.0	—
Defeated candidate for president or vice president	—	4.5	1.1	2.90	—	—
Total elective	68.1	72.5	11.0	21.75	15.0	20.0
Administrative						
Federal cabinet	9.1	4.5	8.9	4.35	10.0	33.3
Federal subcabinet	—	—	11.1	20.30	—	—
Federal administration	4.5	13.6	25.6	21.70	—	6.7
State administration	—	—	—	2.90	—	—
Total administrative	13.6	18.1	45.6	49.25	10.0	40.0
Court system						
Federal judge	4.5	—	—	2.90	35.0	20.0
State judge	—	4.5	1.1	1.45	25.0	—
Federal lawyer	—	—	2.2	5.80	15.0	6.7
Total court	4.5	4.5	3.3	10.15	75.0	26.7
Others						
Major party administration	—	—	7.8	11.60	—	—
Defeated governor or senator	—	4.5	3.3	—	—	—
Local elective officer	—	—	1.1	1.45	—	—
No recent public office or nomination	13.6	—	27.8	5.80	—	13.3
Total other	13.6	4.5	40.0	18.85	0.0	13.3
N	22	22	90	69	20	15

Source: Schlesinger 1966, 34.

**TABLE 3.6.   Officials of Presidential Complex without
Prior Office in the Control of the States (1900–1985)**

States from which Leaders Came	Number of Leaders	Percentage of Total
New York	21	25.93
Illinois	8	9.88
Ohio	6 ⎫	
Missouri	6 ⎬	22.23
Pennsylvania	6 ⎭	
Iowa	5	6.17
Massachusetts	4	4.94
California	3 ⎫	
Michigan	3	
Maryland	3 ⎬	18.50
Colorado	3	
Virginia	3 ⎭	
Texas	2	2.47
Kansas	1 ⎫	
Minnesota	1	
New Jersey	1	
New Mexico	1	
Utah	1 ⎬	9.88
North Carolina	1	
Tennessee	1	
Connecticut	1 ⎭	
Total	81	100.00

Source: Schlesinger 1966, 30.

taged, Kentucky, South Carolina, Wyoming, Vermont, Oregon, and New Jersey; only one, Colorado, lost its advantaged position. Massachusetts, which ranked first before, was even more advantaged. We are therefore led to infer that its standing probably derived more from its politics than its position as a commercial and financial center. The advantage of the border states, as well as that of the Western-Southwestern bloc, was also enhanced. While New York lost slightly in importance, it remained strongly advantaged.[2]

The Stages of Officeholders' Careers

The shape of the national structure of political opportunities emerges further when we plot the careers of the states' most important officeholders, governors and senators, in three stages: (1) first public office held; (2) type of office

2. For a detailed discussion of the variations in the states' structures of political opportunities, see Schlesinger 1966, chaps. 5 and 6.

experience; (3) penultimate office, or the office held just before the office of governor or senator. I have plotted these stages of gubernatorial and senatorial careers on frequency trees, a device that allows me to summarize a great deal of data.

The governors' tree (fig. 3.1) summarizes the careers of the 641 governors elected from 1900 through 1958. Reading from right to left, we find that the largest proportion, 19.7 percent, had as their penultimate office another statewide elective office, 19.34 percent came directly from a law enforcement position, 18.88 percent from the state legislature, and so on. Moving to the left, we find under "office experience" the proportion of governors with a particular penultimate office who had one or more of six types of office experience. Of the governors who had statewide elective office as their penultimate office, 61.7 percent had state legislative experience. This was true for only 37.9 percent of the governors who came directly from a law enforcement position. Moving still further to the left, we find in the "first office" column the percentage of governors with a particular penultimate office and office experience who had a particular first office. Sixty-two percent of the governors who had statewide elective office as their penultimate office and state legislative experience had state legislative office as their first office. Finally, the column at the extreme left records the percentage of governors who held each particular set of offices. Twelve percent of the governors had state legislative office as their first office, their penultimate office, and, therefore, as their office experience; 7.64 percent had state legislative office as their first office and office experience and statewide elective office as their penultimate office.

The tree therefore demonstrates that the careers of the states' governors followed some pattern. If we isolate the dominant career patterns, that is, those used by at least 2.5 percent of the governors, we find twelve dominant patterns out of a possible thirty-seven. These twelve patterns were used by 69.57 percent of the governors. Moreover, more than half the governors (52.4 percent) had complex careers, that is their penultimate office differed from their first office. The distinctive patterns of gubernatorial careers also revealed the importance of offices that enjoyed a manifest relationship with the office of governor. Nearly 40 percent of the governors came either from another statewide elective office such as lieutenant governor or from the state legislature. Some 62 percent of the former statewide elective officials had previously been in the legislature.

Senatorial careers revealed an even stronger concentration of career patterns. The senatorial tree summarizes the careers of the 450 senators elected between 1914 and 1958 (see fig. 3.2). When we isolate the dominant senatorial career patterns, we find that 77.23 percent of the senators used only thirteen career patterns. Moreover, 60 percent of the senators had complex

% of N following path	First Office		Office Experience	Penultimate Office
12.01	Legis.	63.6	100.0	
2.02	Law enf.	68.4	15.7	State Legislative
0.00	Statewide	0.0	0.0	18.88
0.00	Congress	0.0	0.8	
1.56	Admin.	58.8	14.1	
2.64	Local elect.	80.8	17.3	
4.67	Legis.	63.7	37.9	
10.77	Law enf.	55.7	100.0	Law Enforcement
0.15	Statewide	33.3	2.4	19.34
0.00	Congress	0.0	1.6	
1.87	Admin.	75.0	12.9	
0.94	Local elect.	60.0	8.9	
7.64	Legis.	62.0	61.7	
2.81	Law enf.	81.9	17.2	Statewide Elective
3.12	Statewide	15.6	100.0	19.97
0.31	Congress	33.3	4.7	
3.45	Admin.	63.0	27.4	
1.88	Local elect.	54.6	17.2	
8.11				No prior office 8.11
2.65	Legis.	54.8	50.8	
3.12	Law enf.	80.0	41.0	
0.00	Statewide	0.0	1.6	Congress
1.88	Congress	18.7	100.0	9.52
1.09	Admin.	78.0	14.7	
0.62	Local elect.	66.6	9.8	
1.38	Legis.	40.3	25.9	
2.35	Law enf.	71.5	24.7	
0.00	Statewide	0.0	3.5	Administrative
0.00	Congress	0.0	5.9	13.26
7.65	Admin.	57.7	100.0	
1.25	Local elect.	47.0	20.0	
0.94	Legis.	54.5	25.0	
0.47	Law enf.	50.0	13.6	Local Elective
0.00	Statewide	0.0	4.5	6.86
0.00	Congress	0.0	0.0	
1.25	Admin.	80.0	22.7	
4.05	Local elect.	59.1	100.0	
92.65	Total			

Governors (N = 641)

Fig. 3.1. Prior offices of governors, 1900–1958. (From Schlesinger 1966, 91.)

% of N following path	First Office		Office Experience	Penultimate Office	
5.11	Legis.	57.5	100.0		
2.22	Law enf.	100.0	25.0	State Legislative 8.89	
0.00	Statewide	0.0	0.0		
0.00	Congress	0.0	0.0		
1.11	Admin.	50.0	25.0		
0.44	Local elect.	40.0	12.5		
2.67	Legis.	63.2	33.3		
8.22	Law enf.	65.0	100.0	Law Enforcement 12.67	
0.00	Statewide	0.0	3.5		
0.23	Congress	50.0	3.5		
1.34	Admin.	50.0	21.1		
0.23	Local elect.	50.0	3.5		
7.33	Legis.	62.3	53.0		
6.00	Law enf.	62.8	43.0	Statewide Elective 22.22	
2.44	Statewide	11.0	100.0		
0.22	Congress	7.7	13.0		
3.78	Admin.	43.6	39.0		
1.34	Local elect.	37.5	16.0		
8.22				No prior office 8.22	Senators (N = 450)
4.45	Legis.	51.3	32.5		
7.56	Law enf.	64.2	44.2	Congress 26.67	
0.22	Statewide	20.0	4.2		
4.67	Congress	17.5	100.0		
6.00	Admin.	62.8	35.9		
3.11	Local elect.	100.0	11.7		
1.78	Legis.	61.5	20.0		
1.23	Law enf.	63.6	16.9	Administrative 14.44	
0.45	Statewide	20.6	10.8		
0.67	Congress	60.0	7.7		
9.11	Admin.	63.1	100.0		
0.89	Local elect.	50.0	12.3		
0.22	Legis.	33.3	14.3		
0.67	Law enf.	60.0	23.8	Local Elective 4.67	
0.00	Statewide	0.0	0.0		
0.00	Congress	0.0	0.0		
1.33	Admin.	100.0	28.6		
2.22	Local elect.	47.6	100.0		
95.48	Total				

Fig. 3.2. Prior offices of senators, 1914–58. (From Schlesinger 1966, 92.)

careers in which their penultimate offices differed from their first offices. At the same time, the importance of manifest office in senatorial careers was even stronger than in gubernatorial careers. Among the senators, nearly half came directly either from a statewide office, the governorship for the most part, or from the lower house of Congress.

Our analysis of the careers of national officials during the first six decades of the twentieth century, then, points to a hierarchical national structure of political opportunities. Four offices were at the pinnacle, United States representative, governor, senator, and president. Their order in the hierarchy was established by their career patterns. Of the representatives serving in 1951, a majority had been either public attorneys or state legislators; only 18.20 percent had had no prior office experience. The careers of the governors were even more circumscribed. Of the gubernatorial careers we analyzed, only 8.11 percent showed no prior office experience; as we have seen, almost 40 percent of the governors came from manifest offices. As we have also seen, senators' careers were still more focused. If we compare the senatorial figures with the still higher proportion of presidents and vice presidents who came from the manifest positions of governor and senator, we find a hierarchical structure of political opportunities established by increasingly stringent office requirements for advancement.

The Shape of the Opportunity Structure and Political Ambitions

In the United States, then, a hierarchical structure of political opportunities stimulates and directs political ambitions. The base of the structure is broad, consisting of numerous state and local offices to which a wide range of individuals may reasonably aspire. The structure, however, narrows. For the offices of governor, representative, senator, and president realistic opportunities decline sharply. This is a situation that no individual ambitious for these offices can ignore.

Nor can the politically ambitious ignore the variations in political opportunities from state to state. States advantaged in the presidential complex provide more outlets for advancement than those that are disadvantaged. The opportunity structures of advantaged states support the national structure of political opportunities. Therefore, they stimulate a broader range of progressive ambitions, which include ambition for advancement to office within the presidential complex. During the first six decades of the twentieth century, officeholders in Ohio, Massachusetts, and New York had always to be conscious of this possibility. Even those who claimed no desire to advance to the presidential complex had to take account of others around them who surely harbored such ambitions. In contrast, states with no representation in the presidential complex had truncated structures of political opportunities. Since the politically ambitious in these states had to satisfy their ambitions either within the states or in Congress, discrete and static ambitions were most likely to prevail.

At the same time, it is important to remember that the hierarchical structure of political opportunities never totally discouraged political ambition because the structure was not hard and fast. It did not rule out the opportunity for any office because customary requirements were not fulfilled. The impression of openness was encouraged by the structure's broad base. Yet even the highest positions in the structure could be assaulted by individuals who did not hold the limited manifest positions. A structure of political opportunities that arouses a broad range of political ambitions and, at the same time, restrains them has major implications for party organization in democracies, which I shall discuss in subsequent chapters.

REFERENCES

Hunter, Floyd. 1959. *Top Leadership, U.S.A.* Chapel Hill: University of North Carolina Press.
Matthews, Donald R. 1960. *U.S. Senators and Their World.* New York: Vintage.
Mills, C. Wright. 1956. *The Power Elite.* New York: Oxford University Press.
Schlesinger, Joseph A. 1966. *Ambition and Politics.* Chicago: Rand McNally.

CHAPTER 4

The Structure of Political Opportunities: The Age Factor

In the preceding chapter I laid out the size and the shape of the structure of political opportunities in the United States and discussed the consequences for political ambitions. I did not, however, discuss one significant aspect of the structure, the ages at which officeholders typically win election to office. Because the age factor has a considerable impact on political ambitions, it deserves consideration on its own. Nothing can be a greater stimulant to an individual's political ambitions than being the right age for the right office at the right time. Nothing can be a greater deterrent than finding oneself the wrong age for the office to which one aspires. The appropriate age for any office is only slightly determined by legal requirements. Far more important are the age patterns that emerge from the aggregate data on the ages candidates win or fail to win elections.

Aggregate data on the ages at which both successful and defeated candidates try for elective office are easy to assemble, undoubtedly because politicians and political journalists frequently worry in public about the timetables of political careers. Political scientists, on the other hand, have made little use of such data. They have chosen, for the most part, to treat age, along with social and economic status, education, and occupation, as another characteristic of the officeholder's background. They have, therefore, neglected age as an important independent variable affecting elective office careers, primarily by arousing or dampening political ambitions. In this chapter, I shall discuss the age patterns that emerge from the aggregate data. I shall also show how these patterns affect both the size and the shape of the structure of political opportunities and, therefore, political ambitions.

The timetables disclosed by the careers of elective officials reveal an important aspect of a democracy's structure of political opportunities. For the numerous elective offices in the United States, from city councillor to president, timetables do exist. As we have already seen, amidst the apparent chaos there is indeed an officeholding hierarchy; without the prescripts of law, individuals ascend from one office to another. Moreover, without legal prescripts, they often do so in orderly time progression. We should, of course, be aware that age patterns for office in the United States have not hardened, any more than have the patterns of movement from office to office that we discerned in the preceding chapter. Taking into account minimal legal age requirements, we can easily demonstrate that a variety of elective offices have been achieved at a variety of ages. Nevertheless, as we have seen, political opportunities are not random. In this chapter, we shall see that the structure that we found imposed in the preceding chapter derives, in part, also from the frequent disposition of particular offices to particular age groups.

To establish age as an aspect of the structure of political opportunities, we need to demonstrate the relationship between age and office careers. To demonstrate this relationship in the United States, I examined the ages at which major officeholders began their office careers, as well as the ages at which they achieved major office, during the first six decades of the twentieth century. Since we saw the importance of the states' contributions to the national structure of political opportunities in the preceding chapter, it was also necessary to examine variations in the states' age patterns for elective office.

The hierarchy of office in the United States, which emerged in the preceding chapter, is an accurate guide to the typical age timetables of elective officeholders. When I divided the membership of the House of Representatives elected in 1956 into five-year age-groups, I found that the largest single block entered the House between the ages of thirty-five and forty (see fig. 4.1). Of the governors first elected between 1900 and 1958, the largest number were between forty-five and fifty years of age. Of the senators elected for the first time between 1914 and 1958, the largest number were between the ages of fifty and fifty-five. The same was true of the men elected president between 1900 and 1956, although the age at election was much more sharply focused. Five of the ten presidents during the period were first elected in their early fifties.

Based on this experience, individuals ambitious for office in the United States during the first six decades of the twentieth century could easily detect when their best opportunities would occur. It was best to seek the office of representative in the fifteen-year age-span between thirty-five and fifty, and better to seek it earlier than later. The years between forty-five and fifty were the most opportune time for individuals to seek the governorship, the years between forty-five and sixty, the best time to seek the office of senator. Certainly the fifties emerged as the best years for seeking the presidency; of the ten presidents elected between 1900 and 1958, only three did not fall into this age group. Although these figures were by no means binding, they indicated that, in the period from 1900 through 1958, all four major offices in the opportunity structure were most attainable in the fifteen-year span between the

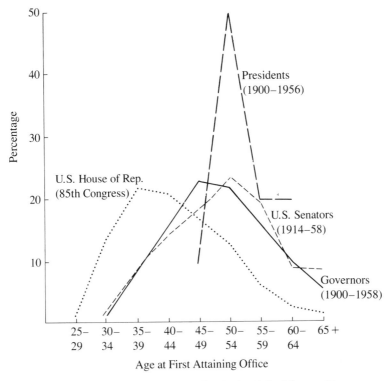

Fig. 4.1. Age and achievement of major office in the United States. (From Schlesinger 1966, 175.)

ages of thirty-five and fifty, a fact to which individuals with hopes for advancement needed to pay close attention.

Age at Entry into Elective Office

We get a better view of age requirements as an aspect of the structure of political opportunities by dissecting the careers of the nominees for major office. The appropriate place to begin is the age at which these individuals began their office careers. Among other things, the younger individuals are when they enter politics, the more likely they are to harbor a broad range of political ambitions and a career commitment to public officeholding. Those who embark on a political career before the age of thirty are the most likely to consider politics their primary occupation; they are the least likely to owe their interest to failure in some other endeavor. Attainment of public office at an early age also represents a less costly investment than later entry to a public office career. Requiring no long and arduous formal training like medicine, politics is an inexpensive trial run for those whose interests may still be diffuse. We can speculate, then, that success at an early age produces a firm commitment to a political career. Unfortunately we do not know how many young people make their trial run and drop out. On the other hand, we do know that, of the major party candidates for governor and senator in the periods 1900 through 1958 and 1914 through 1958 respectively, 37 percent had begun their office careers before the age of thirty.

At the same time, we should recognize that individuals who begin their public office careers in their thirties have undoubtedly made a more conscious and deliberate choice than those who make the choice in their twenties. The choice may well be an expression of failure in some other field, a dwindling law practice or an unprofitable business venture. But it is also possible for individuals to use their positions outside politics to gain entry into politics. Their extrapolitical accomplishments may well bring them to the attention of those seeking candidates for elective office or earn them a public office appointment. Whatever the cause, individuals beginning their office careers in their thirties, unlike those in their twenties, arrive from some other occupation; they are Jane Smith, lawyer, Bill Jones, insurance salesman, Mary Williams, social worker. Nevertheless they are still young enough to achieve higher office. Among the candidates for major office whose careers I examined, 39 percent had started their public office careers between the ages of thirty and thirty-nine.

Entry into public office after forty means that opportunities for a public office career have narrowed, although they by no means disappear. Some of my observations about the office careers of individuals who start in their thirties also pertain to those who start in their forties. Politics, for them, is certainly a secondary occupation or subsequent career. We should expect these individuals to enjoy even more clearly established positions in society, and more often success rather than failure. In this group, extrapolitical accomplishment is required, more often than not, to give added luster to a political candidacy. At the same time, it is very likely that, for these late starters, the opportunities to establish political careers by advancing in politics are fewer. Of our candidates for major office, 76 percent had begun their public office careers before the age of forty; only one-fourth had started their careers after the age of forty.

The age at which individuals enter public office, therefore, helps determine their entire political career. At one extreme, the young bring little to politics except their raw talents and the advantages that their social and economic background provide. Should they be successful they can expect to become the true careerists; if they fail, they lose little by dropping out. At the other extreme, individuals in their forties or older are likely to bring talents and accomplishments tested outside of politics; they are also the most likely to be the political dilettantes. Only individuals who start their careers in their thirties can bring to politics both extrapolitical experience and a serious long-term commitment.

Age of Entry and Occupation

There is a significant relationship between the ages at which individuals begin their public office careers and their extrapolitical occupations. Even for those in their twenties whose career aspirations focus on elective office, the career is so fraught with risk that few can aspire to it exclusively. Thus, even those in their twenties must resort to an occupational sideline. Nevertheless, would-be officeholders are not free to adopt any trade or profession. Unless they enjoy independent wealth, they do best to follow a compatible trade, an occupation in which political activity may well be an aid and, at least, will not be a liability. Of all occupations, the practice of law is clearly the most compatible, if only because the practice requires more or less involvement with the polity (Schlesinger 1957).

Among the candidates for major office whose careers I examined, the relation between early entry into public office and the practice of law was striking. Among the early entrants, those who started their office careers before the age of thirty, lawyers dominated almost to the exclusion of all other occupations (see table 4.1). Of those in the twenty-five through twenty-nine age-group, three out of every four were lawyers. After twenty-nine, the proportion of lawyers declined with age. As the age of entry rose, businessmen became more prominent. Among those who embarked on their office careers after forty, businessmen outnumbered lawyers. As the age of entry rose, the number of those practicing such nonlegal professions as medicine and education also rose, although they represented no large share of the total. Among those starting their careers in full maturity, over the age of fifty, however, individuals practicing the nonlegal professions approached the number of lawyers. In contrast, farmers and journalists were poorly represented and were no more conspicuous in one age-group than another.

The distribution of occupations among our officeholders by age-groups supports my statement about the significance of the age at which officeholders start their careers. Lawyers' overwhelming domination of the under-thirty age-group confirms my suggestion that this group consists of individuals willing and able to try their hand at a political career. Short of no occupation at all, the practice of law allows the greatest flexibility. Not only is a political fling unlikely to harm a law practice, it may well advance it, just as legal training and apprenticeship may well advance a political career. Young law-

TABLE 4.1. Age at First Office and Occupation of Candidates for Major Office in the States, 1900–1958

Age at Entry	Lawyers	Businessmen	Farmers	Communications	Nonlegal Professions	No Information or Other	Total (N)	
Under 25	68.67%	16.27%	3.61%	6.03%	1.80%	3.62%	100%	(166)
25–29	74.16	11.24	3.82	4.72	3.14	2.92	100	(445)
30–34	58.76	22.42	6.95	5.16	5.67	1.04	100	(388)
35–39	40.49	33.47	8.26	7.02	9.52	1.24	100	(242)
40–44	36.70	37.97	5.06	8.23	8.87	3.17	100	(158)
45–49	31.03	45.68	5.17	5.17	10.35	2.60	100	(116)
50+	20.71	47.74	6.30	4.55	18.01	2.69	100	(111)

Source: Schlesinger 1966, 178.

yers, then, have the least to lose and the most to gain from testing the political waters. On the other hand, the steady decline in the number of lawyers as the age of entry rises indicates that, even for lawyers, an office career becomes less compatible as they become more established in their profession. All the same, the very low proportion of businessmen who started a political career before thirty, as well as the nonexistence of other professionals who debuted in this age-group, demonstrates that individuals committed to these occupations are not likely to be political careerists. The true careerists not only make their commitment to an office career early, they commit themselves, at the same time, to the most compatible occupation, the law.

The distribution of occupations among our officeholders by age-groups also confirms the other observations I made about the relationship between age and office careers. I observed that individuals in their thirties become increasingly more settled in their occupations, while marks of occupational success or failure become clearer, thus making the impact of nonpolitical accomplishment upon political decisions more weighty. In line with this observation, I found that the occupations of the major officeholders starting their careers in their thirties were more evenly distributed. Among those starting their office careers in their early thirties, lawyers were still dominant, although the other occupations had increased their representation. By the late thirties, there was a sharp increase in the number of representatives from all the other occupations. After thirty-five, businessmen, nonlegal professionals, farmers, and members of the news media appeared in greater numbers among those starting their office careers. In this respect, they clearly signaled the occupational patterns of the late starters. Of those starting their office careers after forty, two-thirds came from occupations other than the law, thus supporting the observation that those for whom public office is an afterthought dominate among the late starters.

Age of Entry and Political Offices

The age at which individuals enter public office is related not only to their nonpolitical occupation, but also to the type of career they have in politics. As we have seen, the structure of political opportunities in the United States provides a variety of points of entry to a public office career. To a large extent, the point of entry depends upon the age at which the individual enters office. In the preceding chapter, I pointed out that, in the period 1900–1958, the most common points of entry to major office careers in the states were offices low in the office hierarchy, whose numbers were large and whose turnover rates were likely to be high. These offices included the office of state legislator, the law enforcement offices of state and local district and prosecuting attorneys, elective and appointive, and the appointed administrative positions at all levels of government. Of the candidates for major office that I examined, those who started their public office careers early were the most conspicuous users of these three major entry points.

But there were interesting variations among the early entrants. For the youngest entrants, those under twenty-five, administration was the major point of entry.[1] Undoubtedly most of the law enforcement officeholders in this age-group owed their positions to appointment as well. The earliest entrants into public office, then, were individuals mostly coopted into public office, individuals whose political connections were strong enough to gain a public office appointment. After the early twenties, use of the administrative entry point dropped sharply, becoming important again only for the age-group over forty. In this age-group, however, the administrative entry point was undoubtedly at a higher level. After administration, law enforcement office was the most important entry point for young starters, reaching its peak importance for those in their late twenties. The importance of law enforcement office for this group reflected the importance of lawyers among them. As a point of entry, the state legislature was consistently conspicuous until individuals reached the age of fifty. But there were differences worth noting. State legislative office was the most significant point of entry from the age of thirty on, although its absolute importance declined as individuals grew older. After fifty, the decline in its importance was marked.

Certainly we should expect from my general statements about age and office careers that the late starters would try for major office from different entry points than their younger colleagues. Given my comments about the value of prestige achieved in nonpolitical occupations for the late starter's public career, we would expect more late starters to try for top positions without prior office experience. We might also expect that, with the advantage of prestige achieved elsewhere, late starters could try for major office, having begun their careers at higher levels in the office hierarchy. Indeed, as the age of entry into public office rose, there was a sharp increase in the number of individuals nominated for major office without previous office experience. In the age-group over fifty, individuals without prior office experience were dominant. As the age level rose, there was also an increase in the number of major office nominees whose first offices were the prestigious positions of statewide elective official and U.S. representative.

Of course an important question is whether the age at which individuals start their public office career determines the speed with which they advance and the intensity of their careers. Are early starters advantaged or, as I specu-

---

1. For detailed evidence on the relationship between ages and political careers, see Schlesinger 1966, 172–93.

lated earlier, are there advantages to starting a political career after acquiring some experience outside politics? My evidence tends to support the inference that, as far as the rate of advancement is concerned, extrapolitical accomplishment can more than compensate for an early start in public office. Among our nominees for major office, the earliest starters, those entering public office before the age of twenty-five, were not the fastest climbers up the political ladder. A higher proportion of those starting their office careers in their early forties received their major nominations before the age of fifty-five than those who had started their careers in their early twenties. The fastest moving group were those who started their careers in their early thirties; of these, 56 percent received their major nomination before the age of fifty. In the years 1900–1958, then, the structure of political opportunities in the United States did not advantage the precocious in politics. If anything, the early starter was at a slight disadvantage in the race for higher office.

On the other hand, my evidence does support the inference that the early starter is the true career officeholder. A public office career is not only more open than most professions; it is often more risky and sporadic. The age at which individuals enter politics and the age at which they receive their major nominations do not necessarily, therefore, convey their total office experience. An early entry into public office could well be followed by periods of non-officeholding. My evidence reveals, however, a positive relation between early entry into public office and the total number of years spent in office. Twenty years in public office constitutes a substantial career. Of the earliest starters, those under twenty-five, fully one-third held office twenty years or more before receiving their major nominations. Over half of those who started their careers before thirty spent at least ten years in office (not necessarily consecutively) before receiving their major nominations. After the age of thirty, the total time in office dropped; among those who started their office careers after forty, at least three out of four spent less than ten years in public office before receiving their nominations.

The youngest entrants were also careerists in the sense that they advanced through more public offices. Among those who entered public office before the age of twenty-five, a higher proportion became judges and state legislative leaders before receiving their major nominations than those who entered office later. On the other hand, a later start did not rule out advancement through intermediary offices. Although the earlier entrants held the greater number of intermediary offices, the number of intermediary offices held by the older age-groups did not decline sharply. Indeed, the proportion of mayors increased in the twenty-five to thirty-five age-group, while the proportion of legislative leaders rose among those between the ages of thirty-five and forty-five.

Age and Penultimate Office

While age of entry into public office certainly has significance for a public office career, my evidence indicates that the age at which the penultimate office is achieved has greater significance for those who win major office, especially if the penultimate office is a manifest office. In general, manifest officeholders set the typical age pattern for those elected to the offices of governor and senator. Of the manifest officeholders who became governor, most of the statewide elective officials won election in their forties and early fifties, most of the state legislators in the years between forty-five and fifty-five. Of the manifest officeholders who became senator, most were elected in the years between forty-five and fifty-nine. Representatives usually achieved the office five years earlier than governors.

Among the nonmanifest officeholders who became governor, those in more conspicuous offices arrived earlier than those in lesser offices or those without office experience. Holders of law enforcement offices were among the youngest to win gubernatorial office, typically in the years between thirty-five and forty-five. Of the few representatives who became governor, the largest number were elected in their late forties. In contrast, local officials and administrators became governor mostly after they had reached their fifties. The same was true of individuals elected to the governorship without prior office experience.

Among the nonmanifest officeholders who became senator, the age pattern was somewhat different. There was a marked contrast between those who became governor and those who became senator without prior office experience, although the number in each case was small and the proportions about the same for each office. While those who became governor typically came from the fifty to fifty-five age-group, those who became senator were not conspicuous in any one age-group, though they were more likely to win election before they were fifty. Thus, while those from nonpolitical occupations usually became governor later than those who had served in public office, the reverse was true for those who became senators. Furthermore, state legislators elected to the Senate usually won election at an earlier age than those elected from the manifest offices. Local officials were elected to the Senate both earlier and later.

This difference in age patterns between the two offices confirmed the difference in their position in the national structure of political opportunities. The position of the governorship was intermediate, conspicuously placed for advancement. For those to whom the office was a milestone on a well-mapped office career, then, the assault was made sooner rather than later. For the relatively few who had to compensate for the lack of manifest office, assault on the office took more time. The office of senator, in contrast, could well be the final and lengthy stage of a public office career. The relative few who took a deviant path to this office, therefore, were under pressure to act early.

The difference in the position of the two offices was also confirmed by differences in tenure. Governors enjoyed relatively brief careers, senators more lengthy ones. From 1900 to 1959, gubernatorial tenure rose slowly to an average of 4.6 years. In contrast, senatorial service rose from 1914 to 1939 to an average of 8.5 years, after which it remained relatively stable. The increase in senatorial tenure paralleled that of the House. By 1931, the average length of service for representatives was 8.96 years, by 1951, 9.46 years.

Age and Political Office: Regional and State Variations

As we saw in the preceding chapter, a true view of the structure of political opportunities in the United States must include the recognition of regional and state differences. Generally, throughout the United States, the age-groups that achieved major office became older and more restrictive with higher office. Throughout the states, the age level tended to rise progressively and the age focus to narrow from the office of U.S. representative to the office of governor, from the office of governor to the office of senator.

At the same time, this overall pattern masked important regional and state differences. The national norm of age progression for the three major offices of representative, governor, and senator was set in New England and the border states, confirming their well-defined structures of political opportunities (see fig. 4.2). In both these regions, representatives were usually elected in their forties, governors in their late forties, and senators in their early fifties. The age patterns in the Midwest and middle Atlantic states were similar, but not as neat. The age distributions were flatter in the Midwest; the differences in the ages of governors and senators were much smaller than elsewhere. Individuals also went to the House of Representatives later, typically in their late forties.

In contrast, the South had its own distinctive age pattern that also confirmed well-defined structures of political opportunities. This pattern was marked by the election of senators at an earlier age than governors. Representatives were also conspicuously younger than in the other regions. The age pattern was clearly related to the treatment of the office of senator as a career office. In the one-party South of the period, the strong assurance of long tenure in office undoubtedly favored the selection of younger senatorial candidates. A similar pattern emerged in the far West. In this sense, the regions' opportunity structures had an important impact on the national structure by helping to shift power within Congress to the southern and western states.

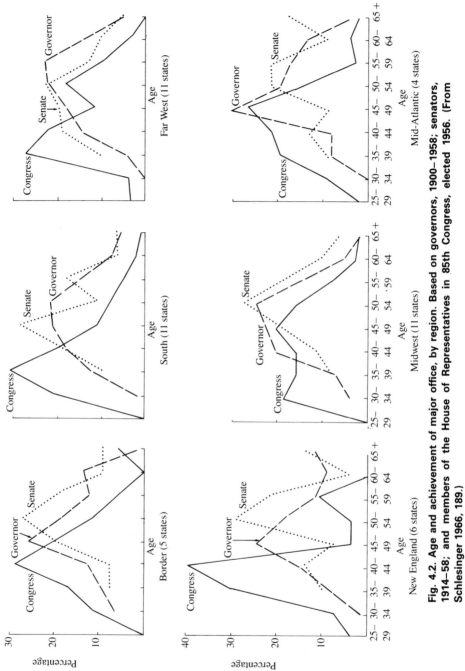

Fig. 4.2. Age and achievement of major office, by region. Based on governors, 1900–1958; senators, 1914–58; and members of the House of Representatives in 85th Congress, elected 1956. (From Schlesinger 1966, 189.)

Distinctive age patterns also emerged when I examined, by state, the age of entry into public office of the nominees for governor and senator.[2] When I ranked the states according to the proportion of their nominees who were careerists, that is, had begun their public office careers before thirty, the range was considerable, from a high of 61 percent in South Carolina to a low of 11 percent in Delaware. An early start was most characteristic of the southern states. In eight of the southern states, one-half or more of the nominees had begun their public office careers before thirty. The states whose nominees were predominantly later starters, that is, more than three-fourths of their nominees had started their office careers after thirty, showed little regional concentration. They consisted of rural states in New England and the Midwest, Vermont and New Hampshire, Kansas and the Dakotas; included also were urban industrial states in the East, New York, New Jersey, and Pennsylvania. I should add that the later starters were seriously handicapped in very few states. In only three states, Arkansas, Mississippi, and Minnesota, did fewer than 10 percent of the nominees start their public office career after the age of forty; only in Mississippi did no one embark on a major office career after forty (see table 4.2). These variations in rankings confirmed the states' distinctive structures of political opportunities.

The states' distinctive opportunity structures were also confirmed by the variations in age patterns for their lesser offices. Figure 4.3 shows the age patterns for five selected state legislatures. Of the five, only the age patterns of the lower houses of the Pennsylvania and South Dakota legislatures resembled that of the U.S. House of Representatives. In contrast, members of the lower house of the Michigan legislature fitted a bimodal age curve; the largest number of legislators first won election either in their early thirties or in their early fifties. The Connecticut House had a larger number of older neophytes, the Vermont House even more. In Vermont, the age pattern deviated from a normal age distribution; the number of new arrivals to the lower house increased with each succeeding age-group from the early twenties on, the largest number of new arrivals coming from the group over sixty-five.

Along with the variations in age patterns went variations in the length of state legislative careers, though tenure in all five legislatures increased. Tenure in the Vermont legislature was the briefest. In the years 1931 to 1940, the average proportion of new legislators each term was 84.3 percent; in the years 1951 to 1960, the average proportion of new legislators each term declined to 57.3 percent. The comparable figures for Connecticut were 56.2 and 49 percent, for South Dakota 59.3 and 42.1 percent, for Pennsylvania 51 and

---

2. For the South, only Democratic nominees were included.

TABLE 4.2. Age at First Public Office of Candidates for Major Office, 1900–1958

| | Percentage in Each Age Group | | |
State	Under 30	30–39	40 and Over
	Group I—Early Starters Dominant		
South Carolina	61%	28%	11%
North Carolina	59	26	15
Mississippi	59	41	0
Florida	56	26	18
Iowa	53	30	17
Texas	53	27	20
Alabama	52	38	10
Louisiana	52	30	18
Minnesota	51	40	9
Georgia	50	30	20
Ohio	50	37	13
Michigan	49	19	32
Maryland	47	32	21
Illinois	46	28	26
Arizona	45	27	28
California	45	33	22
Wisconsin	44	31	25
Rhode Island	43	38	19
Kentucky	42	42	16
Missouri	41	35	24
Tennessee	41	39	20
	Group II—Secondary Starters Dominant		
South Dakota	18	60	22
North Dakota	22	56	22
Arkansas	36	56	8
Nevada	32	54	14
Utah	31	50	19
New Mexico	31	50	19
Maine	28	50	32
Virginia	27	50	23
Washington	38	48	14
New Hampshire	31	48	14
Massachusetts	36	47	17
Nebraska	31	47	22
Colorado	28	46	26
West Virginia	34	45	21
New Jersey	20	44	36
Kansas	21	43	36
Idaho	22	42	36
Montana	34	41	25
New York	31	40	29

TABLE 4.2—*Continued*

	Percentage in Each Age Group		
State	Under 30	30–39	40 and Over
Group III—Tertiary Starters Dominant			
Oklahoma	20	25	55
Delaware	11	41	48
Connecticut	35	24	41
Group IV—Relatively Even Distribution			
Wyoming	39	30	31
Oregon	35	32	33
Vermont	27	39	34
Indiana	32	37	31
Pennsylvania	31	31	39

Source: Schlesinger 1966, 190.

30.4 percent, and for Michigan 46.5 and 26.3 percent (Shin and Jackson 1979).[3]

Age patterns confirmed both the size and the shape of the states' structures of political opportunities. We should expect a high rate of opportunity to be associated with a low level of careerism in public office. This is indeed the case. I found an inverse relation between a state's per capita chances for major office and the proportion of the state's nominees for major office who began their public office careers before the age of thirty (rank-order correlation = −.54). The fewer the state's political opportunities, the more likely the state's nominees for major office were early starters. In contrast, Delaware, which provided the largest number of opportunities for major office, had the smallest number of early starters.

Similarly, we should expect to find that the more well defined a state's structure of political opportunities in terms of movement from office to office, the greater the level of careerism or early entry into office. The evidence points in that direction. In all the states where more than half the nominees started their office careers in their twenties, there was some type of office career pattern. In contrast, ten of the thirteen states whose opportunity structures I classified as diffuse were among the states whose early entrants num-

---

3. The age and tenure patterns of the Vermont and Connecticut legislatures undoubtedly reflected the character of several New England legislatures, including the legislatures of Maine and New Hampshire. These were so-called citizen legislatures, outsize bodies meeting in brief sessions with low remuneration (Schlesinger and Schlesinger 1981, 231–32).

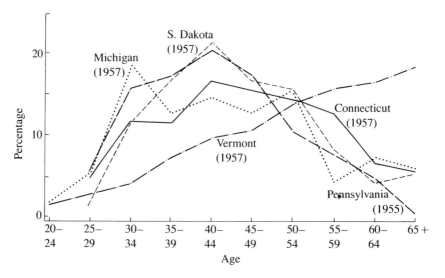

Fig. 4.3. Age at first attaining legislative office. (From Schlesinger and Schlesinger 1981, 214.)

bered under 35 percent. The less orderly structures appeared to advantage the late entrants into public office.[4]

Overall my analysis of the timetables of office careers in the United States during the period 1900–1958 reinforces the hierarchical structure of political opportunities we discerned in the preceding chapter. As offices were located higher in the opportunity structure, so too the ages at which they were won increased. More important, the age focus was sharper in the higher offices. The focus was also sharper where there were fewer political opportunities. Well-defined age patterns were also associated with careerism in public office.

Age Patterns and Changes in the Structure of Political Opportunities

I based the preceding discussion of the opportunity structure's age patterns on the patterns that emerged in the United States between 1900 and 1958. But changes in age patterns are also of interest. Changes in age patterns alert us to the changes in the structure that are most significant for elective officeholding. It is useful, therefore, to break down age patterns according to time periods.

---

4. For a more detailed discussion of the states' structures of political opportunities, see Schlesinger 1966, chaps. 5 and 6.

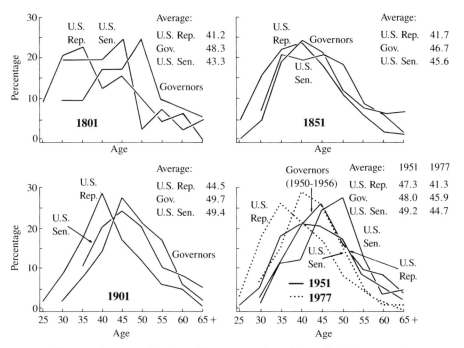

Fig. 4.4. Age at achieving office, 1801–1977. (From Schlesinger and Schlesinger 1981, 210.)

During the first decades of the Republic, the opportune ages for the achievement of elective office were by no means clear. While the modal age distributions for the achievement of major state and federal offices were distinct, the distribution of ages for each office lacked focus and was widely dispersed (see fig. 4.4). Thus, from 1800 to 1809, the largest group of U.S. representatives were first elected in their late thirties, the largest group of senators in their late forties, the largest group of governors in their early fifties. At the same time, the modal age-group for each office was not conspicuously dominant.

From the mid-nineteenth century to the turn of the century, the age distribution for each office became more focused. By 1851, not only was the focus clearer, but the age distribution for the three offices looked very much the same. At either end of the age-scale, fewer individuals achieved office than those in the middle; for all three offices the modal age-groups were in their forties. By 1901, the focus of age distributions was even sharper: representatives were winning their first elections predominantly in their early forties, senators and governors in their late forties.

Given the changing age patterns throughout the nineteenth century, the length of office careers was also in flux. Throughout the nineteenth century the overall length of service in each of the three offices was relatively brief. No office emerged as a potential career office until after the turn of the century, when the average senatorial term approached 8 years (Ripley 1969, 43). In the first years of the Republic, despite the official six-year term, the average length of service in the Senate was a mere 2.5 years, well below that of service in the House, which was averaging 5.66 years, or 2.83 official terms. During the nineteenth century, Senate service rose slowly to an average of 4.0 years in the 1830s. Only in the 1870s did it begin to rise again, but the average length of service did not exceed the official six-year term until 1900. Meanwhile, service in the House took a somewhat reverse course, though it too noticeably increased after 1900. After the high of 5.66 years in 1811, the average length of service in the House dropped to a low of 3.38 years in the 32d Congress of 1853. It then rose slowly until 1901, when it reached 6.22 years (Polsby 1968, 146). Gubernatorial service followed a course similar to that of service in the House. Initially, the average length of service was 4.90 years, although official terms varied from 1 to 4 years, with one-year terms prevailing (Kallenbach 1966, 187). By 1850–59, average gubernatorial service had dropped to 2.94 years, after which it rose to 3.39 years in the decade 1900–1909 (Schlesinger 1970). By the end of the nineteenth century, then, the possibilities for extended elective office careers had not yet emerged.[5]

After the turn of the century and for the next five decades, age patterns for elective office were quite clear. It was for this period that I established the national structure of political opportunities as a hierarchy of offices requiring increasingly stringent qualifications, including age qualifications. During this period, too, the federal legislature emerged as something of a haven for careerists.

Starting in 1960, age and tenure patterns began to alter. For the major offices of representative, governor, and senator the trend was toward younger officeholders. This was especially true of the Congress. By the 1970s, the optimal age for election to the House was the late thirties, for the Senate the late forties (see fig. 4.4). This trend was accompanied by a small increase in the number of individuals entering congress without prior office experience. The marked change was the increased number of senators and representatives with state legislative experience, a change that represented a return to the nineteenth-century practice (see table 4.3). It also implied a change in the age patterns of state legislatures toward younger personnel. Also noteworthy was the change in the age rankings of the offices of governor and senator that was

---

5. According to the evidence available, which is sparse, the nineteenth century saw an even sharper rise in turnover in state legislatures. In Connecticut, for example, the percentage of legislators reelected from the previous year was 54.0 percent in 1800, 22.6 percent in 1830, 12.7 percent in 1860, 9.3 percent in 1880, and a mere 5.2 percent in 1889 (Luce 1924, 356).

accompanied by a decline in the number of senators coming from the governorship. As in the nineteenth century, in the 1970s, senators were typically winning their first elections at a similar or somewhat earlier age than governors, although the evidence also shows a decline in the average age of governors (Sabato 1978, 32). At the same time, the proportion of senators coming from the governorship declined from 28.6 percent in the 1950s to 15.0 percent in the 1970s, while the importance of the House as the manifest office for the Senate rose (see table 4.3).

The trend toward younger legislators was accompanied by an increasing number of retirements in the Congress. In the House, the number of voluntary retirements increased from twelve in 1966 to thirty in 1978. Between 1966 and 1974, 25.4 percent of the House retired; of these more than half retired before the age of sixty-five. A disproportionate number of retirees were late

TABLE 4.3. Selected Prior Public Office Experience of Federal Legislators and Governors, 1800–1976

Prior Office	Congress Served (year elected)				
	7th (1800)	32d (1850)	57th (1900)	82d (1950)	95th (1976)
	U.S. Representatives				
None	14.7%	14.6%	15.6%	18.2%	21.1%
State legislature	74.1	59.4	40.5	33.3	43.9
	U.S. Senators				
None	2.4	4.1	4.3	7.1	11.0
State legislature	78.1	74.0	55.4	38.1	45.0
U.S. Representative	34.2	39.7	38.0	28.6	32.0
Governor	4.9	16.4	19.6	27.6	15.0
	Governors[a]				
	1800–1809	1850–59	1900–1909	1950–59	1970–75[b]
None	7.0	1.6	9.4	5.3	14.0
State legislature	75.4	69.8	57.0	43.6	40.0
U.S. Representative	38.6	23.8	16.8	9.8	14.0
U.S. Senator	15.8	5.6	0.7	4.5	—

Source: Schlesinger and Schlesinger 1981, 217.

[a]Elected governors only.

[b]1970–75 data are from Sabato 1978. The percentages differ in that they reflect the penultimate office rather than total experience. This understates the amount of state legislative experience in the latter group of governors. In the period 1900–1949, only 17.8 percent of the governors had the state legislature as a penultimate office.

starters: over 40 percent had not entered the House until after fifty, while fewer than 25 percent of the entire House had entered at this late age (Frantzich 1978). At the same time, between 1940 and 1970, the percentage of senior representatives, those with ten or more terms, who died in office declined from 34.8 percent to 23.5 percent, while those who retired because of electoral defeat increased from 15.2 percent to 39.6 percent (Bullock 1972). Similarly, the unprecedented turnover in Senate personnel in the elections of 1976 and 1978 marked the end of a number of long senatorial careers.[6]

Younger legislators and increasing retirements were accompanied by some turmoil in congressional tenure. After 1960, tenure rose in both houses of Congress. In 1961 the average length of service in the House reached 11.3 years. In the Senate, the average length of service rose to 10.0 years in 1965 and to 10.5 years in 1967. In 1978, however, the average length of service in the House dropped to 9.37 years, below the 1951 figure, while the average length of service in the Senate dropped to 10.27 years, below the 1967 figure.[7]

Meanwhile, tenure continued to increase in the state legislatures, paralleling the increased importance of state legislative experience in congressional careers. In 1971–76, the national average for the number of new legislators dropped to 37.3. The average also dropped in the five legislatures whose age and tenure patterns I discussed earlier. The largest decline came in Vermont, where the average proportion of new legislators per term dropped to 37.3 percent. But the number fell in the other legislatures as well: in Connecticut to 40.2 percent, in South Dakota to 38.5 percent, in Michigan to 24.6 percent, in Pennsylvania to 23.4 percent.

How should we account for the changes in the age and tenure patterns that I have sketched over the course of the Republic? The most obvious explanation for changes in age patterns in an elite group are the changes in the age composition of the general population. This does not, however, seem to help much. Thus, the increase in life expectancy over the history of the United States did not increase the chances of older citizens for elective office. If anything, those chances appear to have been greatest when life expectancy and the median age of the population was lowest, at the beginning of the nineteenth century.

If demographic factors affect age patterns for elective office, it is most likely due to short-run variations in birth rates, as well as to generational

---

6. Treas (1977), applying a life-table analysis to Senate careers between 1945 and 1970, concluded that increasing seniority did not make senators less liable to electoral defeat.

7. By 1988, however, the average length of service had again risen perceptibly in both houses of Congress: in the House the average rose to 11.74 years, in the Senate to 11.85 years.

differences in morbidity, education, income, and political experience. Thus, variations in the size of birth cohorts may influence the relative chances of their members. The era of the Great Depression saw a decline in the birth rate. Someone born in 1935, then, was thirty-five in 1970 and a central figure in the age-group capturing positions in the congress and in state capitals in unprecedented numbers. Indeed, expanding opportunities in all fields would appear to have reduced the competition for positions of prominence faced by this relatively small birth cohort (Neugarten and Hagestad 1976, 45).

More directly related to the changes in the age and tenure patterns I have noted are other changes in the structure of political opportunities. The period of unfocused age distributions and short tenure coincided with the period of unsettled institutional arrangements that characterized much of the nineteenth century. During the early years of the Republic, the number and status of state and federal offices had yet to be determined. Washington had not yet become the nation's political mecca. Few federal elective officials chose to remain there the entire year. Most senators and representatives did not bring their families to live in the capital (Young 1966). Moreover, after service in the Congress, it was by no means unusual for senators to return to the House or the governorship, and for senators and representatives to return to the state legislatures where most had begun their political careers. Like senators and representatives, governors did not rule out a return to the legislature, from which ranks they had also often risen.

Perhaps no politician's career better demonstrates the unsettled nature of the opportunity structure of the period than that of Henry Clay. Elected to his first public office at twenty-six, Clay was elected to his last public office at the age of seventy-two, appropriately dying in office on 29 June 1852. Between his first and last election, he had a remarkably long but unstructured office career. Elected first to the Kentucky legislature in 1803, three years later he was chosen by the legislature to fill an unexpired term in the U.S. Senate, although he was just shy of the age requirement of thirty. Serving a brief few months, he returned to the Kentucky state House of Representatives where he was immediately chosen speaker. Once again elected to fill an unexpired term in the U.S. Senate, he served one year from 1810–11, following which he was immediately elected to the U.S. House of Representatives. During his first term in the House he was elected Speaker. Resigning briefly from the House in 1814, during which time he served as one of the commissioners negotiating the peace treaty with Great Britain, he returned to the House serving again as Speaker. In 1825 he once again resigned from the House, this time to become John Quincy Adams's secretary of state. In 1831 he was elected to the U.S. Senate, again to fill an unexpired term. This time he was reelected by the legislature and served until he resigned in 1842. During his first term, he served as chairman of the Committee on Foreign Relations.

Unsuccessful candidate for the presidency from the House in 1824, from the Senate in 1832, and as a former officeholder in 1844, he was again elected to the U.S. Senate in 1849 (Biographical Directory 1989; Polsby 1968). Even granting Clay extraordinary political talents, such a career was only possible given the structure of political opportunities of the time.

The relative status of offices was kept uncertain well into the nineteenth century because of the political ethic that triumphed during the 1830s under Andrew Jackson. This ethic equated democracy with the widespread distribution of elected offices enforced by their frequent rotation. Seats in the House of Representatives were frequently viewed as offices to be rotated among the various counties comprising a House district (Kernell 1976). In such an ethos, no well-ordered committee system or methodical progression to the leadership developed in Congress to encourage long service. The brief service that could bring Henry Clay to positions of power, first in the Kentucky House of Representatives, then in the U.S. House of Representatives, and finally in the U.S. Senate, continued to reward others during these years. Similarly, expectations, if not always the law, limited gubernatorial service to two terms. But official terms were also brief, mostly one-year terms in 1820, two-year terms in 1860. Not until 1900 were gubernatorial terms almost equally divided between two- and four-year terms.

While institutional practices were contributing to high turnover, thereby blurring the relative importance of offices, the institutions themselves were expanding in size with something of the same effect. The steady entry of new states meant new positions at the state and federal level. The growth in population also had its effect, most noticeably on the U.S. House of Representatives. The House grew from 142 members in 1800 to 391 members in 1900. At the same time, the states' elective executive positions were expanding to include not only the governorship but such positions as secretary of state, state treasurer, and state attorney general. Thus, the relatively broad distribution of age and tenure patterns that I traced during much of the nineteenth century alerts us to the factors responsible for the expansion of political opportunities and the free movement from office to office during the same period.

The more settled age and tenure patterns that I traced during the first six decades of the twentieth century reflect the settling of institutional arrangements as well as institutional changes that worked to limit the size of the structure of political opportunities and clarify its shape.[8] Affirmation of the

---

8. Important changes were made during the first two decades of the twentieth century in the structure of electoral competition. They were the direct election of senators, the adoption of the direct primary, the widespread adoption of the Australian ballot, and women's suffrage. The significance of these changes will be discussed in subsequent chapters. The effect of nominating procedures on the ages and office experience of candidates is also discussed in Snowiss 1966 and Tobin 1975.

increased power of the Senate contributed to the Senate's establishment as the major elective position beneath the presidency (Rothman 1966; Ripley 1969). Within the Senate, the power of seniority, established by the end of the nineteenth century, was confirmed (Ripley 1969). Evidence of the appreciation in value of senatorial office during the first half of the twentieth century was the increase in the number of senators whose political careers ended in Senate service. In 1851, less than half (47.9 percent) ended their careers in the Senate; in 1951, 81 percent did so. After 1900, there was also a precipitous decline in the number of senators willing to accept federal cabinet posts (Huntington 1965). Movement from the Senate to the governorship ended, too. On the other hand, the number of governors going on to the Senate increased. The number rose from 16.4 percent in 1851 and 19.6 percent in 1901, to 27.6 percent in 1951. Thus, it was during this period, as we have seen, that the governorship established itself as an intermediate office, the Senate more of an end office in the national structure of political opportunities.

During the same period, the House established its position as both a career office and a manifest office for the Senate. By 1910, the number of House seats stabilized at 435. Shortly thereafter, the slow decline in turnover that came at the end of the nineteenth century was given impetus by important internal reforms, notably those weakening the power of the Speaker, which strengthened the importance of seniority and orderly advancement (Polsby 1968). As a result, the proportion of representatives whose public careers ended in the House increased from 39.7 percent in 1851 to 76.8 percent in 1951. At the same time, the proportion of senators who had first served as representatives declined from 39.7 percent in 1851 to 28.6 percent. Nevertheless, the House remained the single most important manifest office for the Senate.

While the changes in the age and tenure patterns after the turn of the century alert us to a reduction in the size of the structure of political opportunities and a clarification of its shape, changes in these patterns after the 1950s alert us to important alterations once again. One of these alterations was the change in the term of gubernatorial office, which reduced the number of opportunities for becoming governor. After the 1950s, an increasing number of states adopted the four-year term for governor. By 1968, only twelve states did not have the four-year term (Kallenbach 1966); by 1976, this number had been reduced to four. The lengthening of the gubernatorial term coincided with the decline in the number of senators whose penultimate office was the governorship, as well as a decline in the age at which senators typically first won election to the Senate. Another alteration was the trend within Congress to reduce the importance of seniority that contributed to the changes in congressional tenure and retirements that we noted (Ornstein and Rohde 1978).

Changes in the presidency's age and tenure patterns over the course of the Republic also reflected the opportunity structure's changing institutional arrangements. Established from the onset as the office of supreme importance in the Republic's opportunity structure, the presidency, unlike other federal offices, emerged in the early years with highly focused age and tenure patterns. The first six presidents all won their first election in the narrow age range of fifty-seven to sixty-one (see table 4.4). Four of the six served the two terms for which Washington had set the precedent. The tightly focused age and tenure patterns of the early years of the Republic reflected a well-defined promotional system. Presidential nominees came from two states, Virginia and Massachusetts, although the Virginia dynasty dominated. Only the two Adamses of Massachusetts were unable to win second terms. Washington's first two successors came from the vice presidency; the next two individuals to repeat this feat came 36 years and almost 200 years after Jefferson, Van Buren in 1836, George Bush in 1988. Jefferson's three successors, Madison, Monroe, and John Quincy Adams, came from the office of secretary of state, a promotional pattern never used again.

With the election of Andrew Jackson, the presidency, until the Civil War, demonstrated the unfocused age and tenure patterns that other offices had experienced previously. The presidential patterns, too, reflected efforts to alter institutional relationships to accommodate the republic's expanding territory and population. The ages at which presidents first won election diverged widely, from William Henry Harrison's sixty-eight to Franklin Pierce's forty-eight. This was also a period of one-term presidencies. Of the nine presidents who served between 1829 and 1857, only Andrew Jackson served two terms. While Harrison and Taylor died in office, their vice presidents, Tyler and Fillmore, could not win election in their own right. During this period, presidents not only varied in age, they came to the presidency from new and varied sources, the Senate, the governorship, the military, and from a variety of states, Tennessee, New York, Indiana, Pennsylvania, and New Hampshire.

After the Civil War, age and tenure patterns became more settled, as they had for the other offices I examined. The age range narrowed: the five post–Civil War presidents elected in their own right won their first elections between the ages of forty-five and fifty-four. Two of the seven post–Civil War presidents were able to win reelection, though Cleveland's two terms were interrupted. Still, neither of the two vice presidents who acceded to the presidency, Johnson and Arthur, could win election in their own right. These age and tenure patterns indicate some clarification of the paths to the presidency. Of the five presidents elected in their own right, only Grant failed to come either from the Senate or a governorship. There was also some evidence of geographical concentration. Four of the five presidents came from the Midwest; only Cleveland came from outside the region.

TABLE 4.4. President's Age at First Inauguration

	Age	Mean	Standard Deviation
1789–1824		57.8	1.5
Washington	57		
J. Adams	61		
Jefferson	57		
Madison	57		
Monroe	58		
J. Q. Adams	57		
1832–56		57.8	7.1
Jackson	61		
Van Buren	54		
W. H. Harrison	68		
Tyler	51		
Polk	49		
Taylor	64		
Fillmore	50		
Buchanan	65		
1860–88		51.3	3.5
Lincoln	52		
A. Johnson	56		
Grant	46		
Hayes	54		
Garfield	49		
Arthur	51		
Cleveland	47		
B. Harrison	55		
1896–1952		53.6	5.2
McKinley	54		
T. Roosevelt	42		
Taft	51		
Wilson	56		
Harding	55		
Coolidge	51		
Hoover	54		
F. D. Roosevelt	51		
Truman	60		
Eisenhower	62		
1960–88		57.1	7.9
Kennedy	43		
L. Johnson	55		
Nixon	56		
Ford	61		
Carter	52		
Reagan	69		
Bush	64		

The age and tenure patterns for the presidents from 1900 through 1958 confirmed the period of relative institutional stability I identified earlier. The age patterns were narrowly focused. Of the eight presidents from McKinley through Franklin Roosevelt, seven first won election in the very narrow range of ages between fifty-one and fifty-six. Of the ten presidents from McKinley through Eisenhower, only Taft and Hoover could not win reelection. Also in contrast to the nineteenth century, the three vice presidents who acceded to the presidency, Theodore Roosevelt, Calvin Coolidge, and Harry Truman, were all able to win election in their own right. During the period 1900–1958, too, the importance of manifest offices for the presidency was established, especially the governorship. Of the ten presidents elected between 1900 and 1958, five were governors and two senators. Of the three who held no elective office before acceding to the presidency, two, Taft and Hoover, failed to win reelection. A geographical focus was also confirmed; of the ten presidents, six came from two states, New York and Ohio.

Again the age and tenure patterns of the presidency after the 1950s confirm a period of lesser stability. The older presidents, Truman and Eisenhower, were followed in 1960 by the election of Kennedy, the youngest president ever elected. While Johnson, Nixon, and Carter were all first elected in their mid-fifties, they were succeeded by two of the oldest presidents in the history of the United States. Ronald Reagan at 69 was the oldest man ever elected. His successor, Bush, at 64 was the next oldest since the Civil War. There was also some disruption in tenure patterns. Ford, the first individual chosen to accede to the presidency after a presidential resignation, failed to win election in his own right, while his successor, Carter, was the first president since Hoover unable to win a second term. Disruptions in age and tenure patterns coincided with some fluctuation in promotional patterns. Nixon, Carter, and Reagan all acceded to the presidency having held manifest offices. But all were former officeholders, demonstrating that nonincumbency could also be an advantage in post-1960s national politics. Geographical backgrounds were more varied too, ranging from Massachusetts to Texas, from California to Georgia, reflecting the new importance of the South and West.

The Impact of Age Patterns on Political Ambitions

Ultimately, our interest in the age requirements imposed by the structure of political opportunities rests with their impact upon political ambitions. The close relation between age and office patterns, which we have examined, intensifies the impact of the structure of political opportunities on political ambitions by controlling the long-range behavior of numerous politicians. Both patterns impose order upon opportunity and reduce the field of the reasonably ambitious. True, nowhere in the United States can any one individual be assured of advancement because office or age patterns have so restricted the field. But this situation merely serves to intensify the impact of ambition; by definition, certainty reduces or eliminates its effect. Rather, my evidence reveals that the opportunity structure in the United States acts as a clearinghouse for political ambitions.

My analysis of the data on political careers in the United States demonstrates that there is an office hierarchy, defined by the movement from office to office, and age timetables, and that ambition intensifies as one rises in the hierarchy. We infer, therefore, that the impact of ambition upon the behavior of public officeholders will be greater on those in higher office, greater upon U.S. representatives than upon state legislators, and greater upon senators than upon U.S. representatives. This, indeed, is one of the controls democracies should provide over the behavior of their officeholders, the control of progressive ambitions as officeholders gain more power.

Do we have any direct evidence that age patterns arouse or dampen political ambitions? For most of the period we have been examining we have no direct test of the relation of ambition to age patterns. Studies have been done, however, of the ages and ambitions of selected state legislators and city councillors during the late 1950s and early 1960s (Wahlke et al. 1962; Prewitt and Nowlin 1969; Prewitt 1970; Hain 1974; Dutton 1975). The striking finding of these studies was the decline in the percentage of officeholders expressing ambition for higher office with each advancing age-group. A sizeable majority of the younger legislators (those under forty-six) in New Jersey, California, Tennessee, and Ohio expressed ambitions for higher office (Hain 1974). This was also true of the majority of the city councillors in the San Francisco Bay area under the age of thirty-six (Prewitt 1970). In contrast, among legislators who had reached the age of fifty-six, only one-third expressed progressive ambitions; only 10 percent of the city councillors in this age-group did so. Hain (1974) also demonstrated in his follow-up of careers of the legislators a strong positive relationship between those who expressed ambition for higher office and those who subsequently took action to achieve it.

At the same time, it is important to note that each office attracted ambitious individuals in different proportions. In each age-group, a larger proportion of state legislators expressed ambitions for higher office than did city councillors. These studies indicate that there is a strong tendency for age patterns to reinforce themselves by focusing the ambitions of political aspirants. Nevertheless, ambitions do not uniformly decline with age. The office itself draws those with progressive ambitions to greater or lesser degree.[9]

As a democratic control, then, the progressive age pattern is especially

9. For the relation between age, ambition, and women's careers in politics, see Schlesinger and Schlesinger 1981, 230–34.

useful, for it channels the tensions created by the ambitions of public office seekers at the height of their political vigor. It makes it acceptable for eminence to come to older individuals, without barring the way to political prodigies. It also makes possible long-range career planning in an otherwise risky business. Thirty-five-year-olds with progressive ambitions, although constitutionally eligible, are not likely to aim directly at the presidency. On the contrary, they know that, under the proper conditions, their chances will improve over the next fifteen to twenty years. In this manner, ambition affects the behavior not only of those in the age-group appropriate for a particular office; it also affects younger individuals, causing them to act in such a way that they will create the proper conditions for subsequent advancement. If, instead, individuals of all ages could assault major offices with an equal chance of success, progressive ambitions would be far less useful as a democratic control.

The structure of political opportunities renders progressive ambitions useful as democratic controls because the structure is as obvious to the members of the political community at large as it is to individuals ambitious for office. In effect, it sets the framework of expectations. In the United States, both the national and the states' structures of political opportunities serve this purpose, despite the variety and exceptions. In the United States there are both manifest offices and manifest ages. When the manifest office and the manifest age coincide, the influential members of the political community, elective and appointed officeholders, party activists, representatives of interest groups, reporters and columnists, begin to treat the officeholder as a potential governor, senator, or president. With such expectations, officeholders gain influence. But they also lose freedom once the goal of their ambition is clearly in focus; they become the creatures of the constituency of the office on which their ambitions are now focused.[10]

To the extent that ambitious office seekers are the focus of party organization, the structure of political opportunities helps determine the nature of political parties in democracies. Of special significance for parties in the United States is the structure's flexibility and its changing character. Flexibility and changes in age and tenure patterns, as well as in patterns of movement from office to office, are of great importance for party organization. A flexible and changing opportunity structure means organizations that must also be flexible and adaptable. The opportunity structure, however, is only one important aspect of the polity to which party organizations must

---

10. In this respect, the 1988 presidential campaign of Governor Michael Dukakis of Massachusetts is instructive. His critics accused him of refusing to make the hard decisions necessary to preserve the fiscal well-being of the state, in order to sustain the image of the "Massachusetts miracle" and further his presidential ambitions.

respond. The other is the structure of electoral competition. It is to the structure of electoral competition that we shall now turn our attention.

REFERENCES

Biographical Directory of the American Congress 1774–1989. 1989. Washington, D.C.: U.S. Government Printing Office.

Bullock, Charles S., III. 1972. "House Careerists: Changing Patterns of Longevity and Attrition." *American Political Science Review* 66:1295–1305.

Dutton, William H. 1975. "The Political Ambitions of Local Legislators: A Comparative Perspective." *Polity* 7:504–19.

Frantzich, Steven E. 1978. "Opting Out: Retirement from the House of Representatives 1966–1974." *American Politics Quarterly* 6:251–74.

Hain, Paul. 1974. "Age, Ambitions, and Political Careers: The Middle-Age Crisis." *Western Political Quarterly* 27:265–74.

Huntington, Samuel P. 1965. "Congressional Responses to the Twentieth Century." In *The Congress and America's Future*, ed. David B. Truman. Englewood Cliffs, N.J.: Prentice-Hall.

Kallenbach, Joseph E. 1966. *The American Chief Executive.* New York: Harper and Row.

Kernell, Samuel. 1976. "Ambition and Politics: An Exploratory Study of Political Careers of Nineteenth-Century Congressmen." Paper presented at the annual meeting of the American Political Science Association, Chicago.

Luce, Robert. 1924. *Legislative Assemblies.* Boston: Houghton Mifflin.

Neugarten, Bernice L., and G. O. Hagestad. 1976. "Age and the Life Course." In *Handbook of Aging and the Social Sciences*, ed. Robert Binstock and Ethel Shanas. New York: Van Nostrand Reinhold.

Ornstein, Norman J., and David W. Rohde. 1978. "Political Parties and Congressional Reform." In *Parties and Elections in an Anti-Party Age*, ed. Jeff Fishel. Bloomington: Indiana University Press.

Polsby, Nelson W. 1968. "The Institutionalization of the U.S. House of Representatives." *American Political Science Review* 62:144–68.

Prewitt, Kenneth. 1970. *The Recruitment of Political Leaders: A Study of Citizen-Politicians.* Indianapolis: Bobbs-Merrill.

Prewitt, Kenneth, and William Nowlin. 1969. "Political Ambitions and the Behavior of Incumbent Politicians." *Western Political Quarterly* 22:298–308.

Ripley, Randall B. 1969. *Power in the Senate.* New York: St. Martins.

Rothman, David J. 1966. *Politics and Power: The United States Senate 1869–1901.* Cambridge, Mass.: Harvard University Press.

Sabato, Larry. 1978. *Goodby to Good-Time Charlie: The American Governor Transformed 1900–1975.* Lexington, Mass.: Lexington Books.

Schlesinger, Joseph A. 1957. "Lawyers and American Politics: A Clarified View." *Midwest Journal of Political Science* 1:26–39.

Schlesinger, Joseph A. 1966. *Ambition and Politics.* Chicago: Rand McNally.

Schlesinger, Joseph A. 1970. "The Governor's Place in American Politics." *Public Administration Review* 30:2–9.

Schlesinger, Joseph A., and Mildred Schlesinger. 1981. "Aging and Opportunities for Elective Office." In *Aging: Social Change,* ed. James G. March. New York: Academic Press.

Shin, Kwang S., and John S. Jackson, III. 1979. "Membership Turnover in U.S. State Legislatures: 1931–1976." *Legislative Studies Quarterly* 4:95–104.

Snowiss, Leo M. 1966. "Congressional Recruitment and Representation." *American Political Science Review* 60:627–39.

Tobin, Richard J. 1975. "The Influence of Nominating Systems on the Political Experiences of State Legislators." *Western Political Quarterly* 18:553–66.

Treas, Judith. 1977. "A Life Table for Postwar Senate Careers: A Research Note." *Social Forces* 56:202–7.

Wahlke, John C., Heinz Eulau, William Buchanan, and Leroy Ferguson. 1962. *The Legislative System.* New York: Wiley.

Young, James S. 1966. *The Washington Community, 1800–1828.* New York: Columbia University Press.

CHAPTER 5

The Structure of Electoral Competition

The structure of political opportunities is one factor that excites and directs political ambitions. Another is the structure of electoral competition. The competitive structure is critical to ambition for office in democracies because it directly affects the chances of success. It is vital in determining whether or not individuals will seek a particular office, and whether or not they will have further aspirations. At the same time, electoral competition is the principal mechanism in democracies for controlling ambitious officeholders. The more competitive a constituency, the more unsure anyone is of election and reelection. It is uncertainty that leads the politically ambitious to respond to the will of the electorate in some manner. Just as the officeholder with no further electoral ambitions is free of electoral controls, the candidate always sure of election is less constrained by the electoral process. Thus, desirably, in democracies, the structure of electoral competition helps inspire and temper political ambitions.

The competitive structure is defined, in part, by electoral rules and procedures. Rules and procedures define the arena or the constituency in which the electoral contest takes place, the timing of the contest, access to the contest, the contest's format, and the measure of winning the contest. All these factors influence the voters' response to candidates for office and, therefore, help shape the structure of electoral competition.

The definition of the office constituency, its size, its demographic composition, and its social and economic makeup clearly have an effect on electoral competition for office. No single electoral rule preoccupies office seekers and officeholders more than the circumscription of their electoral constituencies. The never-ending concern of politicians for the shape of legislative constituencies and the consequences of redistricting reflects their desire to shape competition for individual and partisan advantage. Since the 1960s, most democracies have been affected by pressures to extend the vote to eighteen-year-olds and to revamp legislative districts to eliminate disparities in population. In the United States, civil rights legislation has played a particularly important role in altering the composition of electoral districts and, therefore, the electoral contest.

The timing of elections must also be uppermost in the minds of office seekers and officeholders. A distinguishing feature of the structure in the United States is its predictability. Neither wars, civil or international, nor the accidents of death and resignation have been allowed to alter the electoral schedule. Electoral strategies in such a context are bound to differ from those in parliamentary regimes, where the legislature can be dissolved, or in a presidential system such as the French Fifth Republic, where the death or resignation of the president resets the timetable. The relationship in the timing of elections among offices also affects competition. Offices elected on the same day and ballot are more subject to the same political influences than those elected on different days. The United States, during the nineteenth century, moved consistently toward uniform electoral timing for federal offices, retaining the differences in office terms. Most, but not all, state general elections have come to follow the same schedule, although with variations in office terms that have consequences for electoral competition. Given the level of predictability in the United States, variations in electoral timing are a critical consideration in candidates' electoral strategies too.

Rules for entering the contest or gaining access to the ballot also affect competition. Much depends on how complex these rules are. Does the state make access relatively painless, as in France for those interested in election to the national assembly? Are there financial penalties of some substance for failing to attract a specified number of votes in the general election, as in Great Britain for those interested in election to parliament? Or does the state complicate accessibility by requiring a nominating election, as in the United States after 1900 for those interested in most offices from city councillor to the presidency. Before 1900 in the United States, access to the ballot was not a matter of state interest and procedures varied. They included nomination for the presidency, first by a small and elite legislative caucus, then by the emergence of a party convention. Procedures also varied considerably from state to state for lesser offices. After 1900, the emergence of the direct primary made competition for office an intraparty as well as an interparty affair.

Not only access to, but also the format of, the ballot or electoral contest affect the competitive structure. The number of offices whose candidates appear on the ballot and the amount of information given about each candidate are all factors that can affect the voters' response to candidates and, thereby, the conditions under which candidates compete for office. In the United States during the nineteenth century, the ballot format was in flux. After 1900, the widespread acceptance of the Australian ballot, as adapted to the political structure of the United States, had a considerable impact on electoral competition. It meant that in the United States, in contrast to parliamentary systems such as Great Britain and France, voters were asked to vote for several officials on a ballot that gave the names of all the candidates. In almost all the states the ballot also gave partisan information about the candidates for state and federal offices. Despite the multiple listings, the Australian ballot always allowed voters to make distinct and separate choices for offices, even where the ballot was modified to encourage voters to make a single partisan choice (Rusk 1970). Furthermore, because they are faced with many choices, voters might not complete their ballots; candidates, even on the same ballot, then face different competitive conditions (Walker 1966).

Of course the rules for winning the electoral contest are of considerable importance in determining how candidates compete for office in democracies (Rae 1967; Grofman and Lijphart 1986). Throughout the history of the United States, the rules, following the British precedent, have defined the winner in almost all elections as the candidate with a plurality of the votes. This has been true for legislative candidates running in single-member districts and for presidential candidates seeking the electoral college votes of the states, as well as for most candidates in primary elections. As a consequence, competition for office has generally been limited to a few candidates. There has been no chance to regroup for a second round of elections, as has been true for national legislative elections throughout much of French republican history. In these elections, victory in the first round can come only by receiving an absolute majority of the votes. Only in the second round of elections does a plurality determine the winning candidate (Schlesinger and Schlesinger 1990). Nor have candidates for office in the United States been able to count on winning by attracting a specified proportion of the electorate's support for a list of candidates, as would be true in parliamentary systems that elect their legislatures by proportional representation.

In the United States, then, electoral rules (with few exceptions) require that candidates compete on their own for each office, thereby making the competitive character of each constituency important. Variations in the competitive conditions of offices are therefore critical to an understanding of the operation of political institutions in the United States, especially of parties. Note, for example, how distinctive competitive conditions affect the electoral strategy for the presidency and the Congress differently. The winner-take-all rule for distributing a state's votes in the electoral college means that states certain to vote for one party require less attention from both parties than states that are competitive. I already noted in chapter 3 that competitive states are favored in the presidential complex. In contrast, when overall competition for the Congress is low, members from one-party constituencies have the advantage. Lack of competition assures them the seniority that is the predominant rule for distributing leadership positions. Only if control of the Congress should be threatened are members of Congress from one-party districts, therefore, likely to be concerned about fellow partisans in competitive districts. Within the Congress, the bicameral system provides for distinctive constituencies with their own modes of competition for each legislative house, nationally and in the states, a condition that can produce differences between houses in partisan control and in policy views. Each state within the federal system also develops its own competitive system, a fact that many scholars have used to explain policy differences among the states.

How do we evaluate the competitive conditions for individual offices? The idea of electoral competition is straightforward. It captures the prospects of candidates for each office in a coming election. The more uncertain a candidate is that he or she will be elected, the more competitive the election. In partisan terms, a constituency is competitive if the candidates of more than one party have a good chance at election. It is a one-party constituency, that is, noncompetitive, if only one party is expected to win. Electoral competition can also be defined in terms of relative probabilities. Thus, the chances of a party's winning an office can range from 0.0 (none at all) to 1.0 (perfect). A full range of probabilities from 0.0 to 1.0 can exist. The situation is most competitive when the probabilities for each party are 0.5. Electoral competition has, indeed, become an important concept in analyzing the political history of the United States. The idea of "critical elections," of electoral alignments and realignments, or of different party systems rests on the proposition that the ways parties compete for office take on stable or predictable patterns. A new era or system emerges when the old pattern breaks down and is replaced by a new competitive arrangement or distribution of competitive constituencies that acquires stability.

As is true for the structure of political opportunities, we can deduce the structure of electoral competition empirically; we can construct the structure from electoral data. While electoral data is part of the record easily come by in most democracies, the use one makes of it in determining the competitive conditions for office is very much a matter of judgment. This is especially true for a structure of political opportunities as complex as the structure in the United States, which I have laid out in the two preceding chapters. Electoral competition has long been a critical variable in studies of politics in the United States, including studies of party organizations, as well as studies of the quality of government, and the relationship between political and economic conditions (Key 1949 and 1956, chap. 8; MacRae 1952; Turner 1953; Golembiewski 1958; Lockard 1959). Yet considering the importance of competition for the study of democratic politics, remarkably little has been done to clarify the concept.

Part of our problem derives from the future-oriented character of the idea of electoral competition. The idea rests upon uncertainty and directs our attention toward the next contest, not the last one. The results of past elections are, in contrast, quite certain. Thus to ask, is congressional district X competitive, is to talk about future elections, elections in which the level of competition is bound to be defined by many factors, of which the results of past elections is only one. We can look back at a particular election and estimate that it was or was not competitive by noting whether the election was close, or whether it produced a change in party control of the office. But that evidence does not tell us how those involved before the election actually viewed their prospects. Our figures tell us only how the election turned out.

For example, by every measure taken after the national elections of 1948, the elections were very competitive. Partisan control of Congress shifted from the Republicans to the Democrats. The incumbent president, Harry Truman, was reelected by a narrow margin. A change of 29,294 votes in three states would have made Thomas Dewey president. Yet all accounts before the elections assumed a lopsided Republican victory. Democrats had great difficulty in raising campaign funds and in attracting experienced candidates. How else can one explain the willingness of the Illinois Democratic organization to support such atypical candidates for governor and senator as diplomat Adlai Stevenson and professor-reformer Paul Douglas? In retrospect it was a competitive election; in prospect it was not. Distinguished political reporters refused even to accept the evidence of the first returns for the presidency. Of course the memory of 1948 has reverberated ever since, making candidates, pollsters, and commentators wary. Thus, the experience has made uncertain all subsequent presidential elections, no matter how one-sided the polls before the elections have been. The point is that competition as a factor that influences political behavior is a view of the future and, as such, exists in the eye of the beholder.

Measures of competition, on the other hand, must inevitably rest on the results of past elections. At best, therefore, they can offer a degree of predictability that derives from the stability of voting patterns within a given constituency. By predictability I do not mean electoral forecasting, but rather predictions that depend on consistencies in the electorate's behavior. A constituency may always vote for the same party. If so the constituency can, with some degree of certainty, be classified as safe or noncompetitive. In contrast, a constituency may shift its vote from one party to another with some frequency, allowing it to be classified as uncertain or competitive.

The measurement of competition, then, requires a method that reveals the periods during which the electorate has been consistent over time, the degree of the electorate's consistency during a given time period, and the relative chances of the parties for a particular office during that period. Finding the best definition of a time period rests upon finding eras of relative stability, or consistency in the patterns of constituency voting. Consistency over the selected period in turn allows political actors to make judgments about their relative chances for office. If, over a twenty-year period, each of two parties won half the elections for a particular office, we infer that the probabilities of winning the office for each party's candidate was 0.5. On the other hand, it is also possible that one party dominated the office for ten successive years, the other for the second ten years. In the latter instance, only one election was truly competitive, that in which partisan control shifted. Each situation would lead potential office seekers to different judgments about their relative chances for election.

The Structure of Electoral Competition in the United States: Measuring the Presidential Component

Since the presidency is the focus of the national structure of political opportunities in the United States, first of all we need a means of assessing the presidential component of the structure of electoral competition. At the same time, the states' responses to the parties' presidential candidates are essential to assessing the presidential component of the structure. The states' adoption, early in the Republic, of the winner-take-all practice for assigning their electoral votes in presidential elections has given them the key role in electoral competition for the presidency. Competition for the presidency, therefore, has always rested upon some assessment of a candidate's relative chances in each of the states. Hence our concern with patterns of consistency in presidential voting among the individual states.

The method I have chosen for assessing the presidential component of the structure of electoral competition is scaling (see Guttman 1950). Initially used by psychologists to test for consistency in attitudes, the technique is well adapted to the analysis of presidential voting because it rests upon simple *yes* or *no* responses to questions. In the real world of presidential politics, the states make such responses because they have had to respond, with few exceptions, to the candidates of only two parties. Thus, a state's voting behavior in presidential elections can be framed as a response to the question, Did it vote for or against party X? The answer to the question also tells us whether the state voted for or against party Y.

The idea of consistency implicit in scaling coincides with the sense of consistency in politics. By asking the simple question for each state over a sequence of elections, scaling allows us to discern consistency in voting behavior among the states in presidential elections, as well as incidents of disruption in their presidential voting patterns. While we would not expect all states to vote for a particular party always, we should consider it inconsistent behavior if states that voted Democratic when the party was doing poorly in most states were to vote Republican when the party was doing well in other states. If, for example, in a presidential election during the 1990s the District of Columbia were to vote for the Republican candidate while Arizona voted Democratic, we would say that a significant disruption had occurred. In seven previous consecutive elections the district and the state had behaved in just the opposite manner. It is precisely this sense of consistency and disruption that scaling captures with precision. Scaling also allows us to quantify the level of consistency in any sequence of elections so that we can determine precisely just when and where changes have taken place in the structure of competition.

To perceive consistency in any electoral time period in voting for the presidency, we need to align the states according to their level of support for each of the parties. I have taken the number of states voting Democratic or non-Democratic for president in the electoral college as the basis for defining the states' measure of support. I have chosen the Democratic party because it has the longest continuous history in presidential politics. For most elections since 1792, voting non-Democratic has meant voting first Federalist, then Whig, then Republican.[1] Thus, the elections are aligned from left to right on the scales in order of the increasing numbers of states voting Democratic. I could, of course, construct separate scales for each party. Because, however, presidential elections have been overwhelmingly dominated by two parties, the scale based on the Democratic party is simply the obverse of that for the other party.[2] Consistency, therefore, requires that states that vote Democratic or non-Democratic when the party is doing poorly continue to vote Democratic or non-Democratic when the party is doing better. Inconsistent behavior, or an "error," occurs when a state fails to vote as expected according to this rule. For any set of elections, we can measure the states' general level of consistency by calculating the proportion of errors or the *coefficient of reproducibility* (CR) in all the states' votes in all of the elections in a given time period.

The First Phase of the Presidential Competitive Structure

Scaling reveals the first phase of the presidential competitive structure to be the seven presidential elections between 1792 and 1816 (see table 5.1). Since our concern is with each state's consistency of behavior during the entire period, the placement of the elections from left to right on the scale is not a time-sequence but, rather, a ranking of the elections according to the proportion of states won by the Democratic candidates. Thus the election of 1792,

---

1. I am, of course, aware that granting the Democratic party a continuous history back to 1792 is taking historical liberties. Nevertheless, there are electoral links between the Jeffersonian Republican-Democrats and the Jacksonian Democrats of 1832.

2. My use of the Democratic party as the base may well have consequences for the rare occasions when a third party has won a state because the third party's votes are, in effect, included with all non-Democratic votes. The elections for which this consideration is relevant are 1892 (the Populists), 1912 (the Bull Moose Progressives), 1924 (the Lafollette Progressives), 1948 (the Dixiecrats), and 1968 (the Wallace Independents). On the other hand, since, with the exceptions of 1892 and 1948, these defections cut more into Republican votes, there are few significant effects on the scales due to adopting the Democratic–non-Democratic scheme.

the election in which the Democrats won the fewest states, is placed at the far left. The elections of 1796 and 1800 follow in that order because the Democrats took fewer states in these elections than in subsequent elections. The election of 1804 appears on the far right because, with Jefferson's reelection, the Democrats won their largest number of states in the period. The election of 1812 falls to the left of 1808 and 1804 because the Democrats carried fewer states than in those elections. With seven elections, the states fall into one of eight possible scale positions, from the states at the top that voted Democratic in all seven elections, to those at the bottom of the scale that never voted Democratic.

By any standard, the scale for this phase of the structure of electoral

TABLE 5.1. First Phase of the Presidential Competitive Structure, 1792–1816

Federal Wins		Democratic Wins					
1792[a]	1796	1800	1812	1808	1816	1804	State
X	X	X	X	X	X	X	Virginia
X	X	X	X	X	X	X	North Carolina
X	X	X	X	X	X	X	Georgia
X	X	X	X	X	X	X	Kentucky
X		X		X	X	X	New York
0	X	X	X	X	X	X	Tennessee[b]
	X	X	X	X	X	X	South Carolina
	X	X	X	X	X	X	Pennsylvania
		X	X	X	X	X	Maryland
		X	X	X	X	X	Vermont
0	0	0	X	X	X	X	Ohio[c]
				X	X	X	New Jersey
					X	X	Rhode Island
					X	X	New Hampshire
						X	Massachusetts
							Delaware
							Connecticut
0	0	0	0	0	X	0	Indiana[d]

Notes: X = majority of electors voted for the Democratic candidate; blank = majority of electors voted Federalist; 0 = state did not vote. Coefficient of reproducibility (CR) = 98.26.

[a]Vote in 1792 is based on the second-choice ballots; Washington received all of the first ballots. John Adams was considered the Federalist candidate for vice president. Democratic votes are those for Clinton, Jefferson, and Burr.

[b]First voted in 1796.

[c]First voted in 1804.

[d]First voted in 1816.

competition reveals considerable consistency in the states' voting behavior. We find only two errors or inconsistencies, New York's votes in 1796 and 1812. Having voted Democratic in 1792 (for George Clinton of New York for vice president), we would assume that New York should have also voted Democratic in the elections of 1796 and 1812. In these instances, as in many subsequent cases, inconsistencies often reflect the pull of local or regional candidates, which lead constituencies to behave in ways not otherwise expected of them.[3] The number of errors in a scale also provides us with a simple measure of the strength of the pattern. Thus, 2 errors out of a possible 117 choices (i.e., all of the electoral possibilities for these seven elections) yields a coefficient of reproducibility (CR) of 98.29. This is a very high coefficient in scaling terms.[4]

The Democratic dominance of the first phase of the structure for the presidency is also readily established. It is revealed by the predominance of X's (i.e., Democratic wins in a state) and confirmed by the Democratic victories in all presidential elections after 1800. At the same time, the scale reveals the party's strength as regional. The southern states of Virginia, North Carolina, and Georgia, along with Kentucky, formed the most reliable base of support for the Democrats. On the other hand, Connecticut was unswervingly non-Democratic (i.e., all blanks on the scale), while the other New England states were non-Democratic in varying degrees.

The Second Phase of the Presidential Competitive Structure

Scaling reveals the six elections from 1832 through 1852 as another distinct period of electoral competition for the presidency (see table 5.2), beginning with Andrew Jackson's reelection in 1832 and the development of the Whig opposition. The struggle between Democrats and Whigs continued to dominate the presidency through the election of 1852, after which the Whigs were replaced by the Republicans. Again, scaling reveals distinct patterns of consistency in the ways the states voted for the presidency. The seven scale-positions ranging from most Democratic to most Whig now reveal, in contrast to the first phase, a broad national base for both parties. Among the most consistently Democratic states were the southern states of Arkansas, Ala-

---

3. In the 1960s and 1970s, for example, a number of inconsistencies were clearly the product of specific candidates (see table 5.7). In 1968, Edmund Muskie's vice presidential candidacy produced inconsistencies in Maine's vote. Jimmy Carter's candidacy in 1976 and 1980 was responsible for errors, certainly in Georgia's vote and probably in that of other southern states. Gerald Ford's candidacy in 1976 created an inconsistency in Michigan's vote as well.

4. According to Guttman (1950, 77), "An acceptable approximation to a perfect scale has been arbitrarily set at 90 percent reproducibility."

bama, and Virginia. Now, however, the party's base of support also included the New England state of New Hampshire and Illinois to the west. The most Whiggish states were the New England states of Vermont and Massachusetts. But the Whig states also included Delaware, Maryland, Tennessee, and Kentucky. In all, there were nine inconsistencies, producing a coefficient of re-

TABLE 5.2.   Second Phase of the Presidential Competitive Structure, 1832–52

Whig Wins		Democratic Wins				Average Democratic	
1840	1848	1844	1836	1832	1852	Percentage of Vote[a]	State
X	X	X	X	0	X	60.7	Arkansas
X	X	X	X	X	X	59.2	New Hampshire
X	X	X	X	X	X	57.0	Virginia
X	X	X	X	X	X	56.9	Missouri
X	X	X	X	X	X	56.4	Alabama
X	X	X	X	X	X	54.9	Illinois
X	X	X			X	no popular vote	South Carolina
0	X	0	0	0	X	71.7	Texas
	X	X	X	X	X	53.0	Mississippi
	X	X	X	X	X	52.5	Maine
	X	X	X	0	X	52.0	Michigan
	X	X		X	X	51.1	Indiana
	X			X	X	47.9	Ohio
0	X	0	0	0	X	50.1	Iowa
0	X	0	0	0	X	45.2	Wisconsin
		X		X	X	51.2	Georgia
		X	X	X	X	51.2	Pennsylvania
		X	X	X	X	50.5	Louisiana
		X	X	X	X	46.5	New York
			X	X	X	53.7	North Carolina
			X		X	44.9	Connecticut
			X		X	41.8	Rhode Island
				X	X	49.5	New Jersey
				X		46.6	Tennessee
0		0	0	0	X	50.8	Florida
					X	48.5	Maryland
					X	47.9	Delaware
						44.3	Kentucky
						35.2	Massachusetts
						31.6	Vermont

Notes: X = state voted for the Democratic candidate; blank = state voted for a non-Democrat (Whig); 0 = state did not vote. The scale has 9 "errors" out of 162 choices, CR = 94.44.
[a]Mean = 50.1 percent; standard deviation = 7.7.

producibility of 94.44, not as high as that for the first phase, but still quite respectable by scaling standards. It was also a highly competitive period. The average percentage of the vote received by the Democratic party over the six elections in all the states was 50.1 percent of the total, with most states having close margins (see table 5.2).

The election of 1856 marked the end of the second phase of the structure of electoral competition for the presidency, not merely because the Republican party replaced the Whigs, but mostly because the distribution of Democratic party support shifted enough among the states to introduce a high level of inconsistency. There was a reshaping of state support as the sectional issue of slavery came to dominate the presidential contest. Had I extended the scale to include the election of 1856, enough new inconsistencies would have been introduced to reduce the coefficient of reproducibility to 91.8. The second phase, therefore, provides us with a convenient benchmark. Throughout the period, the coefficient of reproducibility was 94.0 or better. The collapse of the second phase reduced the coefficient to less than 94.0. We can then define a phase of the electoral structure as one that produces a coefficient of reproducibility of 94.0 or more.

The Post–Civil War Era and the Presidential Competitive Structure

Were we to create a single scale based on the states' votes in all the presidential elections between 1872 and 1988, the level of inconsistency would be as high as 20 percent. This high level of inconsistency alerts us to further distinct phases in the presidential component of the structure of electoral competition. We know that students of politics in the United States have found these years characterized by periods of alignments and realignments in the bases of support for the two parties, Republican and Democratic, that have dominated all elections since the Civil War. Again, scaling enables us to see how long a given distribution of support lasted and to measure its degree of consistency with some precision.

In table 5.3 I have laid out the coefficients of reproducibility, based on the states' votes, in sequences of presidential elections from 1872 through 1988. In the table, the first election in a given time sequence is listed on the top diagonal, running from 1872 to 1980. The last election in a time sequence is on the left, along the bottom diagonal, running from 1880 through 1988. Note that the minimum number of elections needed to form a sequence is three. As the table shows, three presidential elections in a row usually (but not always) produce relatively few inconsistencies. Four elections, 1904, 1928, 1964, and 1976, were followed by two elections that scaled perfectly (CR = 100). The table should be read down from the first election in a time sequence

TABLE 5.3. Presidential Competitive Structure Scale Values, 1872–1988

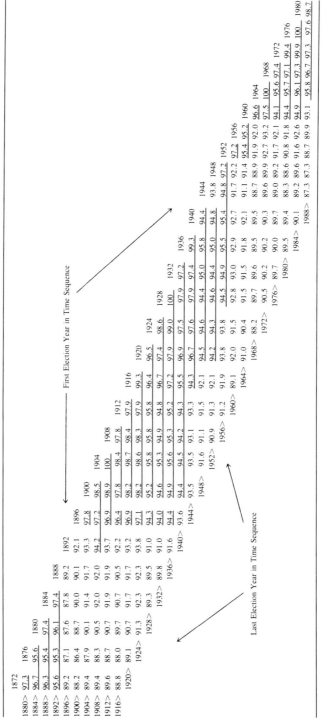

First Election Year in Time Sequence

Last Election Year in Time Sequence

Note: Figures are the coefficients of reproducibility (CR) for scales of state voting (Democratic–non-Democratic) in all presidential elections between the first and last election year in each time sequence. Scales with a value of 94.0 or better have been underlined.

and then across from the last election in the series. Reading downward shows how long a given pattern lasted. Reading from left to right reveals how well the last election in a time series scaled with previous elections. To highlight the longevity of patterns of voting, I have underlined all coefficients that have a value of 94.0 or more.

The full range of scales from 1872 to 1988 reveals that, during these years, the structure of presidential electoral competition went through three distinct phases. The immediate post–Civil War phase ended with the election of 1896. The election of 1896 introduced a phase that lasted, with modifications, through 1956. The election of 1960 ushered in a new phase that lasted clearly through 1984, and, while modified in 1988, allowed for elections that scaled well between 1964 and 1988.

Table 5.3 reveals the strength and longevity of the phase of electoral competition for the presidency that began in 1896. Reading across, we find that the election of 1896 scales poorly with the elections that preceded it. Reading down, we find that the election of 1896 scales well with every succeeding election through 1936, producing a coefficient of at least 94.0. The election of 1900 scales well with every succeeding election through 1940. No sequence produced coefficients of 94.0 or more for more than forty years. Efforts to measure consistency over a longer time-span reveal a persistent weakening of the coefficient. Although the election of 1944 interrupts the pattern begun in 1896, the elections of 1920 and 1928 allow the pattern to continue through 1956. It appears that the distribution of party strength by states that emerged with the presidential election of 1896, while subject to readjustments in 1920 and in 1928, essentially remained consistent through 1956. Of course it is well recognized that the election of 1896 initiated a major realignment in the politics of the United States. Indeed, V. O. Key (1955) deemed the election "critical." Thus, scaling confirms a generally accepted conclusion about the election of 1896 and the subsequent restructuring of presidential politics.

As I have already pointed out, scaling proves to be a sensitive measure not only of the continuity but also of the disruption that has taken place in the politics of the United States. Note that when the election of 1960 is added to any of the previous sequences (reading from left to right), except for the brief trio of 1952, 1956, and 1960, all the sequences drop below the 94.0 level, as was the case with the election of 1896. If, however, we begin the electoral sequence in 1960, we find the coefficients holding up very well until the 1988 election, when the coefficient slips to 93.1. Starting the electoral sequence in 1964, we find that the coefficient remains above the 94.0 benchmark through the election of 1988.

The distinctiveness of the three phases of competition is further borne out when we look at the state-by-state distribution of the vote for the presidency.

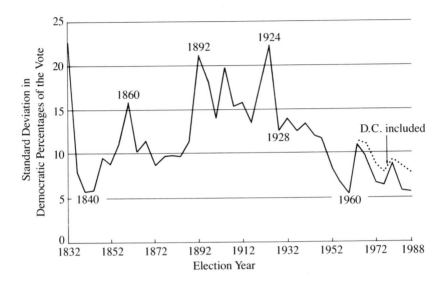

Fig. 5.1. Variation among the states in the Democratic percentage of the popular vote for president, 1832–1988

Figure 5.1 shows the variation among the states of the Democratic percentage of the votes in all the presidential elections from 1828 to 1988. The figure clearly reveals the strong sectionalism of the period from 1896 through 1924, at the same time revealing the modified regionalism of the post-1872 phase that preceded it and the 1928–56 Democratic era that followed. In sharp contrast, the post-1960 phase most clearly resembles the pre–Civil War phase in the diminished variation of the vote.

The Competitive Structure for the Presidency, 1872–92

To reveal the competitive structure for the presidency during each phase, however, we must expose the role of the states in the overall scale laid out in table 5.3. Table 5.4 shows the place of the individual states in the electoral sequence from 1872 through 1892. It reveals the presidency as a competitive office, but with a competitive structure clearly different from that of the preceding phase, as figure 5.1 leads us to expect. A relatively solid block of Democratic states in the top two or three scale-positions is balanced by an equally solid block of non-Democratic (or Republican) states in the bottom

TABLE 5.4. Post–Civil War Presidential Competitive Structure, 1872–92

Republican Wins				Democratic Wins		Average Democratic	
1872	1876	1888	1880	1892ª	1884	Percentage of Voteb	State
X	X	X	X	X	X	64.2	Georgia
X	X	X	X	X	X	63.9	Texas
X	X	X	X	X	X	54.9	Kentucky
X	X	X	X	X	X	53.5	Tennessee
X	X	X	X	X	X	53.2	Missouri
X	X	X	X	X	X	52.7	Maryland
	X	X	X	X	X	63.8	Mississippi
	X	X	X	X	X	59.0	Alabama
0	X	X	X	X	X	56.2	Arkansas
	X	X	X	X	X	54.4	Virginia
	X	X	X	X	X	52.7	Delaware
	X	X	X	X	X	50.7	West Virginia
	X	X	X	X	X	50.0	North Carolina
	X	X	X	X	X	49.6	New Jersey
	X	X		X	X	49.0	Connecticut
	X			X	X	48.6	New York
	X			X	X	48.3	Indiana
		X	X	X	X	62.7	South Carolina
0		X	X	X	X	60.0	Louisiana
		X	X	X	X	57.8	Florida
			X	X		46.2	California
			X	*		39.1	Nevada
				X		46.0	Illinois
				X		45.6	Wisconsin
						47.3	Ohio
						47.0	New Hampshire
						44.3	Pennsylvania
				*		42.8	Colorado
						40.5	Michigan
						40.4	Oregon
						40.3	Massachusetts
						40.3	Iowa
						40.2	Maine
						38.6	Rhode Island
						37.9	Minnesota
				*		31.5	Kansas
						31.3	Nebraska
						27.5	Vermont
0	0	0	0		0		Washington

(*continued*)

TABLE 5.4—*Continued*

Republican Wins				Democratic Wins		Average Democratic Percentage of Vote[b]	State
1872	1876	1888	1880	1892[a]	1884		
0	0	0	0		0		Montana
0	0	0	0	*	0		Idaho
0	0	0	0		0		Wyoming
0	0	0	0		0		North Dakota
0	0	0	0		0		South Dakota

Notes: X = Democratic vote; blank = Republican vote; * = Populist vote; 0 = state did not vote. CR = 95.61.

[a]Adjustments have been made for increases in the number of states as they were admitted by using the percentage of states voting Democratic rather than the actual number. This explains the placement of 1892 before 1884.

[b]Mean = 48.2 percent; standard deviation = 9.3.

three scale-positions. These blocks also show some evidence of a resurgence in regional voting. At the same time, since the two parties were very evenly matched, a few states capable of switching parties and tipping the balance in either party's favor also made this a period of intense competition for the presidency. Inconsistencies in scale-position reveal the strategic competitive position of New York and Indiana. Their position undoubtedly explains both parties' use of the two states as major sources for presidential and vice presidential candidates during this phase of presidential competition. The evenness of the two parties' overall competitive relationship meant also that the loss of a few states could cost either party the election. Thus, the loss of Florida, Louisiana, and South Carolina from the Democratic base of support in 1876 gave the Republican candidate, Hayes, the electoral college victory over Tilden, while the inconsistencies in the voting behavior of Indiana and New York contributed to the Democratic losses of 1880 and 1888.

The Competitive Structure for the Presidency, 1896–1956

The scales for the years 1896 through 1956, based on the states' relative standing from most to least Democratic, indicate that the states' voting patterns for the presidency remained much the same throughout the period. Unlike the preceding phase, this period breaks down into a Republican era from 1896 through 1928, during which Democrats won the presidency only in 1912 and 1916, due to dissension in Republican ranks, and a Democratic era from 1932 through 1956, during which Republicans won only in 1952 and

1956. Table 5.5 lays out the states' voting patterns from 1896 through 1928, table 5.6 the patterns from 1928 through 1956.

As in table 5.3, the election of 1928 emerges as a transitional election. The election ends the Republican era.[5] The election of 1928 also ends the intensely sectional character of the Republican era revealed in figure 5.1. This was an era in which the average range of support for the Democrats ranged from 93.8 percent in South Carolina to 25.5 percent in Vermont, with an average among all the states of 45.5 percent. The standard deviation in the states' votes reached 15.1, the highest of any era in presidential politics before or since (see table 5.5). Note also that 14 of the 24 "errors" that appear in the entire scale are due to the votes of two states (Massachusetts and Rhode Island) for the Democratic candidate in 1928, Al Smith. Up to 1928, the two had been among the strongest Republican states. In contrast, the Democratic era is characterized by a more homogeneous or less sectional vote (standard deviation = 9.06) than the Republican era, as well as by more closely divided votes (average Democratic percentage = 52.9; see fig. 5.1 and table 5.6).

All the same, competition for the presidency was structurally consistent throughout the entire period. Apart from the broad shift toward the Democratic party after 1928, most of the states retained a generally similar relative standing with respect to support for the two parties. The southern states continued to provide the base of support for the Democratic party, reinforced now by enhanced support from the border states of West Virginia and Missouri, and from the state of Illinois. The Republican base of support remained in the northeast, while the western plains states of the Dakotas, Kansas, and Nebraska moved in a more Republican direction. Large states such as New York, Ohio, Pennsylvania, New Jersey, and Michigan retained their same positions during both eras.[6]

This finding is compatible with my findings about the structure of political opportunities during the period from 1900 through 1958. Recall that I characterized the opportunity structure of this period in chapters 3 and 4 as one of stable expectations, for which the patterns of advancement were relatively clear both with respect to movement from office to office and age requirements. As I also noted in chapter 3, the states' relationship to the presidential complex in the structure of political opportunities was greatly

---

5. I have begun the Democratic era in 1928 (see table 5.6) because the coefficient of reproducibility for the scale starting with 1928 is the same as that starting in 1932, and the 1928 election reproduces itself with subsequent elections as well as the 1932 election (see table 5.3).

6. The Spearman rank-order correlation between the states' positions on the Democratic–non-Democratic scales was +.75 for the two post-1896 periods (1896–1928 and 1928–56). In contrast, the correlation was −.35 between the post–Civil War period (1872–92) and its successor (1896–1928). Between the Democratic era (1928–56) and its successor (1960–88) the rank order correlation was −.16.

TABLE 5.5. Republican Era Presidential Competitive Structure, 1896–1928

| Republican Wins | | | | | | | Democratic Wins | | Average Democratic Percentage | |
1928	1920	1924	1904	1908	1900	1896	1916	1912	of Vote[a]	State
X	X	X	X	X	X	X	X	X	93.8	South Carolina
X	X	X	X	X	X	X	X	X	88.5	Mississippi
X	X	X	X	X	X	X	X	X	79.2	Louisiana
X	X	X	X	X	X	X	X	X	67.2	Alabama
X	X	X	X	X	X	X	X	X	66.7	Georgia
X	X	X	X	X	X	X	X	X	61.3	Arkansas
X								X	36.4	Rhode Island
X								X	35.6	Massachusetts
	X	X	X	X	X	X	X	X	67.5	Texas
	X	X	X	X	X	X	X	X	63.6	Florida
	X	X	X	X	X	X	X	X	59.2	Virginia
	X	X	X	X	X	X	X	X	55.4	North Carolina
	X		X	X	X		X	X	48.4	Kentucky
		X	X	X	X		X	X	52.1	Tennessee
		X	0	X	0	0	X	X	45.7	Oklahoma
		X	X				X	X	45.8	Maryland
			X	X	X		X	X	47.2	Colorado
			X	X	X		X	X	46.3	Nevada
			X				X	X	40.9	Nebraska
				X	X		X	X	47.3	Missouri
				X	X		X	X	44.3	Montana
				X	X		X	X	40.1	Idaho
				X	X				45.5	Utah
					X		X	X	37.7	Kansas
					X		X	X	37.1	Wyoming
					X				34.2	South Dakota
					X		X		31.8	Washington
			0	0	0	0	X	X	44.5	Arizona
			0	0	0	0	X	X	44.0	New Mexico
							X	X	40.2	Ohio
							X	X	38.2	New Hampshire
							X		33.9	California
							X	X	32.1	North Dakota
								X	44.0	West Virginia
								X	43.3	Indiana
								X	42.9	Delaware
								X	39.4	New York
								X	37.7	Connecticut
								X	37.1	New Jersey
								X	34.8	Iowa

TABLE 5.5—*Continued*

Republican Wins							Democratic Wins		Average Democratic Percentage of Vote[a]	State
1928	1920	1924	1904	1908	1900	1896	1916	1912		
								X	34.8	Oregon
								X	32.8	Maine
								X	32.3	Illinois
								X	32.2	Wisconsin
									30.7	Michigan
									30.4	Minnesota
									32.0	Pennsylvania
									25.5	Vermont

Notes: X = state voted for the Democratic candidate; blank = state voted for the non-Democratic candidate; 0 = state did not vote. CR = 94.30.
[a]Mean = 45.5 percent; standard deviation = 15.1.

TABLE 5.6. Democratic Era Presidential Competitive Structure, 1928–56

Republican Wins			Democratic Wins					Average Democratic Percentage of Vote[a]	State
1956	1928	1952	1948	1944	1940	1932	1936		
X	X	X	X	X	X	X	X	74.8	Georgia
X	X	X		X	X	X	X	74.1	Mississippi
X	X	X		X	X	X	X	73.9	South Carolina
X	X	X		X	X	X	X	73.7	Alabama
X	X	X	X	X	X	X	X	68.3	Arkansas
X		X	X	X	X	X	X	61.5	North Carolina
X			X	X	X	X	X	53.7	Missouri
	X	X		X	X	X	X	68.7	Louisiana
	X		X	X	X	X	X	52.7	Rhode Island
	X		X	X	X	X	X	49.8	Massachusetts
		X	X	X	X	X	X	52.9	West Virginia
		X	X	X	X	X	X	52.7	Kentucky
			X	X	X	X	X	66.4	Texas
			X	X	X	X	X	59.0	Florida
			X	X	X	X	X	57.1	Tennessee
			X	X	X	X	X	55.6	Virginia
			X	X	X	X	X	55.2	Oklahoma
			X	X	X	X	X	54.5	Arizona

(*continued*)

TABLE 5.6—*Continued*

Republican Wins			Democratic Wins					Average Democratic Percentage of Vote[a]	State
1956	1928	1952	1948	1944	1940	1932	1936		
			X	X	X	X	X	53.9	Nevada
			X	X	X	X	X	53.1	Utah
			X	X	X	X	X	52.4	New Mexico
			X	X	X	X	X	52.2	Montana
			X	X	X	X	X	51.6	Washington
			X	X	X	X	X	51.0	California
			X	X	X	X	X	51.7	Minnesota
			X		X	X	X	49.7	Wisconsin
			X	X	X	X	X	49.1	Illinois
			X	X	X	X	X	48.2	Idaho
			X		X	X	X	47.8	Wyoming
			X		X	X	X	47.0	Ohio
			X			X	X	46.8	Colorado
			X			X	X	46.4	Iowa
				X	X	X	X	51.0	Maryland
				X	X	X	X	49.0	Oregon
				X	X	X	X	49.0	New York
				X	X		X	48.6	Delaware
				X	X		X	47.8	Connecticut
				X	X		X	47.2	Pennsylvania
				X	X	X	X	46.6	New Jersey
				X		X	X	46.6	Michigan
				X	X		X	45.6	New Hampshire
						X	X	47.0	Indiana
						X	X	46.2	North Dakota
						X	X	45.1	South Dakota
						X	X	44.0	Nebraska
						X	X	40.6	Kansas
								39.6	Maine
								37.3	Vermont

Notes: X = state voted for the Democratic candidate; blank = state voted for the non-Democratic candidate. CR = 94.53.
[a]Mean = 52.9 percent; standard deviation = 9.06.

affected by their positions in the structure of competition for the presidency. This relationship is now verified by the data in tables 5.5 and 5.6, which support the logic of the electoral college. The logic requires that parties largely expend such resources as presidential appointments within states that can be most readily shifted in presidential elections, that is, states toward the center of the scales or those with high levels of inconsistencies. The competitive structure referred to in chapter 3 is the one laid out here for the comparable period.

The Post-1956 Competitive Structure for the Presidency

As table 5.3 reveals, a new phase of competition for the presidency emerged with the election of 1960. The full scale from 1960 through 1988 is laid out in table 5.7. While the period from 1960 through 1988 is a period of Republican domination of the presidency (average Democratic vote = 44.3 percent), its competitive structure is not the same as that for the period 1896–1924. Not only are the southern states more Republican than they were in that era; several of the northeastern and midwestern states are more Democratic than they were during the Democratic era of 1928–56. Not only the relative scale positions of these states have shifted. The average Democratic percentage of the vote in Massachusetts, Connecticut, Rhode Island, Maine, Vermont, New York, Pennsylvania, Michigan, Minnesota, and Iowa from 1960 through 1988 is equal to or higher than it was during the Democratic era.

In effect, as figure 5.1 reveals, the competitive structure of the post-1956 phase most closely resembles the structure of the immediate pre–Civil War period in the even distribution of competition for the presidency. Almost all states show a willingness to support either major party in some election. Only Arizona and the District of Columbia do not vote for both parties in this period. Had Barry Goldwater come from any state other than Arizona, it is likely that Arizona would have voted Democratic in 1964 as well. In contrast, in the 1872–92 competitive phase for the presidency, six states never gave their electoral college votes to a Republican, while fourteen never gave their votes to a Democrat. In the 1896–1956 phase, five states never voted Republican, while one never voted Democratic. During the post-1956 phase, competition is also more evenly distributed; there is much less variance in the vote of the two parties than in the two previous phases (see fig. 5.1). The standard deviation in the vote is 5.3 percent, or 7.3 percent when the District of Columbia is included. This degree of homogeneity or lack of sectionalism in presidential voting was equalled only during the Whig-Democratic phase of presidential competition before the Civil War.

The Structure of Electoral Competition: Federal Legislative and Statewide Elective Contests

We looked first at the presidential component of the structure of electoral competition because the presidential contest provides the national focus for the structure in the United States. At the same time, as we saw in chapter 3, the presidency dominates a complex structure of political opportunities. The

TABLE 5.7. Post-1956 Presidential Competitive Structure, 1960–88

Republican Wins					Democratic Wins			Average Democratic Percentage of Vote[a]	State
1972	1984	1980	1988	1968	1960	1976	1964		
X	X	X	X	X	0	X	X	81.4	D. of Columbia
X			X	X	X	X	X	56.6	Massachusetts
	X	X	X	X	X	X	X	52.3	Minnesota
		X	X	X	X	X	X	57.8	Rhode Island
		X	X	X	X	X	X	52.5	Hawaii
		X	X	X	X	X	X	51.4	West Virginia
		X		X	X	X	X	49.4	Maryland
		X			X	X		45.2	Georgia
			X	X	X	X	X	50.6	New York
			X			X	X	48.4	Wisconsin
			X				X	47.3	Oregon
			X				X	46.8	Iowa
			X	X			X	46.6	Washington
				X	X	X	X	48.8	Pennsylvania
				X	X	X	X	45.0	Texas
				X	X		X	47.8	Michigan
				X	X		X	47.8	Connecticut
				X			X	47.8	Maine
					X	X	X	47.4	Missouri
					X	X	X	46.6	Delaware
					X	X	X	45.1	Arkansas
					X	X	X	43.6	North Carolina
					X		X	47.0	Illinois
					X		X	45.6	New Jersey
					X		X	44.6	New Mexico
					X	X		41.3	Louisiana
					X	X		40.9	South Carolina
					X		X	40.9	Nevada
						X	X	45.8	Kentucky
						X	X	45.6	Ohio
						X	X	43.3	Tennessee
						X	X	40.3	Florida
						X		39.1	Alabama
						X		33.3	Mississippi
							X	45.9	California
							X	44.7	Vermont
							X	43.7	Montana
							X	43.6	South Dakota
							X	42.0	Colorado
							X	41.6	Indiana

TABLE 5.7—*Continued*

Republican Wins					Democratic Wins			Average Democratic Percentage of Vote[a]	State
1972	1984	1980	1988	1968	1960	1976	1964		
							X	41.0	New Hampshire
							X	41.0	Virginia
							X	40.7	North Dakota
							X	40.1	Alaska
							X	38.8	Kansas
							X	38.6	Oklahoma
							X	37.7	Wyoming
							X	35.5	Nebraska
							X	34.8	Idaho
							X	34.3	Utah
								37.3	Arizona

Notes: X = state voted for the Democratic candidate; blank = state voted for the non-Democratic candidate; 0 = state did not vote.
aIncluding District of Columbia, mean = 45.0 percent; standard deviation = 7.3. Not including District of Columbia, mean = 44.3 percent; standard deviation = 5.3.

structure of electoral competition, therefore, must be filled out by considering the competitive conditions for other significant elective offices. These are principally the offices of federal legislator and statewide elective official. For this task we need measures of competition that are of comparable utility from office to office. Only such measures can capture the complexity of the structure of electoral competition that exists beneath the presidency. Studies have attempted to capture this complexity by demonstrating divided partisan control of different offices within the same states, for example, divided control of governorships and state legislatures (for a pioneer study see Key and Silverman 1954). Measuring the division of control between offices is, however, different from measuring competition over time for the same office and using a comparable measure to compare the competitive conditions for different offices.

To determine the competitive conditions for winning significant elective offices below the presidency, I devised two measures of competition. These measures were designed to capture the two dimensions of competition that send the clearest messages to candidates about their chances in a given constituency and, when combined, indicate the consistency in a constituency's partisan voting. The measures assess: (1) the extent of the division of control of an office between the parties or the percentage of each party's wins; and (2) the rate of alternation of control, or the percentage of elections in which there was a change of party control of the office. By combining the results of the two measures, an overall view of the competitive conditions for each office that encompasses variations within and among the states emerges.[7] By comparing the results for different offices within and among the states we come close to completing the national structure of electoral competition.

To lay out this aspect of the structure of electoral competition I applied the two measures to the offices from which I derived, in part, the structure of political opportunities. The time period is also comparable, 1914–58.[8] Note also the period coincides with the longest phase of the presidential component of the structure of electoral competition. The offices are the major offices of U.S. senator and governor elected by the state at large, and the lesser administrative offices elected at large by most states, the offices of lieutenant governor, secretary of state, auditor, treasurer, attorney general, and state comptroller. The offices also include the office of U.S. representative elected within the congressional district, which, in most states, encompasses only a part of the state's electorate. For the office of U.S. representative, a composite measure of all the house seats within a state was taken. For the office of senator, the result was a composite of both senate seats within the state.[9]

The two measures form the axes of a scatter diagram (see fig. 5.2). The horizontal axis measures the division of control of each of the selected offices between the two parties, or the percentage of victories for the dominant party defined as the party with the majority of victories over the selected time period. The vertical axis measures the rate of alternation of control of each of the selected offices during the same time period, or the percentage of elections in which the party of the winning candidate differed from that of the incumbent. Together, the two measures reflect the competitive conditions for each of the selected offices: the more centrally located on the horizontal axis, the more competitive the office in terms of division of control; the higher the office on the vertical axis, the more rapid the rate of turnover, the lower the office, the longer the cycles of one party control, regardless of the overall division of control between the two parties. The two external sloping lines of the diagram

---

7. There are other measures of competition, e.g., the closeness of the vote. For the reasons this measure was not used, see Schlesinger 1960, 198–99.

8. I begin the period in 1914 because this was the first election in which U.S. senators were popularly elected.

9. The composite result for the House seats was calculated by totaling the number of House elections during the time-period and then determining the proportion of wins for each party and the proportion of party changes. A problem arose in determining party changes after the redistricting that followed the censuses of 1930, 1940, and 1950. Wherever possible, a district was traced throughout the time-period. When, however, as a result of redistricting, a district changed substantially, the calculation of party change began anew. For the Senate, party change was determined by calculating the result for each Senate seat independently and then combining the totals.

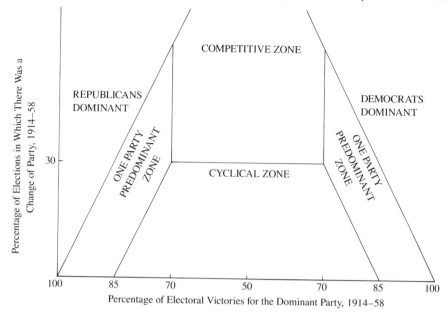

Fig. 5.2. Structure of electoral competition in federal legislative and statewide elective contests, 1914–58

represent the mathematical bounds of possible positions for the two related variables. Thus, we can determine how frequently each party won a particular office and how long the cycles of party control for each office were.

To refine the concept of competitive conditions for office, I have divided the space on the diagram arbitrarily into three zones. The competitive zone is defined by one party's control of a selected office for 70 percent or less of the time and by a turnover rate higher than 30 percent. The cyclical zone is defined by both parties alternating control of a selected office for long periods of time. In the cyclical zone, whose offices fall below the competitive zone, the horizontal base has been extended to include those offices for which minority control extended over lengthy time periods. The one-party zone is defined by one party's control of the selected office more than 70 percent of the time and for a lengthy time period that excludes long periods of control by the minority party.

The two measures reveal a broad range in the level of competition for individual offices. Table 5.8 summarizes these findings, according to the zones laid out in fig. 5.2; figures 5.3–5.10 lay out the zones of competition for the selected offices in each of thirty-six states.[10] Table 5.8 reveals the

10. The figures do not include the twelve southern states, which were one-party states during this period, and Alaska and Hawaii, which had not yet achieved statehood.

offices of governor and senator as the most competitive. At the same time they fall in the two extreme zones: where the offices are not competitive, they are most likely to be dominated by one party. In only a few states do either of the two offices fall in the cyclical zone: in Rhode Island and Nebraska the governorship is in this zone; in Rhode Island, Washington, New Mexico, and New York the office of senator appears there. In these states, either all offices fall in the cyclical zone or party control of the two senate seats is, in all likelihood, divided.

In contrast, the largest proportion of House seats appears in the cyclical zone in most states. This does not mean that the states had alternating periods of one-party control of congressional delegations. It is more likely the product of the composite measure. On the other hand, the position of the office in the cyclical zone does represent a very low rate of alternation between the parties for congressional seats, a reflection of the one-party character of most congressional districts. All the same, a closer look at the range of competition for House seats reveals some differences even for this office. Thus, in Massachusetts, where the division in party victories for the office of U.S. representative is 69 percent to 31 percent, the turnover rate between the parties for the office is only a little over 5 percent. In contrast, Connecticut has about the same pattern division of victories for the office, but a party turnover rate of over 38 percent. Apart from Connecticut, the two other states whose House seats fall in the competitive zone are Delaware and Nevada. Since both states elect only one representative, the effect of the composite calculation for the office is not a factor.

The lesser state offices fall primarily in the one-party or cyclical zones. Among these offices, the office of lieutenant governor tends to be more

TABLE 5.8. Distribution of Offices among the States According to Competitiveness, 1914–58

	Number of States	Percent in Each Zone		
		Competitive	Cyclical	One-Party
Governor	36	50	6	44
Senator	36	42	11	47
Congressman	36	8	61	31
Lieutenant governor	24	21	25	54
Secretary of state	30	13	30	57
Attorney general	26	11	31	58
Auditor	21	14	34	52
Treasurer	26	15	35	50
Comptroller	5	20	0	80

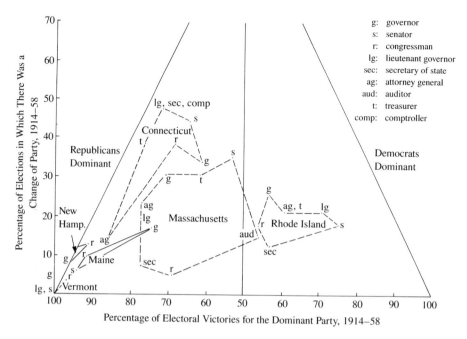

Fig. 5.3. The New England states

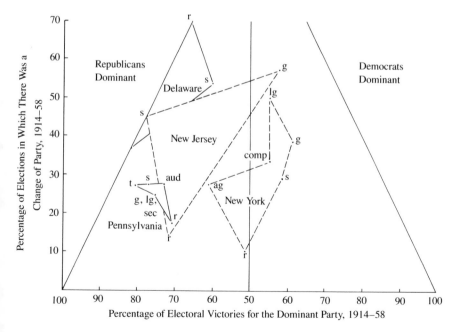

Fig. 5.4. The Mid-Atlantic states

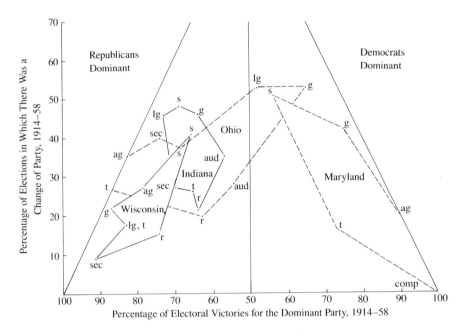

Fig. 5.5. Maryland and the Great Lakes states

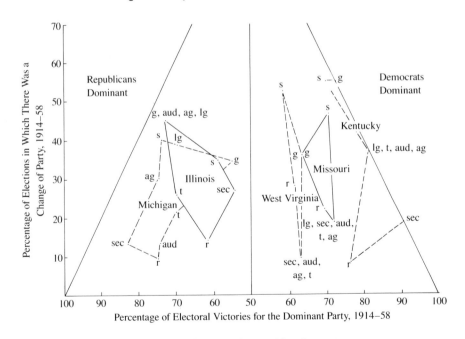

Fig. 5.6. The Great Lakes and border states

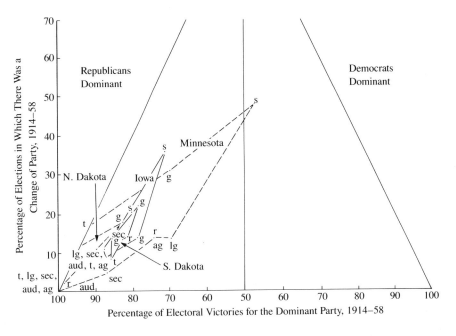

Fig. 5.7. The midwestern states. All Farmer-Labor included with Democrats in Minnesota.

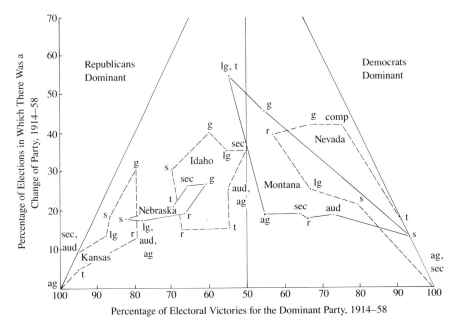

Fig. 5.8. The midwestern and mountain states

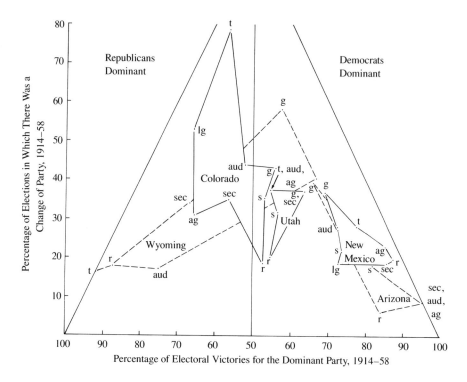

Fig. 5.9. The mountain states

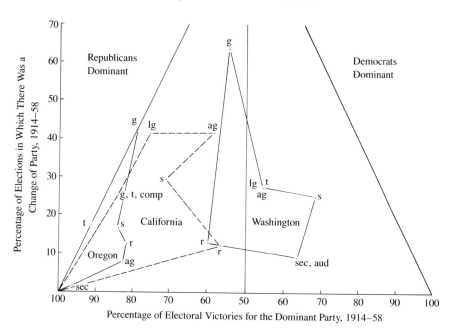

Fig. 5.10. The Pacific Coast states

TABLE 5.9. Range of Competition

Narrow Focus (Group 1)[a]	Cyclically Elongated Focus (Group 2)[b]	Medium-Broad Focus (Group 3)[c]	No Focus (Group 4)[d]
Maine	Colorado	Arizona	California
Nebraska	Connecticut	Massachusetts	Maryland
New Hampshire	Delaware	Michigan	Minnesota
New Mexico	Idaho	New Jersey	Montana
North Dakota	Illinois	Wisconsin	Nevada
Pennsylvania	Indiana		Ohio
Rhode Island	Iowa		Washington
South Dakota	Kansas		Wyoming
Utah	Kentucky		
Vermont	Missouri		
	New York		
	Oregon		
	West Virginia		

Note: Based on the degree of spread among the offices of a state in figures 5.3–5.10.

[a]Maximum horizontal spread of 25 percent, maximum vertical spread of 20 percent.

[b]Maximum horizontal spread of 25 percent, minimum vertical spread of 25 percent.

[c]Approximately 30 percent spread along both axes.

[d]More than 40 percent spread along both axes.

competitive, as is the case in Ohio and New York.[11] Where all lesser state offices fall in the competitive range, as in Utah, the more important offices of governor, senator, and representative are usually also in this range.

The utility of the measures lies in the revelations about the range of competitive conditions for elective office from state to state and within states for a variety of offices. Figures 5.3–5.10 show that competitive conditions for office cannot be assessed by a unilinear measure. Nor is it enough to measure partisan cycles of control of office. We must also be able to measure the differences in the competitive conditions from office to office if we are to gauge their effect on political ambitions properly. Table 5.9 lays out the range for the thirty-six states based on the percentage spread among the selected offices within each state along both the vertical and horizontal axes. In group 1 of the table are the ten states that show little variation in range from office to office. In group 2 are the thirteen states whose offices fall within a narrow range horizontally, in terms of the division of control between the two parties,

---

11. During this period, states elected the lieutenant governor independently of the governor. New York first joined the election of the two offices in 1953 (Kallenbach 1966, 231).

but whose range vertically, as far as cycles of party control are concerned, is broader. In group 3 are the five states with marked variations for each office on both axes. Nevertheless, the variations are not wide enough to leave us without any guidance as to the competitive relationships within these states. Based on the competitive status of all the selected offices, we can assign all the states in groups 1–3 to one of our three zones of competition. In contrast, the eight states in group 4 have such a broad range among offices on both axes that they can be assigned to none of the zones. Their offices range through all three zones of competition, while in some of these states, Ohio, Montana, and Wyoming, each party has some office that it tends to dominate. Thus, the Democrats win practically every senatorial election, while the Republicans have the edge in contests for the office of lieutenant governor in Montana. In Wyoming, the Republicans win almost all the House elections, while the Democrats win almost all the Senate contests. It is, therefore, meaningless to categorize the states in group 4 as either competitive or one-party dominant.

The four groups of states demonstrate the variety of competitive conditions for offices both among and within the states. Even in group 1, where the range in the measures of competition is the narrowest, three states, Rhode Island, New Mexico, and Utah cannot be safely assigned to the total control of either party. The remaining states are strongly Republican. For the thirteen states in group 2, the results are more varied: for some offices control is more evenly divided, for others more cyclical. In West Virginia and Missouri control of the Senate seats is more evenly divided, control of the remaining offices more cyclical. In Iowa conditions are similar, except that in both instances there is a Republican advantage. In Illinois, the high rate of turnover for the offices of governor, auditor, and attorney general means overall Republican dominance with frequent short-run victories for the Democrats. In contrast, while the Republicans also tend to dominate the offices of senator, representative, secretary of state, and treasurer, the cycles of control are longer for both parties. In Kansas and Oregon the Republicans dominate all offices except the governorship. There is a high rate of turnover for this office, the Democrats being unable to hold the office for long periods of time. In Colorado, control of all offices, except that of representative, is more-or-less evenly divided. For the offices of treasurer and lieutenant governor, there is also a very high rate of party turnover. For the states in the remaining two groups, the range in competitive conditions varies greatly from office to office.

My findings for 1914 through 1958 indicate that, in most states, the competitive conditions for office were such that those seeking the selected offices and using the same partisan label did not succeed or fail as a team. In some states, for example, Vermont and the states of the south, the dominance of all offices by one party made the concept of alternating competing teams meaningless. Only six states gave even some semblance of nurturing competing teams. In group 1, Rhode Island, Nebraska, and Utah did not fall entirely within the one-party dominant zone, but only in Utah did all offices fall in the competitive zone. Rhode Island and Nebraska fit the cyclical zone best. In group 2, most offices in Connecticut, New York, and Colorado fell in the competitive zone, although there were cyclical disparities.

My findings also indicate that the differences in competitive conditions for the selected offices could not be ascribed to differences in the voters' response to federal and state offices. In only seven states did the differences separate federal from state offices: the border states of Delaware, West Virginia, Missouri, and Maryland; and the midwestern states of Wisconsin, Iowa, and Minnesota. In each of these states the federal offices of senator and representative fell closer to the competitive zone than the state offices. In most states, the voters commonly voted for candidates of different parties for different offices within the same jurisdictions. While I did not include state legislative offices, observation indicates that the range in competitive conditions would have been even greater had they been included.

The Relation between the Presidential Contest and the Contests for Other Elective Offices

Despite the broad range of competitive conditions among the states for the offices I have just examined, the relationship between these electoral contests and the states' position in the presidential contest is clear. Of the eighteen states in which the Republican party dominated all the federal legislative and statewide elective offices, all but California are found at the bottom, or Republican, part of the two presidential scales covering the years 1896–1956 (see tables 5.5 and 5.6). Even California is only marginally Democratic for the presidency during the Democratic era. In the twenty-one states where the Democratic party dominated all of the federal legislative and statewide elective offices, much the same relationship with the presidency exists. On the other hand, states that allowed each party to dominate different offices, Massachusetts, New York, Ohio, Washington, Montana, Wyoming, and Colorado, were all centrally located on the presidential scales. These were the states that were more competitive for both presidential and federal legislative and statewide elective office.

All the same, the significant conclusion to draw from this analysis is that most state electorates exhibited widely varying partisan behavior in their choices for different offices, even during the longest phase of the structure of electoral competition. That the states could generally be assigned to one or the other parties during this phase should not obscure this conclusion. The conclusion also holds despite the verifiable strength of the partisan electoral ties among offices during this phase. Throughout this phase the party that won the presidency always won control of both houses of Congress, with the exception of the last election, Eisenhower's reelection in 1956. But this election was, after all, the first concrete sign that the structure of electoral competition was about to change. Nevertheless, during the phase of electoral competition that exhibited the closest partisan relationships, we have found significant variations in competition for electoral office.

In contrast, the post-1956 phase of the structure of electoral competition narrowed the differences in the competitive conditions for office, although partisan electoral ties among offices appeared weaker. The election of 1956 marked the beginning of a trend in which control of the presidency and control of the Congress were divided. Through 1988 the Democrats consistently controlled the House of Representatives, while Republicans won the presidency six times. During the same phase, the Republicans held a majority in the Senate for only six years. We have also seen that a significantly different structure of state presidential support for the parties emerged in 1960. Moreover, the disparities we demonstrated in state voting for different offices in the 1914–58 period increased. The significant fact to keep in mind, however, is that these disparities, along with the disparities in the control of the Congress and the presidency, were due to the increase in competition in most office constituencies. The broader distribution of competitive or uncertain office constituencies of all types created a more homogenous competitive structure. Such a competitive structure, as well as the structure characteristic of the preceding phase, had considerable consequences for parties in the United States, which I shall discuss in chapters 7 and 8.

The Impact of the Structure of Electoral Competition on Political Ambition in the United States

The broad range of competitive conditions for office within and between phases of the structure of electoral competition, which I have just laid out, surely affects ambitions for elective office in the United States. It means that different state competitive structures, as well as different offices, can excite, encourage, dampen, or direct different types of political ambitions in different ways at different times. In many states, the lesser state offices and the office of representative encourage static ambitions, while the offices of governor and senator arouse progressive ambitions. In some states, however, competitive conditions may stimulate progressive ambitions in representatives and static ambitions in senators. These situations also alter over time. In other words, competitive conditions are a highly variable statement of an individual's chances to gain, hold, or advance to the offices that comprise the structure of political opportunities.

Our principal interest is, of course, in the way in which various competitive conditions, promoting and controlling different types of political ambition, affect party organization. Surely my findings confirm the observation in chapter 1 that partisan identification within the electorate is a poor indicator of the strength or weakness of partisan organization. Rather, my findings indicate that candidates will more likely vary their organizational behavior within the same party due to varied competitive conditions, including the varied response of the voters to different offices. Among other things, where constituencies tend to be dominated by one or the other party, a situation often characteristic of lesser offices, those who want these offices will be impelled to enter the locally dominant party. While examples abound of successful movement by individuals to more politically auspicious areas, the United States has no tradition of "parachuting" candidates from one area to another, or of grooming candidates by moving them from losing to safe constituencies. Thus, the constituency's competitiveness is of prime importance in directing the movement of political hopefuls at the earliest stages of their careers. In chapters 7 and 8 I shall discuss the effect of the voters' behavior on party organization more fully. Before I do so, I wish to devote the next chapter to another aspect of the structure of electoral opportunities that has consequences for party organization: the various ways of winning that competitive electoral conditions impose upon individuals ambitious for office.

REFERENCES

Golembiewski, Robert T. 1958. "A Taxonomic Approach to State Political Party Strength." *Western Political Quarterly* 11:494–513.
Grofman, Bernard, and Arend Lijphart, eds. 1986. *Electoral Laws and Their Political Consequences.* New York: Agathon Press.
Guttman, Louis. 1950. "The Basis for Scalogram Analysis." In *Measurements and Prediction,* ed. S. A. Stouffer, L. Guttman, E. A. Suchman, P. F. Lazarsfeld, S. A. Star, and J. A. Clausen. New York: Wiley.
Kallenbach, Joseph E. 1966. *The American Chief Executive.* New York: Harper and Row.
Key, V. O., Jr. 1949. *Southern Politics.* New York: Knopf.
Key, V. O., Jr. 1955. "A Theory of Critical Elections." *Journal of Politics* 17:3–18.
Key, V. O., Jr. 1956. *American State Politics.* New York: Knopf.
Key, V. O., Jr., and Corinne Silverman. 1954. "Party and Separation of Powers: A Panorama of Practice in the States." *Public Policy* 5:382–412.
Lockard, Duane. 1959. *New England State Politics.* Princeton: Princeton University Press.
MacRae, Duncan, Jr. 1952. "The Relation between Roll Call Votes and Constituencies in the Massachusetts House of Representatives." *American Political Science Review* 46:1046–55.

Rae, Douglas. 1967. *The Political Consequences of Electoral Laws*. New Haven: Yale University Press.

Rusk, Jerrold G. 1970. "The Effect of the Australian Ballot Reform on Split Ticket Voting." *American Political Science Review* 64:1220–38.

Schlesinger, Joseph A. 1960. "The Structure of Competition for Office in the American States." *Behavioral Science* 5:197–210.

Schlesinger, Joseph A., and Mildred Schlesinger. 1990. "The Reaffirmation of a Multiparty System in France." *American Political Science Review* 84:1077–1101.

Turner, Julius. 1953. "Primary Elections as the Alternative to Party Competition in 'Safe' Districts." *Journal of Politics* 25:197–210.

Walker, Jack L. 1966. "Ballot Forms and Voter Fatigue: An Analysis of the Office Block and Party Column Ballots." *Midwest Journal of Political Science* 10:448–63.

CHAPTER 6

The Concept of Winning

In the preceding chapter I discussed the electoral rules and the competitive electoral conditions that affect the politically ambitious and therefore party organization. In this chapter I shall discuss another aspect of the structure of electoral competition that also has its impact: the different ways of winning elections. Not only can competitive conditions vary from office to office, so too can the nature of the electoral victories won. Among other things, variations in the nature of electoral victories open the way for conflict and tensions within parties. An understanding of these tensions is essential to our understanding of party organization in democracies.

In chapter 1 I associated my theory of party organization with rational choice (positive) theory.[1] Among the most important concepts for party theory discussed by the influential positive theorists Anthony Downs and William Riker is the optimal size of electoral victories. Not the least significant aspect of their concepts is that they are in disagreement. Downs (1957, 11 and 31) states it as axiomatic that parties will seek to maximize their votes in elections. In contrast, Riker's size principle leads him to conclude that a party will seek to win by the smallest margin possible or with a "minimum winning coalition" (1962, 332–33). Riker argues that Downs would have avoided a rationality crisis if he had adopted the minimum winning concept. The crisis arises because parties, in their effort to attract as many votes as possible, put forth ambiguous policies, making it impossible for voters to vote rationally. What is rational behavior for the party leads to irrational behavior on the part of the voter. According to Riker (1962, 98–101) this dilemma can be resolved by having the parties adopt the minimum winning strategy, freeing them from the need to be ambiguous.

Riker's criticism appears to have some validity. Indeed, the proposition that parties try to win by as narrow a margin as possible had previously been made very effectively by E. E. Schattschneider in his influential work, *Party Government.*[2] Certainly for those who prefer to see politics as the work of

---

1. I use the term *positive theory,* in the same way as Riker and Ordeshook (1973), who also synthesized much of the literature on positive theory.

2. Schattschneider (1942, 95–96) clearly anticipated the concept of the minimum winning coalition when he wrote that a party would not want to win 100 percent of the vote because

rational beings it is always a relief to have any rationality crisis resolved.[3] At the same time, it is possible to resolve Downs's rationality crisis in another and more useful manner. If we conclude that Downs and Riker recommend different strategies of winning because they define *party* differently, then it becomes possible that Downs, as well as Riker, is positing a rational strategy for winning.

A personal experience in practical politics opened up this possibility for me. In the fall of 1971 I served as campaign manager for an incumbent running for reelection to the city council. The incumbent faced a difficult situation. The extension of the vote to eighteen-year-olds had more than doubled the electorate in the university town. A well-organized, radical slate was prepared to use the untested youth vote to oust my sixty-year-old candidate, despite his proven liberal credentials. At the same time, as a liberal councilman, he had antagonized many of the older town voters who were supporting a conservative slate. As the centrist, my candidate ultimately squeaked through by the narrow margin of 40 votes out of some 14,000 cast.

In the immediate postelection euphoria, as we expounded on the brilliance of our strategy, we appeared to have demonstrated the value of Riker's minimum winning coalition perfectly. Even if we had fulfilled Riker's condition that perfect execution of the strategy requires perfect information, we would have behaved in exactly the same way. Any more effort, one more sign, one more mailing, one more coffee would have been wasted; any less effort would have meant defeat.

Yet the postelection period also brought a more sobering experience. Individual voters and campaign workers came forth to claim credit for the electoral victory. Individual voters found it plausible to claim they were responsible for the forty-vote margin; individual campaign workers found it plausible to claim they had brought in the essential forty votes. Individual voters and individual campaign workers, therefore, both felt entitled to press upon the candidate some special claim. In retrospect, what had happened became clear. By achieving a minimum winning coalition we had maximized the importance of both the marginal voter and the political activist. The effect of the minimum winning coalition, therefore, was to heighten the expectations of individual payoffs from the officeholder, a situation that might well

---

it is unnecessary and wasteful. Fifty-one percent will give any party all there is of the power to govern. . . . From the point of view of the interests participating in the political venture, it is more profitable to share a victory with a narrow majority than it is to partake of the spoils of victory with a larger number, for the smaller the number of participants, the greater will be the share of each . . . the perfect party victory is to be won by accumulating a relatively narrow majority, the mark of the skillful conduct of politics.

3. Kenneth A. Shepsle (1972) presents a different resolution for Downs's rationality crisis.

jeopardize future chances of reelection. Perhaps, after all, Downs was right; my candidate should have tried to maximize his vote.

Closer examination convinced me that both Riker and Downs were right, depending upon whose point of view one was considering, the candidate's, the voter's, or the activist's. The strategy of the minimum winning coalition certainly made sense for voters and activists. By reducing their numbers to the minimum needed to win, they could maximize their claims upon the successful candidate. Candidates, on the other hand, would be well advised to try to maximize their votes, if only to reduce the claims that any one individual could make upon them. Two rational ways of winning were therefore possible. Riker's was the rational choice for the voter and activist, Downs's was the rational choice for the candidate.[4]

It further appeared that Riker and Downs provided two equally rational ways of winning, because they have two distinct views of party, in particular of party goals and party boundaries. As I pointed out in chapter 1, for Downs a party is a team of office seekers and is dominated by their goal, the winning of office. In that chapter I explained why the Downsian party must exclude the voter. Riker's party, on the other hand, encompasses voters and activists with goals other than that of winning office. Confusion arises only if we assume the two parties are the same.[5] The admission to parties of voters and activists with goals other than winning office alters all of Downs's assumptions. In particular, it reverses the critical proposition that ". . . parties formulate policies in order to win elections rather than win elections in order to formulate policies" (Downs 1957, 28). Voters and activists find no advantage in winning elections per se. The party that encompasses voters and activists, as well as candidates, must derive its interest in winning elections, at least in part, from the hope that it will thereby be able to implement policies or benefits other than officeholding.[6]

By recognizing that Downs's and Riker's differences over optimal win-

---

4. Although a minimizing strategy makes sense for voters, they can hardly be expected to implement it as individual voters. This is a collective strategy and requires organization for its implementation, a point to which I shall return. Candidates, on the other hand, can try to implement a maximizing strategy, as Hershey (1973) has demonstrated.

5. Economist George J. Stigler (1972) has tried to resolve the conflict between the party goals of Downs and Riker. While his argument is interesting, it rests upon an apolitical assumption, the elimination of winning office as a party goal.

6. Riker (1962, 203–10) is aware of the distinction between the payoff to leaders and the payoff to followers. But his resolution of the conflicting claims departs from rationalists' assumptions. To resolve the conflict, he resorts to psychoanalytic explanations of leaders' motives. Thus, he relates Woodrow Wilson's extraordinary efforts to gain office to his need to overcome feelings of inadequacy instilled by his father. In so doing, Riker creates for us another rationality crisis, for he concludes that ". . . leaders may pay out more to win than a victory is objectively worth" (1962, 209).

ning strategies derive from different views of party, we are able to shed considerable light on the basic tensions that beset parties in democracies. In democracies, two kinds of individuals participate in parties for the purpose of achieving two distinct goals: office seekers, whose goal is office; and benefit seekers, whose goals are the benefits derived from the control of office. In turn, the two goals lead to different convictions about what parties should be. We must be very careful, then, not to obscure the differences in goals by subsuming both goals under the term *winning*. Winning is not a goal; it is the means of achieving goals. This is not to deny the participation of individuals who engage in partisan politics, as in amateur competitive sports, for the thrill of winning. For most participants, however, winning means gaining office or the benefits that can be bestowed upon others by those who win office.

In keeping the two goals distinct, we must be especially careful not to obscure the intrinsic value of office, as Riker's view tends to do. Its value is certainly widely acknowledged in all democracies. The acknowledgement is inherent in the common observation that most, if not all, officeholders are "opportunists" whose preoccupation with office and its powers overrides all other concerns, including public policy. At the same time, democracies go to great lengths to raise the independent value of office. The lifetime use of titles such as "Mr. President" or "Governor," graded seating arrangements at state functions, and the privilege of state funerals are among the added distinctions for those who hold or have held public office. Prevalent in democracies, too, are wealthy individuals who spend vast amounts of money in quest of offices that cannot possibly provide them with commensurate material return. We cannot, therefore, ignore the holding of office as an incentive in its own right.

Benefits, on the other hand, encompass all the nonoffice goals that individuals bring to partisan politics. Many of the benefits sought are private: jobs, contracts, favors; others are collective: the national defense or pollution control. Some of the sought-after benefits provide only personal advantage; others provide for the common welfare. Whatever the nonoffice goals, self-seeking or selfless, private or collective, we must recognize that benefit seekers, whatever type of benefit they seek, have more in common with each other than with office seekers.

At the same time, when benefit seekers enter an existing political party or form a new one, they commit themselves to some use of the tactic of electoral politics or the winning of office. It is, of course, possible for benefit seekers to eschew the tactics of electoral politics and form organizations whose only goal is benefit seeking. These organizations are called interest groups, and I discussed their differences with political parties in chapter 1. When, on the other hand, benefit seekers choose to enter parties instead, they tacitly adopt winning office as a tactic for achieving their goals. Thus, labor unions in the United States debated for many years whether or not they could best achieve their goals as an interest group before deciding, in the 1930s, that involvement with Democratic candidates was a useful strategy.[7] This does not mean that winning office becomes essential to the achievement of the benefit seeker's goals. By entering partisan competitive politics, benefit seekers force both competitors to pay attention to their demands. It then becomes possible, if the opposition also accepts their demands and wins the election, for benefit seekers to achieve their goals even though their candidate lost the office.

Nevertheless, winning elections, while not essential to benefit seekers, is a better strategy than not winning. In 1968, George Wallace's American Independent party failed to win the presidential election. While the size of its vote and the threat of its reemergence in 1972 forced the two major parties to make some concessions to the Wallacites, these concessions by no means met all of their demands. Without doubt, Wallace and his supporters would have gained more of their desired benefits had they won the election. Of course, winning elections is essential for office seekers, the sine qua non that forces them to enter or form political parties. Thus it is important to keep in mind that, while winning is the optimal strategy for those whose goals are benefits, it is the mandatory strategy for those whose goal is office. Still, winning elections is the best strategy for the achievement of both goals.

If winning is the best strategy for both the office seeker and the benefit seeker, why is it useful to distinguish between their goals? Surely office seekers as well as benefit seekers must be sensitive to the other's goals. I have already pointed out that benefit seekers realize their maximum gains either by winning office or supporting those who do. But office seekers must also be concerned with benefits; otherwise no one would have any reason to provide the assistance essential to their getting elected. True, one's means appears to be the other's end: the benefit seeker sees winning office as the means of obtaining benefits; the office seeker sees concern for benefits as the means of winning office. But in practical politics, is it really possible to distinguish means from ends? My experience with practical politics leads me to contend it is both possible and useful, because the distinction leads to distinct types of political behavior. While both office seekers and benefit seekers find winning instrumental to their goals, they seek to win in different ways. In distinguishing between the two strategies, Downs's and Riker's theories provide guidance.

Before making use of their guidance, I should mention an important refinement that has been added to their work. As we saw earlier, both theorists are concerned with the size of the electoral victory. But Hinich and Ordeshook (1970) have pointed out that Downs and others fail to distinguish between

---

7. The debate within the labor movement and the impact of direct involvement upon the unions' political flexibility are discussed in Greenstone 1969.

maximizing one's vote and maximizing one's plurality. Yet the distinction is critical because the two can differ considerably, depending on the degree of voters' abstention, thereby opening up other strategic choices. Thus, the ability of voters to choose not to participate in an election makes it possible to try to maximize the plurality or the distance between one candidate and the nearest competitor, while at the same time minimizing the total vote. Or it is possible to try to maximize the vote, while minimizing the plurality. In any event, only if all those eligible to vote do so can we say that vote maximizing and plurality maximizing are one and the same strategy.

Recent political history provides us with ready evidence that vote maximizing and plurality maximizing are different. In 1960, based on the vote cast, Richard Nixon barely lost to John Kennedy; Kennedy's plurality was a mere 0.2 percent. Nixon's percentage of the *potential* vote was 31.6 percent. In 1972, Nixon achieved a landslide plurality over McGovern of 23.2 percent. Yet because the turnout rate was well below that of 1960, Nixon's percentage of the potential vote had risen only a little over two points to 33.7 percent.[8] We can say then that Kennedy won in 1960 with a strategy that involved maximizing the vote while minimizing his plurality. In contrast, Nixon won in 1972 with a strategy that involved minimizing the vote, while maximizing his plurality.

By adding to Riker's and Downs's minimizing and maximizing strategies, then, the consideration of pluralities, we find that parties have four distinct ways of winning open to them. The size of an electoral victory has two components: the size of the vote cast and the size of the plurality. Logically they are independent of one another. A candidate can win all of the votes cast and gain a plurality of 100 percent while winning hardly any of the potential vote, a situation characteristic of uncontested elections. Any combination of the two components is at least possible. To clarify the strategic options open to parties, however, it is best to focus upon maximizing and minimizing the two components.

The Four Strategies for Winning

The first strategy requires the party to try to minimize both the vote and its own plurality. This is the preferred strategy of the benefit seeker. It is also identical with Riker's minimum winning coalition, for it seeks to reduce support to the bare minimum. Benefit seekers wish to minimize the vote or, in other words, seek a low turnout election in order to minimize the number of claimants to the spoils. Benefit seekers also want to minimize the plurality of

---

8. One positive theorist has addressed the problem of the relationship between turnout and pluralities. See Kramer 1966.

the victory for the reason I pointed out earlier: the narrower the victory, the greater the claim of each supporter upon the successful candidate. Reducing the number of voters reduces the number of people among whom the benefits must be shared; reducing the plurality strengthens the hold of each supporter upon the officeholder. Again I must emphasize that this is the optimal strategy for benefit seekers, no matter what type of benefits they are seeking. Patronage seekers hanging around the party's headquarters are chary of newcomers. Ideologues watch their candidates for signs that they are broadening their appeal, or in their words, "selling out." Both recognize the value of minimizing the candidate's support in order to maximize their benefits.

The second strategy requires the party to maximize the votes cast as well as its own plurality. This is the office seeker's preferred strategy. Victories that reflect large turnouts and large pluralities enhance an office's inherent value by insuring the holder of the maximum independence from any single individual or group. Large victories also improve the officeholder's chances of continuing in the same office or advancing to another. The greater the officeholder's freedom from past supporters, the greater the ability to maneuver to advantage in future elections. Those who aspire to public office as a career must be future oriented. They must be continuously concerned about securing some office, whether it be the one they hold or another. They can best position themselves for future elections by being relatively free of the burdens imposed by past elections. Thus, the successful candidates who have maximized both the vote and their plurality are most free to change as political conditions change.

Maximum victories also serve as a type of political currency for office seekers. The political community, consisting of party officials, financial contributors, and other office seekers, as well as newspaper, radio, and television observers, is impressed by large victories. This is important to office seekers because the members of this community are responsible for singling out and promoting potential presidents, governors, or senators. More often than not they will single out those who have been able to demonstrate broad electoral support.

The remaining strategies are mixed strategies or compromises. One strategy requires the party to maximize its plurality while minimizing the vote. If office seekers must compromise, this is the strategy they prefer. Davis, Hinich, and Ordeshook (1970, 438) present plurality maximization as the best strategy for candidates. I feel they are also served by maximizing the vote. But if office seekers cannot do both, I agree they will prefer to sacrifice the size of the vote. I assume, for example, that John Kennedy would have preferred to win in 1960 as Nixon won in 1972, that is by a large plurality in a low-turnout election rather than by a narrow plurality in a high-turnout election. Narrow pluralities not only reduce the maneuverability of the winner, they place winning office itself in jeopardy. Of course, that would not be the case under conditions of perfect information. Given the normal level of uncertainty, however, we can expect reasonable office seekers to worry first about their pluralities. By concentrating on their pluralities alone, office seekers can also assuage their benefit-seeking supporters who, as I have pointed out, are not interested in seeing their claims diluted any more than necessary.

The Nixon campaign of 1972 exemplifies the strategy of plurality maximizing and vote minimizing. Nixon's large plurality was produced by sizable shifts of traditionally Democratic voters—southern whites, blue-collar workers, and ethnic minorities—all of whom were disaffected by the direction the Democratic party had been taking since 1964. Nixon, however, made few appeals to new voters, particularly to those who characteristically turn out in low numbers—poor whites, blacks, and the young. Indeed, Nixon himself did hardly any campaigning at all. In the southern states, where he was to register enormous pluralities, he avoided, for the most part, involvement in other races. A brisk campaign would undoubtedly have relieved much of the tedium observers noted among the electorate and would surely have produced a larger turnout. In retrospect at least, Nixon's campaign strategy was well designed to maximize his plurality, while keeping the overall vote low. Here I should point out that the two components of the electoral victory, the size of the vote cast and the plurality received, are only technically independent of each other. A candidate like Nixon in 1972 might reasonably conclude that his chances for a sizable plurality rested on a low turnout of voters. John Kennedy in 1960, on the other hand, explicitly waged a "get out the vote" campaign because he saw a large turnout as crucial to his chances for a large plurality.

The other compromise strategy requires the party to minimize its plurality while maximizing the vote. This strategy fits the needs of the benefit seeker better than those of the office seeker. The office seeker would find the value of the large vote wiped out by the small plurality. A large vote would mean that the number of marginal voters had been maximized, placing the officeholder in the weakest position. On the other hand, benefit seekers committed to maximum voter participation would find this a desirable compromise, since they could still retain a strong claim on the successful candidate. The League of Women Voters, many political scientists, and advocates of greater participatory democracy would be among the benefit seekers favoring this compromise strategy.

Depending upon the circumstances, each party must decide which of the four strategies is the best strategy to follow. Depending upon the reasons for abstention, variations in turnout will not affect the parties equally. Thus, depending upon the candidate and the issues, each party must decide whether a large or small voter turnout is desirable, as well as a large or small plurality.

This in no way vitiates my central point, however, that the preferred strategy of the benefit seeker is to minimize both turnout and plurality, the preferred strategy of the office seeker is to maximize both. The distinction among different strategies for winning elections has certainly not been ignored. We are indebted to Hinich and Ordeshook (1970) for their distinction between vote and plurality maximization. Hinich and Ordeshook, however, treat these maximizing strategies as if they were the goals of parties and candidates rather than a means to achieve goals. The authors do so because they are concerned only with winning; they do not ask what it is the candidate wins. Their failure to probe further and define the goals of parties as benefits and office leads them to ignore the principle of the minimum winning coalition as a possible electoral strategy. As a result, they fail to consider not only minimizing strategies, but the compromise strategies I have posited as well. Yet in order to incorporate the principle of the minimum winning coalition into a theory of parties, one of whose aspects is electoral competition, we must recognize that parties and candidates can follow minimizing and maximizing strategies, as well as combinations of both.[9]

It is one thing, of course, to posit a theoretical statement of electoral strategies for parties and candidates, and another to perceive differences in behavior in actual competitive situations. How can one possibly distinguish between the goals of office and benefits in a two-party system where both parties accept winning as the optimal means of achieving their goals under conditions of uncertainty about what will influence the outcome? Within each party, competition forces both office seekers and benefit seekers to woo a similar electorate; uncertainty forces them to broaden their appeal. As a result, any conclusions about real goals is subject to dispute. I wish to point out, then, that conclusions about goals will be drawn not from direct evidence but from our perceptions of the strategies parties appear to follow.

---

9. There can be no doubt that Riker means his size principle to be a statement about the objectives of candidates and parties. However, in the work in which he and Ordeshook seek to synthesize positive political theory (1973), the size principle and the discussion of electoral competition are handled as though they were entirely unrelated. If parties do seek to achieve a minimum winning coalition, as they argue in chap. 7, then one might expect the coalition to play a major part in their discussion of candidates' objectives that appears in chap. 11. Instead, candidates' use of the coalition is relegated to a footnote that asserts that, under certain conditions, the minimum winning coalition leads to results identical to those of plurality maximization. While it is true that the results can be identical, Riker and Ordeshook fail to point out that candidates who are trying to maximize their pluralities can hardly be trying to minimize their coalitions.

They also discuss possible goals for parties and candidates other than plurality and vote maximization. They mention briefly such goals as maximizing the proportion of the vote, the probability of winning, and the probability of securing a fixed percentage of the vote (1973, 336). None of these, however, is identical with the minimum winning coalition.

This is also true because the two goals of parties, as well as the two types of individuals who press these goals within parties, are, of course, abstractions. For that reason, the strategies of compromise may be the most realistic. Our ambitious office seekers are unlikely to be concerned solely with office. Inevitably, office seekers are also citizens concerned with the policies of government. Office seekers, then, are also benefit seekers. As office seekers they want to free themselves by maximizing their victories. Only a sizable victory can free them to consider the range of policies most likely to insure their continuation in office or their advancement. On the other hand, as benefit seekers they may well wish to reduce their maneuverability. Thus, they may well be drawn to a minimizing strategy. Like the southern legislators who could do pretty much as they wished as long as they voted the southern position on racial legislation, the benefit seekers in office want to be held by their supporters to policies whose benefits they also want. The claims of their supporters provide the best defense against the requests for trade-offs made by other officeholders.[10] And yet, as perpetual office seekers, they want to be able to make the trades when they can help further their careers.

In reality, therefore, the individuals who constitute political parties are inevitably subject to the pressures of both goals, making it difficult to determine which goal dominates parties. The tensions created by the goals of benefits and office, as well as the confusion over whether offices and benefits are ends or means, make it nearly impossible to determine which goal is dominant on the basis of direct evidence. On the other hand, we are able to observe differences in strategies that allow us to draw conclusions about the dominant goal.[11]

On what basis, for example, do most observers conclude that the two major parties in the United States are predominantly concerned with winning

---

10. The benefit-seeking officeholder's position is not unlike that of the bargainer's, analyzed by Schelling (1962), where a bargainer is able to increase his strength by proving his inability to change his position.

11. Positive theorists have examined the possibility that candidates and parties are subject to internal restraints, i.e., their ability to respond to electoral competition may be affected by the need to respond to activists or benefit seekers either in obtaining nominations or campaign resources. Riker and Ordeshook (1973, 361–62) raise the problem briefly. It is also raised by Davis, Hinich, and Ordeshook (1970) and Coleman (1971). The argument made by these authors is, however, quite distinct from the one I am making, since it treats benefit seekers or activists as individuals who have preferences, assigning strategies only to candidates or parties. In this respect, their analysis resembles James Q. Wilson's distinction between amateurs and professionals. My contention is that the benefit seekers or activists are also capable of making strategic judgments to achieve their goals.

Analyses that do treat the activist as a potential strategist are Aronson and Ordeshook 1972 and Coleman 1972. These analyses do not, however, make my point that the activist as benefit seeker attempts to win with a strategy different from that of the office seeker.

office? This conclusion rests not on overt statements in the parties' platforms or on the campaign oratory of the parties' candidates. The conclusion follows, instead, from our observation that the parties generally pursue strategies of vote and plurality maximizing, which make sense only if the quest for office is uppermost. We conclude, on the other hand, that U.S. parties are allowing the goal of benefits to dominate when we observe them, on some occasions, adopting strategies that are exclusionary. We came to this conclusion as we watched Barry Goldwater impose upon the Republican party the strategy of courting only pure conservatives and George McGovern's supporters reject as worthy practitioners of Democratic politics large segments of the traditional Democratic electorate.

Implications of the Two Goals for Party Organization

The usefulness of the distinction between the goals of office and benefits ultimately lies not in predicting party behavior but in determining how parties in democracies are organized. It is precisely because positive theorists have failed to distinguish between the two goals that their impact upon the study of political parties has been limited. Riker believes that his view of party is the same as Downs's, and students of parties generally have concluded that both of their views lead to a narrowly conceived view of party organization, the office-seeking party, deriving from their observations primarily of parties in the United States. Thus William Wright (1971, 17–54) has classified parties and party theorists along a continuum ranging from "rational efficient" to "party democracy." At one end of the continuum he places the major U.S. parties and theorists such as Downs; at the other end of the continuum are the European Socialist parties and such theorists as Maurice Duverger. Were he to understand the distinction between Riker and Downs, he would recognize that the rational-efficient view of party is capable of encompassing all parties in democracies, including the Socialist parties of Western Europe. Observers of the French, Italian, and Spanish Socialist parties during the 1980s should have little difficulty in accepting this position. For the Riker-Downs distinction allows us to see that, contrary to Duverger's belief, we are not talking about different kinds of parties but the same kinds of parties subject internally to the tensions provoked by the conflicting goals of office and benefits.

Once we appreciate the Riker-Downs distinction we do not need to assign rational behavior only to the office seeker. The assumption that only office seekers are rational calculators is a bias that runs deeply through the study of politics. Thus, James Q. Wilson's (1962) influential distinction between amateurs and professionals rests on the notion that only the latter are capable of treating issues and votes in a detached manner. Interested in winning office, they can compromise and bargain. Amateurs, on the other hand, hold policies preeminent. They feel that decisions should always be based on principle; thus, they are driven toward extremist positions. The difference is one of style and personality. The professional is the shrewd, rational, calculating politician; the amateur is the impassioned individual irrevocably committed to principles.

Once we accept the distinction in goals, however, we no longer need to reject rationalist assumptions in interpreting the behavior of policy-oriented participants in parties. No a priori reason exists for assuming them to be less capable of treating issues in a detached, calculating manner than those whose goal is office. Robert Putnam (1971, 669), in his careful study of British and Italian members of parliament, certainly found no inability on the part of ideologically committed legislators to compromise. Rather, what we must recognize is that each goal implies its own strategy. Behavior that is rational for the individual whose principal goal is office can be irrational for the individual whose principal goals are benefits.

In considering the implications of the two goals for party organization, we must keep in mind that winning an election means something quite different to one whose principal goal is office and one whose principal goals are benefits. For this reason, each goal requires a distinct approach to party organization.[12] The difference in organizational effort made by the dedicated benefit seeker and the dedicated office seeker derives primarily from the different value winning has for each. For the office seeker, winning provides immediate satisfaction. The state, according to its rules, hands over the prize. The benefit seeker, on the other hand, must await the decisions of the officeholder. Thus, benefit seekers need some mechanism to assert their claims. Indeed, before they make any claims at all they must be able to prove their support. This is not as easy as it may appear under a voting arrangement where the ballot is secret. One of the principal arguments for the secret ballot is that it makes it difficult for benefit seekers to prove their support and be paid for their vote. What good is it, then, for voters to forge minimum winning coalitions if there is no way they can prove their support to successful candidates? For all the candidates know, they might have voted for an opponent.[13]

---

12. Ordeshook (1970) applies positive theory to one concept usually associated with problems of internal party organization. His discussion of the concept of the responsible party, however, deals entirely with the question of whether or not parties present clear and distinct electoral choices.

13. In many political situations, open voting does exist, making the type of organization required by voters with a secret ballot unnecessary. Quite naturally, the concept of the minimum coalition has been applied most successfully in these situations. Brams and Riker (1972) applied the concept to presidential nominating conventions. The concept has also been readily applied to legislative voting, which is also open. The volume edited by Groennings, Kelly, and Leiserson (1970) contains a number of studies of open legislative voting in various countries, the common feature of which is that individuals form minimum winning coalitions overtly.

There are, of course, ways in which voters can prove their support. Giving money has been institutionalized in the United States to the extent that the office seeker must officially report each contribution, thereby giving legal assurance to voters who become contributors that their support will be recorded. Working for a candidate is another way, and only a foolish voter would do so anonymously. Interest groups such as labor unions are careful to identify their support and even devise ways to keep their activities on behalf of the candidate distinct so that their contribution is clear. All of these methods are available to groups and individuals interested in overcoming the anonymity imposed on the voting contribution by the secret ballot.

For voters who cannot or wish not to employ these methods, another way to make claims upon candidates is to become an explicit member of the political party that sponsors the candidates. This alternative provides the rationale for parties as membership organizations. It rests on the proposition that a party is, or should be, concerned with distributing benefits. The people for whom the party seeks benefits, therefore, must be identifiable. Voters must be turned into party members. Only in this way can the minimizing strategy become effective. Thus, ideological movements that become political parties must carefully define their boundaries with explicit organizational structures and techniques, such as the membership card. Similarly, a party theorist such as Duverger (1963), who conceives of a party as the representative of interests, that is, benefit seekers, has to conclude that the mass membership party is the last stage of party evolution. Explicit membership, along with an explicit organization to enforce the membership's claim, emerge in democracies to perform the essential function of keeping officeholders in line.

On the other hand, those whose dominant goal is office will naturally prefer not to be burdened with mechanisms designed to keep them in line once they have achieved their goal. Their preference is for light organizational baggage, for a loose structure with vaguely defined participants. They, of course, want a large body of voters who identify with their party and can be relied upon for support. But there are costs to putting names to these voters. Obviously, office seekers need help. Inevitably there will be individuals upon whom they will depend and who will therefore be able to make claims. But office seekers want to keep such individuals at a minimum and easy to replace. Only in this way can they achieve the maneuverability that is one of their most valuable assets.

The maneuverability that office seekers gain from loosely organized parties does not free them from all controls. All the same, the controls to which they are subject differ from those exerted over leaders of organizations whose goals are purely benefits. Albert O. Hirschman (1970) has distinguished between voice and exit as types of organizational controls. In an organization where office is the dominant goal, exit, that is the willingness of participants—officeholders, candidates, potential candidates, and voters—to leave controls behavior. In an organization where the goal of benefits predominates, voice, or the internal expression of dissatisfaction, is the means of control.

The distinctive controls of exit and voice reinforce the two models of party organization that I have just outlined. Control through exit requires no elaborate structure. The departure of voters, candidates, and contributors can become painfully obvious. Office seekers in the Republican party after 1964 and in the Democratic party after 1972 needed no referenda among party members or the convocation of party organs to determine that the parties had done something wrong and needed to alter their course. Control through voice, on the other hand, requires an apparatus through which party members can express their sentiments and exert their claims. Continuous forums must be provided, whether through committees, clubs, or conventions. Once these forums exist, it follows that the party's officeholders are expected to carry out the demands that these forums make explicit.

In reality, neither model exists in democratic politics. On the other hand, the two models offer a plausible explanation of the tensions that plague all parties serious about achieving power in democracies. In democratic politics, no party consists solely of office seekers or benefit seekers. Rather, conflicts arise within parties because the two goals can impose conflicting views of how to win elections and, ultimately, conflicting views of how parties should be organized.

Nevertheless, I assert that no matter how intense the struggle, the goal of office and the office seeker will ultimately prevail. Because office seekers must win elections to achieve their goal, while benefit seekers find winning elections only the best alternative, the former will always tend to dominate parties in democracies. Lacking an alternative, office seekers must either keep pressing their strategy, give up their goal, or move on to another party. Benefit seekers, because their goals are likely to be realized in some measure, are under less pressure to insist on their strategy. They can even withdraw from partisan activity and seek their goals by some other means, an alternative that office seekers do not have.

The goal of office also prevails because, as I pointed out in chapter 1, its realization is readily observable. When the goal of office is realized, not only office seekers but everyone else is aware of it. The achievement of benefits, on the other hand, is by no means clear. The implementation of policies especially, involving as it often does compromise, may well leave benefit seekers in doubt about the value of what they have received. This means that while office seekers have an easy test of organizational proficiency, benefit seekers do not. One goal, then, office, is simple and observable, its achievement easily gauged, and the performance of the organization in achieving the goal easily evaluated. The other goal, benefits, is often ambiguous, its realization difficult to assess, the performance of the organization in realizing the goal subject to dispute. These differences provide further reasons why the goal of office ultimately dominates parties in democracies. It is quite possible for parties to satisfy office seekers. If they do not, the remedy for their dissatisfaction is clear. On the other hand, it may well be ultimately impossible for parties ever to satisfy benefit seekers.

In chapter 1 I laid out a theory of party organization that described parties as unique organizations tethered to the electoral market and to those who compete in that market. I then went on to describe the factors affecting this unique organization, the structure of political opportunities and the structure of electoral competition. In this chapter, one aspect of the electoral structure, possible strategies for winning, introduced a characteristic of parties in democracies that is crucial to our understanding of these unique organizations as I have described them. These are organizations continuously subject to tensions brought on by potentially conflicting goals, the goals of office and benefits. By introducing the conflict of goals and electoral strategies, I hope I have made it clear that my theory of party does not disallow the use of such devices as membership rolls, doctrinal positions, and clearly defined apparatus by parties in democracies, devices imposed upon them by the goal of benefits. At the same time, by demonstrating that the goal of office must eventually triumph, I reinforced the concept of party I described in chapter 1. In the next chapter, therefore, I shall describe the content of the party organization in which the goal of office dominates.

REFERENCES

Aranson, Peter H., and Peter C. Ordeshook. 1972. "Spatial Strategies for Sequential Elections." In *Probability Models of Collective Decision Making,* ed. Richard G. Niemi and Herbert F. Weisberg. Columbus, Ohio: Merrill.

Brams, Steven T., and William Riker. 1972. "Models of Coalition Formation in Voting Bodies." In *Mathematical Applications in Political Science.* Vol. 6, ed. James F. Herndon and Joseph L. Bernd. Charlottesville: University Press of Virginia.

Coleman, James S. 1971. "Internal Processes Governing Party Positions in Elections." *Public Choice* 11:35–60.

Coleman, James S. 1972. "The Positions of Political Parties in Elections." In *Probability Models of Collective Decision Making,* ed. Richard G. Niemi and Herbert F. Weisberg. Columbus, Ohio: Merrill.

Davis, Otto A., Melvin J. Hinich, and Peter C. Ordeshook. 1970. "An Expository Development of a Mathematical Model of the Electoral Process." *American Political Science Review* 64:426–48.

Downs, Anthony. 1957. *An Economic Theory of Democracy.* New York: Harper and Row.

Duverger, Maurice. 1963. *Political Parties*. New York: Wiley.

Greenstone, David J. 1969. *Labor in American Politics*. New York: Knopf.

Groennings, Sven, E. W. Kelley, and Michael Leiserson, eds. 1970. *The Study of Coalition Behavior*. New York: Holt, Rinehart and Winston.

Hershey, Marjorie R. 1973. "Incumbency and the Minimum Winning Coalition." *American Journal of Political Science* 17:631–37.

Hinich, Melvin J., and Peter C. Ordeshook. 1970. "Plurality Maximization vs. Vote Maximization: A Spatial Analysis with Variable Participation." *American Political Science Review* 64:772–91.

Hirschman, Albert O. 1970. *Exit, Voice, and Loyalty*. Cambridge, Mass.: Harvard University Press.

Kramer, Gerald H. 1966. "A Decision-Theoretic Analysis of a Problem in Political Campaigning." In *Mathematical Applications in Political Science*. Vol. 2, ed. Joseph L. Bernd. Dallas: Southern Methodist University Press.

Ordeshook, Peter C. 1970. "Extensions to a Model of the Electoral Process and Implications for the Theory of Responsible Parties." *Midwest Journal of Political Science* 14:43–70.

Putnam, Robert D. 1971. "Studying Elite Political Cultures: The Case of Ideology." *American Political Science Review* 65:651–81.

Riker, William H., and Peter C. Ordeshook. 1973. *An Introduction to Positive Political Theory*. Englewood Cliffs, N.J.: Prentice-Hall.

Riker, William H., and Peter C. Ordeshook. 1973. *An Introduction to Positive Political Theory*. Englewood Cliffs, N.J.: Prentice-Hall.

Schattschneider, E. E. 1942. *Party Government*. New York: Holt, Rinehart and Winston.

Schelling, Thomas C. 1962. *The Strategy of Conflict*. New York: Oxford University Press.

Shepsle, Kenneth A. 1972. "The Strategy of Ambiguity: Uncertainty and Electoral Competition." *American Political Science Review* 66:555–68.

Stigler, George J. 1972. "Economic Competition and Political Competition." *Public Choice* 13:91–106.

Wilson, James Q. 1962. *The Amateur Democrat*. Chicago: University of Chicago Press.

Wright, William E. 1971. *A Comparative Study of Party Organization*. Columbus, Ohio: Merrill.

CHAPTER 7

Party Organization

In the preceding chapters I laid out the structures of political opportunities and electoral competition. Because these are the principal factors that stimulate and direct political ambition, the motive force in politics, they must be the principal determinants of party organization in democracies. In chapter 6, I also sought to demonstrate that party organization in democracies is subject to considerable tension due to the potentially conflicting goals of office and benefits. All the same, I argued that the goal of office must always prevail. In this chapter, therefore, I am concerned with the ways in which the opportunity and electoral structures, by stimulating and directing ambition, define the outline and content of party organization dominated by the goal of office.

The Basic Unit of Party Organization

I call the basic unit of party organization the *nucleus*. The nucleus represents the simplest implementation of political ambition, the systematic effort to capture a single office. The effort may be as minimal as one candidate circulating his or her own nominating petition for a seat on a local school board. Or it may be the multiple activities involved in an assault on the presidency of the United States. Complex party organizations emerge out of the relationships among nuclear organizations that I shall discuss below. Here, we should note that the nucleus is not the same thing as a formal unit of organization. Thus, in the United States, the nucleus is not the same as a precinct organization. The precinct organization is frequently described as the smallest party unit, which it is in the structure ascribed to the party by the state. Where a precinct controls a desirable elective office, the nucleus and the precinct organization are identical. But the need to record votes or to fill out the legal party structure does not assure party organization in the precinct. For a true nucleus to exist, there must be the expectation that at some time, if not in the immediate future, organizational activity will lead to the capture of the nuclear office.

The number and distribution of nuclei depend on a democracy's structures of political opportunities and electoral competition. Both the existence of desirable offices and the rules for their election define the extent to which separate nuclei for each office can develop. As I have already pointed out, in the United States, there is an extraordinary number of independently elected public officials, ranging from the president to the ward alderman, each of whom can develop an independent organization. On the other hand, no separate party nucleus can emerge around the vice presidency because its election is tied to that of the president. The situation is the same for the offices of governor and lieutenant governor in several states. It is true that candidates for vice president may develop their own independent organizations, but these organizations have, as their goal, influence within the presidential nucleus and depend entirely for their success upon that influence. Most offices in the United States, however, are elected independently, making separate party nuclei possible.

The electoral situation also defines the number and distribution of party nuclei. A true party nucleus will emerge only in those constituencies where a party has a short- or long-run chance of winning the office. It is, of course, possible for a candidate to run for an office without any expectation that the office can be won. In this instance, candidates and their supporters form not a true, but a *mock nucleus*. This was frequently the case for Republican candidates during the period of Democratic control of the South in the United States. This does not prevent candidates of mock nuclei from contributing to other nuclear organizations, most commonly in the United States to the presidential nucleus of their parties. But their activities will be aimed, not at the offices for which they are the ostensible candidates, but at such offices as postmasterships and judgeships that are in the control of the presidential nucleus.

Contributions and Party Organization

To describe the content of the party nucleus, I have followed Herbert Simon's suggestion (1951, 112) and used the concept of *contributions* rather than *membership,* the term most commonly used about participation in parties. The concept of contributions is most compatible with the Downsian definition of party I adopted in chapter 1. It allows us to maintain the narrow yet imprecise boundaries for party organization set by the image of the team seeking office. The concept of membership, on the other hand, connotes a degree of substance that is misleading in political parties in democracies. It is by no means easy to determine who is a member and what membership involves. In chapter 1, I discussed my reasons for excluding from parties the voter as a member defined by self-identification. Yet even more exacting tests of party membership are of little utility in giving the term meaning. In the United States, the legal control of formal party structure has produced a variety of tests of membership that tell us little about what it means to be a member of a party (see, for example, Berdahl 1942). The same may be said for the parties of Western Europe, where the term is far more commonly used. It is not unusual for researchers to express reservations about the extent of party activity based on the parties' self-reported membership figures.

Identification of Contributions

One way the concept of contributions alerts us to the imprecision of party organization is by calling our attention to the varied sources of nuclear activity. It is easy enough to identify the contributions of those who take part in party activities that are clearly labeled as such: running for office with the party's name, serving as party chairmen or delegates to party conclaves, or paying dues regularly to a party unit. But the newspaper publisher, the interest-group leader, the financial donor, and the voter in a primary in the United States can and do make contributions to party organization without necessarily clearly identifying with a political party.

The use of contributions from individuals whose connection to the party is tenuous gives the party considerable flexibility. It need depend on the contributions of committed participants for little. Workers for the nucleus of any office can be drawn temporarily from elsewhere, from interest groups such as unions or from corporations. At the other extreme, it is always possible to draw upon apolitical luminaries as candidates for high office. Thus in the United States, the partisan identification of Wendell Willkie and Dwight Eisenhower became clear only after they had become active candidates for the Republican presidential nomination.

At the same time, the tenuous connection allows those who contribute considerable flexibility, ultimately including the opportunity to transfer their contributions to another party. The more circumspect their identification, the easier such transfers. Thus, to the extent the New Deal wrought a realignment in politics, it was accomplished by those least strongly identified with either party. Financial donors, newspaper publishers, and ultimately ordinary voters found it easiest to switch their contributions from the Republican to the Democratic party. Even minor party officials, as a study of Pittsburgh precinct workers showed (Keefe and Seyler 1960), were able to make the change.

On the other hand, the contributors most clearly identified with the party nuclei, the officeholders themselves, are most restricted. Only during periods of major electoral realignment or restructuring of parties are officeholders likely to change parties. In the partisan turmoil that preceded the Civil War, Abraham Lincoln was among the most prominent of a number of officeholders who switched from the Whig to the Republican party. From then until the 1960s there was remarkably little switching by officeholders in the United States. The Bull Moose Progressives all returned to the Republican party once their crusade ended. During the New Deal, dissident Republican officeholders, like George Norris and Fiorello LaGuardia, made their accommodations within their own party. Alfred Smith, the failed Democratic presidential nominee who became disgruntled with his party in the 1930s, found solace in the conservative Liberty League, a nonparty association (Schlesinger 1960, 519).

Evidence of the far more extensive electoral realignment that began after the New Deal in the late 1950s was the increase in the number of officeholders who successfully switched parties. While in the North Republicans Wayne Morse of Oregon, Donald Riegle of Michigan, and John Lindsay of New York became Democrats, in the South, Strom Thurmond started the more significant transfer of Democratic officeholders to the Republican party. Nevertheless, compared with the movement of other contributors, especially voters, the movement of officeholders is limited.

Types of Contributions

The concept of contribution also allows us to identify the types of activity in which party nuclei engage. A useful distinction is that between minimal and secondary contributions. The basic, or minimal, contribution to any nucleus is the selection of the candidate. All nuclei must have candidates with some expectation of winning office, immediately or in the foreseeable future. Without them there would be no nucleus; with them the nucleus can be self-sufficient. All the same, nuclear activity usually involves additional contributions. While these contributions are not essential to the existence of the nucleus, they are aimed at helping it achieve its principal goal, the winning of office. I call these secondary contributions. Secondary contributions differ from minimal contributions in that their impact is more difficult to assess. The most important secondary contributions are the selection of issues and the formulation of policies, information, technical services, and money.

Minimal Contributions

Recruitment
The most important task performed by the nuclear organization is the selection of its candidate for office. The first stage of this process is the recruitment of candidates. At this stage, the office-seeking theory implies that the initiative rests with those seeking office. Recruitment takes place within the context of the structure of political opportunities. In the United States, for lower offices in the structure, particularly the potential starting points of public office careers, positions on local councils and in state legislatures, people emerge as candidates in a variety of ways. Studies of individuals holding these offices, however, confirm our inference about the candidates' initiative. They show

that a high proportion had one or more relatives active in politics, had already developed an interest in politics during adolescence, and saw themselves as "self-starters" rather than as individuals having to be pushed to run for office (Rosenzweig 1957; Seligman 1959 and 1961; Wahlke et al. 1962).

The structure of electoral competition also has much to do with recruitment, because it is critical to defining the costs and risks of any candidacy. For the minority party in a constituency where the candidate has little chance of winning, there may be a need for other office seekers to conscript a candidate (Seligman 1961). The greater the likelihood that a party will win an office, the greater the number of willing candidates. As Jacobson and Kernell (1981) have also demonstrated for congressional office, the greater a party's chances of victory, the more likely the party will have a "quality" or politically experienced candidate. The process of self-recruitment becomes even clearer within the nuclear organization surrounding higher offices. As I pointed out in examining the shape of the structure of political opportunities, the higher the office, the more likely the victors have come from a few manifest positions.

Choice

The most critical stage of the selection process is the choice of a single candidate for a particular office. No nuclear organization is likely to succeed in winning election if it must divide its vote for an office in a general election with other nuclei bearing the same party label. Thus, the selection of the candidate must combine the encouragement of one individual with the dissuasion of others. Again, the aspirants for office are themselves largely responsible for the process. The party provides the prize, its label. The ultimate victor is the one most capable of discouraging others' ambitions. But the victor should also be capable of linking the ambitions of the defeated aspirants to his or her own. Ideally then, the party label is won by the individual who can impose upon his or her competitors the maximum of discouragement with a minimum of public disgrace. Discouragement is facilitated by rules that allow only one person the designation "candidate" of the party. In the United States, this vital partisan accomplishment is protected by state laws.

Rival aspirants can use many resources to discourage their competitors. They can use the outright threat of sanctions, economic, social, or political. The aspirant whose supporters control such sanctions is in a strong position to discourage others. An aspirant can also block the acquisition of resources necessary to compete effectively for the party label. This is particularly successful when the contest requires substantial financing, as it does for statewide and national office in the United States. An aspiring candidate can also use more benign techniques, offers of alternative outlets for ambition, for example. The most powerful resource is undoubtedly situational, the obviously superior strength of one aspirant to that of all the others. This resource is normally available to an incumbent, seeking renomination, who has not aroused great opposition. But it is also available to the manifest officeholder who, having demonstrated prowess in obtaining one office, seeks to advance to another. All resources are, of course, not equally available to each aspirant. We can say, however, that the situational factor is critical; with that resource in hand, the other resources for discouragement are likely to follow. The scent of victory creates the "bandwagon effect" or fear of not being with the winner.

However the selection of the candidate is made, whether by the discouragement of rivals or their open defeat, the contribution is dysfunctional if it leaves the candidate too weak to win the general election. The contribution must be made so that all of the defeated aspirants who continue to harbor office ambitions will feel not merely constrained from opposing but induced to supporting the candidate in some way. The most effective control a party nucleus has is the defeated aspirant's hope for preferment in another situation at some later date. It is peculiar to the office-seeking party in democracies that, at one and the same time, it encourages people to open conflict and then forces them to curb animosity to achieve a subsequent goal. Much of what external observers see as the hypocrisy of political activity in democracies comes from this inherent characteristic of the office-seeking party. Even in democratic politics, burying the hatchet is not easy and frequently is not done or done grudgingly. Still, those who would rise in democratic politics must be capable of eliminating one's opponents with some grace, as well as of accepting elimination in the same fashion.

An important aspect of the contribution of selection, therefore, is the ability of self-interest to transform the potentially divisive and corroding effects of political ambition into a force for cooperation. In this sense, we should distinguish between the pure power seeker and the individual with ambitions for public office in democracies. In his earlier work, Harold Lasswell (1948) emphasized the dominance of power drives in the personality of political leaders. In later writings (Lasswell 1954), he noted that such persons do not rise to the top in democracies (see also Lane 1959, 124–28). The pure power seeker, as distinct from the person with office ambitions, can probably find more satisfactory outlets than democratic politics.

In democracies, then, the party leader is the office seeker, playing a role much akin to that of the business entrepreneur. Certainly the risks and potential gains are commensurate. As we have seen, office seekers themselves bear the prime responsibility for the all important contribution of candidate selection. As I have also pointed out, even for the many offices where a party will have neither an incumbent nor an overt candidate, the contribution will come temporarily from the candidates or incumbents of other party nuclei who stand to benefit from cross-nuclear activity. Once active candidates emerge, the contribution will come from them. Most others involved in the activities surrounding the selection process contribute on a voluntary and, therefore, fluctuating and ephemeral basis. Thus it becomes essential for someone to move people to participate, to oversee the assembling of needed resources, and to handle negotiations with other aspirants. No one has a greater interest in doing this than the office seekers themselves. Moreover, once the candidate has been selected, it is the candidate who is most interested in seeing that those secondary contributions are made that can help insure election.

Secondary Contributions

Issues and Policies

Once the candidate is selected, the nucleus must seek support for reasons other than the candidate's ambition for office. To succeed, the nucleus must offer voters reasons for supporting its candidate, its positions, or policies on issues that concern them. Who helps select the issues and frame the policies for the nucleus? To a great extent the process of candidate selection decides the issues and the policies on which the nucleus will stand. Once again, the office seeker is probably the prime contributor. But, in addition to the candidates, there are individuals who more or less specialize in political issues and policies, political journalists, college professors, and other specialists in public affairs, who are part of institutions aimed at making policy recommendations. A host of organized interest groups, using policy specialists, will also seek to contribute to the formulation of policies.

To what extent do party nuclei rely on specialists to determine what issues they will emphasize and what policies they will offer to resolve these issues? The specialists' contribution is very much limited by the ways in which office-seeking parties must devise policy in government. A party in control of government can make choices, but its range of alternatives is usually narrow. Only under conditions of crisis such as severe economic depression, hyperinflation, war, or great social unrest can a government make significant policy alterations. Even then it is constrained. It must respond incrementally within an existing administrative and economic framework. The important consideration is that the voters' perceptions of party policy rest predominantly on their experiences with parties in government. It is true that a long and continuing controversy among students of voting behavior revolves around just how competent voters are to judge the parties' policy positions and how consistent the voters themselves are over a range of policies in any event. Nevertheless, retrospective voting, or judgments about what kind of policies are associated with this or that party, severely limits the independent contribution of the policy specialist.

In effect, the specialist's role is often reduced to that of apologist for the office seekers who select and implement policy. Most of all, party nuclei need ideas from specialists that can make the virtues of their candidates' positions clear to the political community and especially to the voters. Thus, Keynesians provided the rationale for a variety of governmental programs put forth by the Democratic presidential nucleus during and after the New Deal. Subsequently, monetarists and supply-side theorists provided the rationale for the retrenchment programs implemented by the Republican presidential nucleus in the 1980s.

Information

Along with the selection of issues and the formulation of policies, information is another important secondary contribution to which the candidate must attend within the party nucleus. Given the individualistic, transitory, and uncertain character of much of the nuclear organization's activity, information that can modify this situation is a valuable commodity. Nevertheless, the contribution of information often reflects the dominant purpose of nuclear activity. Within the nucleus, the gathering and storing of information is undertaken primarily by succeeding candidates, for their own advantage. In a situation where much is fleeting, any record becomes a precious raw material that is not to be casually passed on. Especially valuable are data about financial donors and volunteer workers. So too is information about voters' reactions to personalities and issues as well as to types of campaign appeals, information vital to decisions about electoral strategy, as well as about future career choices. In this instance, candidates rely mainly on the contribution of professional polltakers who have mostly eliminated the candidates' dependence on face-to-face canvassing within the nucleus (Pool and Abelson 1961). Ultimately, however, information serves the candidates, and the responsibility for gathering and using it rests with them.

At the same time, the party nucleus must face the reality that some vital information can be disseminated by groups that have no identification with the nucleus and may even be hostile. Thus, the most ubiquitous polltakers and disseminators of their results are newspapers and the electronic media. The media also gather and disseminate other information, such as polls of convention delegates and the announcements of individual candidacies. The resources of the media may well be superior to any that the nucleus has for gathering and distributing such information. These external groups, therefore, have a powerful means of influencing the nucleus, for they provide some of its most important channels of information.

The nucleus will, therefore, try to exert some control over independent channels of information. The media are under some restraint to present information truthfully, particularly when its accuracy can be tested. Thus, newspaper and television polls are more successful, the more accurately they predict the electoral results. On the other hand, where tests of accuracy are less refined, as for reporting about factional conflicts, partisan preferences may well affect the flow of information. As a consequence, the nucleus will attempt to influence what gets reported in the news media. If the nucleus has any hired staff at all, it is likely to be a press agent or public relations expert (Ebel 1960).

Much of the responsibility for minimizing the adverse effects of the independent channel of information, however, rests with the office seekers themselves. When individuals plan to seek a particular office, it is advisable that they at least inform other prominent party figures before the public announcement, even if they know they will be opposed. To make party luminaries dependent upon the press for information is to infer their demotion. The surest sign that an individual is unimportant within the nucleus is the failure of a potential candidate to consult with or even inform the individual about the critical decision of candidacy. It is also advisable to keep prominent party figures, especially former competitors for the party's nomination, well informed during the electoral campaign. With an external source always capable of exposing ignorance, the giving and withholding of information become a political strategy and its reception an indication of status and importance.

Technical Services
Characteristically, technical contributions within the nucleus are made by small permanent staffs that exhibit no tendency to develop a sense of direction independent of candidates and officeholders. They gain influence through their relations with the candidates, not as a separate bureaucracy (Ebel 1960). Professional staffs blossom mostly during the campaign. Every campaign creates a surge of tasks for which volunteers must be recruited. Each party affair, rally, or coffee hour involves bringing together as many people as possible to give the appearance that the party enjoys popular support. On election day there are many things that the nucleus can do to make sure that committed voters get to the polls and have their votes tallied.

We should note, however, that some nuclei have more professional substance than others. In the United States, civil service traditions have not prevented public officials from using their staff for continuous electoral purposes. Most major officeholders enjoy, at public expense, the services of individuals who write their newsletters and act as their agents in their constituencies. Such paid staff engage in what is essentially activity designed to keep the officeholder in office. This activity must, therefore, be counted as an important technical contribution to the nuclear organization, one that gives great advantages to incumbent officeholders.

Money

For the party nucleus, money is undoubtedly the most important secondary contribution. Money represents "instant" organization, the means of purchasing many of the other contributions to the nucleus. In an era when political campaigns depend heavily on the use of paid commercial advertising and on computer programs for pinpointing a candidate's appeal, money is essential to the nuclear organization. Money can also be stored, amassed, quantified, and transferred, all qualities that are especially useful to the nucleus operating in an uncertain competitive climate and forced to deal with other nuclei. As I pointed out in the discussion of the selection of candidates, simply having a large and well-advertised campaign fund is one way of fending off competitors. The active nucleus, therefore, puts much effort into gathering money.

Government intervention has increasingly affected the way in which this contribution is made. The impact of money on politics has long been a matter of concern in democracies. Government efforts to make campaign expenditures public, to limit expenditures, and even to provide public financing affect the ways party nuclei gather and spend money. While government regulations have made the contribution of money more overt, they have also heightened the importance of the fund-raising function within each party nucleus. The public reporting of expenditures requires that someone within the nucleus be responsible for the reporting. More important, gathering money in small amounts requires more effort than soliciting relatively fewer large contributions.

The Multinuclear Party

Thus far I have discussed the party nucleus, the organization designed to capture a single office. Yet it is the multinuclear party that the party label evokes and that, at the same time, has proved most elusive to analysis. Few nuclei that share the same partisan label can be totally independent of others. In particular, cooperation is desirable among successful nuclei whose officeholders are in government. Yet as the examination of the nucleus has revealed, all nuclei do not share the same fate, nor do they provide the same career prospects. Cooperation among nuclei, then, proceeds neither in the same way nor at the same pace. This, in turn, means the substance of the multinuclear party will never be fixed. I assume that, for the multinuclear party, as for the party nucleus, ambition for office is the motive force and the capture of office the central goal. There is, however, an important distinction between the two units of party organization. Within a single nucleus the office goal is simple and straightforward; in the multinuclear party, office goals are complex and the possible source of conflict as well as cooperation. It is within the multinuclear party that discrete, static, and progressive ambitions, in a variety of possible combinations, come into full play. Cooperation among nuclei may be pro forma or substantial, but nucleus A will be willing to cooperate with nucleus B only to the extent that A finds cooperation useful in achieving its own goals. Thus, the substance of the multinuclear party depends on the way the most favorable strategic conditions for each nucleus meld.

As with the number and distribution of party nuclei, the structures of political opportunities and electoral competition are critical in determining the substance of the multinuclear party. The opportunity structure is critical because it determines the expectations of the politically ambitious. As we have seen, the opportunity structure provides the guidelines for public office careers. Among other things, it indicates at each stage of an office seeker's career the best possible allies, those whose office ambitions are in harmony with the office seeker's. At the same time, the structure of electoral competition sets the conditions for multinuclear cooperation. It defines the competitive as well as the noncompetitive nuclei within the multinuclear party. In so doing, it defines the needs of each nucleus as it competes for office. I infer that nuclei in competitive constituencies need the most assistance and, therefore, will be most likely to cooperate with other nuclei of their party. On the other hand, nuclei in safe constituencies need little or no help and thus are less likely to cooperate with others. Thus, the greater the number of competitive constituencies, the greater the level of cooperation among nuclei, and the more clearly defined the multinuclear party.

The structures of political opportunity and electoral competition in effect define the regular cycle of activities in which the multinuclear party must engage to achieve its dominant goal. The multinuclear party, then, emerges from this cycle of activities whose three phases require varying organizational efforts and varying degrees of cooperation among party nuclei. Although the goal of gaining and retaining office is central in each phase, the nature of the effort and the degree of cooperation vary in each phase. During the first or *nominating* phase, each nucleus strives to capture the same party label for a particular office. During the nominating phase, this is the principal means by which the multinuclear party acquires some presence. In the second or *electoral* phase, the use of a common label by all party nuclei continues to sustain the multinuclear party. Further substantive cooperation among nuclei will depend upon the competitive conditions each nucleus faces in the general election. In the electoral phase, the organizational task of each nucleus is that of winning the general election by whatever means the competitive conditions require. The party nuclei that win in the general election enter the third or the *governmental* phase. In this phase, the use of the common label is likely to be supplemented by cooperation that will allow the nuclei in government to survive the next nominating and electoral phases. I shall now examine the way in which the multinuclear party emerges during each of these three phases in greater detail.

The Nominating Phase

The nominating phase is crucial to the emergence of the multinuclear party. The nomination of candidates for multiple offices using the same party label is essential to the multinuclear party's credence with the political community and the electorate. To achieve this minimal but necessary degree of credibility, the multinuclear party is dependent upon the rules and procedures established by the structure of electoral opportunities for nomination. In most democracies, nominating procedures are unregulated by public law. This was true in the United States during the nineteenth century and has remained true, in large part, for presidential nominations during much of the twentieth century. When they are private associations, party nuclei are free to select and nominate candidates for public office in any way they please. They are, however, constrained by their need to produce a candidate who is perceived by the political community, by the competitors for the nomination, and ultimately by the electorate as the sole legitimate nominee of the party. Thus, early on, parties in democracies develop devices such as caucuses, conventions, or well-defined meetings to nominate candidates for public office. Consisting of party activists, these gatherings, following formal procedures devised by the parties themselves, publicly bestow the common label upon candidates for particular offices.[1] In no democracy have these devices been totally successful in preventing dissident candidacies, in forestalling dissatisfied aspirants from running with the same party label. Dissident candidacies are potentially damaging to the multinuclear party in the subsequent phases of activity.

In the United States, the alteration of the structure of electoral competition during the twentieth century to extend the state's role into the nominating phase has been of considerable value to the multinuclear party. During this time, the direct primary has been nearly universally adopted as the method of nominating candidates for public office (Merriam and Overacker 1928; Key 1956). This has substantially contributed to the multinuclear party's legitimacy. State-run primary elections for nominations have solved the problem of producing one legitimate candidate for each nucleus, while assuring the multinuclear party that its labeling will be uniform.

By solving this problem, the primary has guaranteed the multinuclear

---

1. Dallinger 1897 is a useful source on early nominating procedures in the United States. David, Goldman, and Bain 1960 provides a thorough history and analysis of presidential nominating conventions.

party continuity. Whether there is much or little partisan activity, the primary guarantees each party, over time, a sole nominee for each office, whose right to the nomination is protected by law. Also protected by law is the nominee's use of a uniform party label. The continuity of the multinuclear party is therefore assured, as long as the demands of the primary, including the need to run with the common label, do not deter aspirants for a particular office from participating. By making all of the technical arrangements and certifying the outcome as fair, the state certainly eases the organizational burden of individual party nuclei. But it does so by requiring them to accept a minimal organizational bond.

To the extent that the primary underwrites the multinuclear party in the United States, it underwrites the Democratic and Republican parties (Turner 1953; Key 1956; Standing and Robinson 1958). In this respect it goes beyond the effect of the rules for the general election, election in single-member districts by a plurality vote, in fostering two dominant parties. The primary strengthens the two existing dominant parties because it alters the relative costs and benefits to politically ambitious individuals of choosing between a dominant party's nomination and that of an existent or new minor party. Trying for a place on the primary ballot reserved for the two dominant parties is far less costly than participating in a lesser party's efforts to get its candidates' names on the ballot in the general election. Moreover, a major party nomination, given the name familiarity of the party's label, is likely to bestow benefits (in terms of votes in the general election) far greater than those a lesser party's nomination can provide. Little wonder, then, that following the adoption of the primary in the early twentieth century, minor party candidacies in the United States declined sharply.

To say that the primary provides the multinuclear party with a modicum of uniformity and continuity is not to say that it removes the need for party nuclei to act during the nominating phase. Nor does it mean that they must act uniformly. On the contrary, by creating two successive elections necessary for winning office, the primary makes nuclear activity, including nuclear cooperation, dependent, as in the general election, on the competitive situation peculiar to each nucleus.

Among other things, the creation of two elections gives unequal advantage to the nuclei of incumbent officeholders, as well as to those of manifest officeholders. We have already seen that incumbents and manifest officeholders control the situational advantage in making the contribution of candidate selection in the nucleus. During the nominating phase, primaries magnify their advantage because they are familiar names to the primaries' electorate. This alone gives them a degree of support that they would not necessarily receive from the more restricted electorate of activists who attend party conventions or caucuses. Activists have more information than the primary's electorate about competing aspirants. They are also more likely to be the active allies of one or the other of the aspirants competing for the nomination. Thus, by shifting the arena of nomination from the restricted conclave of the activists to the broader arena provided by the voting booth, the primary helps those who have well-known names and who bear the obvious credentials for holding elective office.[2]

Indeed, the use of the primary in the nominating phase reopens the question I raised in chapter 1: Should we include voters in the multinuclear party? I argue there that voters are choosers, not members, and that confusion can only result from considering multinuclear parties as organizations composed of voters as well as office seekers and their supporters. This argument is valid for the primary as well as for the general electorate. Voters in primaries approach their task in much the same way as voters in general elections. Some undoubtedly see their task as nominating the candidate most likely to win in the general election, others as expressing a preference among the choices presented. Whatever the basis for their choice, few primary voters feel constrained by their participation in the nomination to vote for the nominee in the general election. This is certainly true if, over the course of the campaign for the general election, they come to find the opposing party's candidate more attractive. They do not consider themselves to be, nor do they behave as, party "members." Rather, they continue to behave as "voters," that is, as choosers who treat primary elections as simply the first of a pair of elections in which they choose among the options presented to them.

For the multinuclear party, however, primary elections are not the first of a pair of identical elections. Therefore, they have different consequences for the party than general elections. Primary electorates are usually smaller than general electorates. This is encouraged by the legal requirement that voters can vote in only one party's primary. Thus, the composition of the primary electorate tends to exaggerate the differences that exist between voters and nonvoters in general elections. Even more than voters in general elections, primary voters are older, wealthier, more educated, more interested in politics, more associated with organized interest groups, and more concerned about issues. As a result, candidates in primaries contest before a drastically reduced electorate that can respond to them and the issues in a very different manner than the general electorate. Forced to please the primary electorate, party nuclei may well contribute to the formation of a multinuclear party in the nominating phase that is quite different from the party that emerges during the electoral phase.

---

2. In this respect, it is worthwhile noting that the U.S. vice presidency has emerged as a major stepping stone to the presidency in the era of presidential primaries and public opinion polls, both tests in which the standing of contestants is greatly affected by name recognition.

The multinuclear party that emerges during the nominating phase will depend, in part, on the kind of legal and political constraints placed on primary electorates. These constraints vary markedly among the states. The more constrained the electorate, the more clearly it is identified by the party label, the greater the reality and legitimacy of the multinuclear party in the nominating phase. This is so because voters as well as contestants must acknowledge the party label. The closed primary, therefore, is most supportive of the multinuclear party because it requires voters to preregister on a party's list. Also supportive are legal procedures that acknowledge a candidate endorsed by the party on the primary ballot with a favorable position or mark of endorsement (Jewell and Olson 1982, 114–16).

Less supportive of the multinuclear party are the different versions of the open primary. These primaries range from the so-called challenge primary, where voters need not preregister but must publicly take only one party's ballot, to the open primary where voters receive both parties' ballots, making the choice of which party's primary to participate in secretly. The "blanket" primary encourages broader voter participation; voters can vote in both parties' primaries, although not for the same office. "Nonpartisan" primaries, which dispense with the partisan label for both contestants and voters, provide no support at all for the multinuclear party. The salient feature of all the less restrictive primaries is that they permit candidates competing for different offices to distinguish themselves from each other, as they seek support from an electorate with no clear partisan identification.

Whether the primary electorate is more or less restricted, the multinuclear party will be affected by the number of nominees to be chosen in any single primary. Primaries can range from those devoted to a single office, the presidency, to those that combine the nominations for several offices, from president, governor, and senator, to the state legislature. Primaries that combine the nominations for several offices force each nucleus to take into account the effect on its nomination of the other nominating contests within the party. The consequences for the multinuclear party are clearest in primaries that include the contested nomination for a major office. In such primaries, turnout is likely to be highest. Moreover, if the contest exists in only one party, voters may well decide to participate in the contested primary, thereby affecting not only that nomination but the nominations for all other offices in both parties as well. Faced with such a primary, the nuclei within both parties can do anything but ignore each other.

Whatever the effect of nominating procedures on the relations among party nuclei during the nominating phase, relations are most delicate during this phase. The principal reason is that intervention by one nucleus in the nomination of another may, particularly if it is unsuccessful, cause difficulties in the succeeding phases. Intervention by larger nuclei in the affairs of smaller ones is likely to be the least fruitful. Efforts by presidents in the United States to oust troublesome incumbents of their own party by denying them re-nomination, such as Roosevelt's attempted "purge" of Congress in 1938, have usually met with little success. This is not to say that one nucleus can never step in and prod another. This is more likely when a nucleus has no incumbent or is inactive. It is especially likely when there is a close contest for partisan control of state or national legislatures. Then, coalitions of legislative nuclei may well seek to recruit and support candidates for inactive nuclei whom they deem capable of winning in the general election. Intervention by lesser nuclei in the nominations for higher offices is also not unusual. Indeed, the interplay of ambitions will often direct such action as those in lower offices seek to open up positions above them. Thus in the United States, candidates for president, senator, or governor can often count on support in the nominating phase from members of Congress and state legislators interested in improving their own prospects. At the same time, since this phase is short and uncertain, of-ficeholders with static or progressive ambitions may well find it advantageous to preserve their flexibility by abstaining from intervention in the nominating activities of other nuclei.

The Electoral Phase

Once the task of nomination is completed, the party enters the electoral phase. Multinuclear formation in this phase, as in the others, depends upon the advantages each nucleus finds in cooperation to achieve its own ambitions. The fundamental factor determining multinuclear cooperation in this phase is the way in which the constituency of each nucleus relates to the constituency of another. Constituency relationships are determined by four aspects of the structure of electoral competition: the ballot format, electoral timing, voters' attitudes, and the geography of constituencies.

The Ballot Format

In determining the relationship among the nuclei of a party, much depends on how the choice is presented to the voter, or the ballot format. In the United States where voters choose many different officials, at least some run on the same ballot with the same partisan label. Listings on the same ballot with the same label naturally provide an association between party nuclei. In some states, the rules may allow and, indeed, even encourage the voter to vote for all the candidates of the same party or engage in straight-ticket voting. In others, the rules may make it easier to pick and choose different partisan candidates for different offices, or to practice split-ticket voting. Given the possible consequences of the ballot format for voting, it has not been unusual for officeholders to seek to alter the format to their own advantage (Key 1958).

Electoral Timing

Also relevant to nuclear cooperation is electoral timing. Elections held for different offices at the same time will naturally be more conducive to nuclear cooperation than elections held for different offices at different times. Different timing produces different sets of voters, qualitatively as well as numerically. Thus, congressional elections held in presidential years encourage multinuclear cooperation absent from midterm elections for Congress. The more prevalent fall elections are likely to bring nuclei closer than the less frequent elections scheduled in the spring. Even-year elections combine choices for more offices than do odd-year elections. Electoral timing, then, is an additional factor working for nuclear cooperation or independence.

Voters' Attitudes

Since office constituencies consist of individual voters who have distinct attitudes toward the offices and the parties, the voters' attitudes go a long way toward bringing about or discouraging nuclear cooperation. This is true because voters' attitudes determine whether or not constituencies are competitive. A vital difference between voters is whether their vote is based on a long- or short-term view of the parties. Voters develop long-term attitudes toward parties on the basis of past experiences with the parties and their candidates in and out of office. These experiences may extend over several decades and the attitudes that evolve from them may be passed from one generation of voters to another. The strength of the voters' identification with one or another party best captures long-term attitudes. The stronger the voters' partisan identification, the more likely they will vote consistently for all the offices of the same party from election to election. Since their votes are predictable, a constituency composed entirely of strong party-identifiers is least likely to be competitive. It will be competitive only if there are variations from election to election in the turnout of the voters who identify strongly with one or the other party.

In contrast, voters' short-term views of parties rest on the parties' actions in the current election. They are based only on the parties' current candidates and these candidates' current stands on the issues. Voters who take a short-term view of the parties are most likely to vary their partisan choices from candidate to candidate and from election to election. Because their votes are least predictable, a constituency composed entirely of voters with short-term attitudes toward the parties is most likely to be competitive.

Since no constituency consists entirely of voters with short- or long-term views, the mix of voter attitudes determines the constituency's competitiveness. Every constituency includes, to a greater or lesser degree, both types of voters. Individual voters themselves respond to elections with varying degrees of long- and short-run concerns, depending on the times and the offices. Moreover, the parties' current actions may reinforce or weaken long-run attitudes toward the parties. Nevertheless, we can conclude that where voters' attitudes are predominantly short term, competition will be high. In such districts, parties will find the best opportunity to alter the voters' previous decisions. Where voters predominantly take a long-term view of the parties, competition is likely to be low. In such districts, the parties will see little opportunity for altering the voters' previous partisan preferences.

The level of competitiveness sends the crucial message to party nuclei of just how much effort, including nuclear cooperation, is needed to win the general election. No organizational effort is required by the dominant nucleus to win in a noncompetitive constituency; much organized effort is needed to win in competitive constituencies. For any pair of nuclei, then, we can predict the direction and intensity of the transfer of contributions. If we assume that each constituency is either competitive or noncompetitive, each pair of nuclei will face one of three sets of conditions with consequences for nuclear cooperation. If both nuclei are in competitive constituencies, both have common needs and both can find advantages in cross-nuclear activity. Both can benefit from appealing candidates sharing the same partisan label, both can profit from offering appealing policies as solutions to cogent issues under the same partisan sponsorship, and both can benefit from the favorable voter turnout mutually appealing candidates and policies can produce. At the other extreme is the relationship between two dominant nuclei in noncompetitive constituencies. In the electoral phase these nuclei have no organizational needs at all. Thus we should expect little in the way of transfers. This is the condition described by Key (1949) in his study of one-party states in the southern United States. He found the Democratic organizations there weak and fractionalized because of their unfailing support by the electorate. When one nucleus faces competition and the other nucleus does not, the situation is imbalanced. The nucleus facing competition will seek support from the nucleus without competition. Support, however, will depend on needs defined in the governmental phase. Thus, a candidate in a one-party nucleus will be concerned for the success of other nuclei of the party if their election will subsequently affect his or her chances of gaining a desired position during the governmental phase.

The Geography of Constituencies
The relationship between two nuclei during the electoral phase is dependent finally upon the geographic outlines of their constituencies. In the United States there are three basic types of relationships imposed by the geography of constituencies. Party nuclei have a *congruent* relationship. Both nuclei share the same set of voters, as gubernatorial and senatorial candidates of the same state. Nuclei have an *enclaved* relationship, that is, the voters of one nucleus are a subset of the voters of another, as with the presidential and senatorial nuclei, or the senatorial nuclei and the nuclei of representatives of the same

state. Nuclei have a *disjoint* relationship, that is, they share no voters. Most nuclei have this type of relationship. Thus, no U.S. representatives from the same or different states, and no senators, governors, and state legislatures of different states share the same electorates.[3]

The Congruent Relationship

Formal party organization in the United States has developed around congruent constituencies. Each level of government, the municipality, the county, and the state, has its network of party committees, chairmen, and conventions. Cooperation between party nuclei, that is, the transfer of contributions from one nucleus to another, is also likely to be greater between congruent constituencies, since the discrepancy in voting from office to office is likely to be smaller. Because party nuclei face the same electorates, albeit for different offices, they can expect the voters to treat them similarly. Thus, the congruent relationship is not affected by the barriers to nuclear cooperation that arise when each nucleus faces an electorate with a different mix of long-term and short-term attitudes toward the party.

Nevertheless, in the congruent relationship, ballot rules, electoral timing, and voter attitudes will also affect nuclear cooperation. Thus, the congruent relationship between two nuclei will most likely lead to nuclear cooperation if nuclear candidates run at the same time on a ballot encouraging straight-ticket voting. Where two congruent nuclei face an electorate closely divided between strong party-identifiers, they will also be encouraged to cooperate. Where, on the other hand, congruent nuclei run at different times, or at the same time on a ballot that encourages split-ticket voting, cooperation will be less likely during the electoral phase. Where the electorates are able and willing to split their tickets, we would also expect a more ambiguous relationship. Both nuclei need help and, thus, we should expect transfers of contributions. But cooperation is likely to be more discreet, campaign tactics more varied. Finally, where two congruent nuclei share an electorate dominated by voters strongly committed to their party, cooperation during the electoral phase will be minimal. If the two nuclei do cooperate, it will be due to mutual needs imposed by the governmental phase of the cycle.

The Enclaved Relationship

In elections in which one nucleus is an enclave of the other, nuclear cooperation will be modified by the same factors affecting the congruent relationship. Where cooperation is expected, the enclaved relationship raises the question of the type of contributions that each nucleus can make best. In the enclaved

---

3. For an analysis of the impact of constituency relationships on state party organization, see Schwartz 1990.

as in the congruent relationship, cooperation between nuclei will be greatest for elections held at the same time where the ballot encourages straight-ticket voting and where voters' attitudes toward the parties produce competitive conditions. In contrast to the congruent relationship where both nuclei can make similar contributions, in the enclaved relationship, the substance of the organizational transfers need not be the same. In the enclaved relationship, the larger nucleus can contribute the greater visibility of attractive candidates and policies on which the lesser nucleus can hope to ride to victory. The smaller nucleus or enclave can most easily provide information about the voters in its constituency and reach out to the supporters it has identified on election day.

The uneven transfer of contributions between nuclei in the enclaved relationship is therefore responsible for the specialization among nuclei in the multinuclear party of the United States. Although all nuclei are concerned with turning out sympathetic voters, the smaller nucleus is best situated to perform this task. Thus, in the enclaved relationship, the larger national and state nuclei look to their enclaves to bring out the vote. In turn, the smaller nuclei need the resources with which to attract voters. These are best provided by the larger nuclei in the form of attractive national and state candidates with policies that appeal to voters. Of the two factors that decide elections, turnout and partisan division of the vote, the smaller nucleus can best affect the former, the larger nucleus the latter.

Much attention has been paid to the value of the enclave's contribution for the multinuclear party (see, for example, Eldersveld 1956; Frost 1961). For turning out voters, direct canvassing appears to be superior to other methods, such as computer-based mailings and televised appeals. The problem is one of having and maintaining a local work force willing to engage in direct canvassing. Studies of two midwestern cities before the development of television and computer mailings showed the value to the larger nucleus of having an active nuclear organization in the enclave or local constituency (Cutright and Rossi 1958; Katz and Eldersveld 1961). Both studies demonstrated a significant difference in the vote, depending upon whether the local organizations were or were not active. For a presidential candidate, an active local organization was worth between 5 and 10 percent of the vote, a margin that could well mean victory or defeat in a close election. Both these studies did make the point that the marginal increment due to increased local activity was larger for the weaker party. In part this may have been due to the ability of direct contact to counteract the phenomenon of "breakage" (Berelson, Lazarsfeld, and McPhee 1954), or "clustering" (Katz and Eldersveld 1961), that is, the tendency for the dominant party to attract a higher proportion of the vote than would be expected from the composition of the electorate. While television and computer-based mailings have certainly altered the nature of nuclear activity, there is no evidence that they have eliminated the value of close contacts with voters. In every election, the turnout of voters sympathetic to the party's candidates remains a major problem that television and targeted mailing certainly have not solved.

Thus, a larger nucleus that contains few active smaller nuclei must either arrange for local contacts with the voters or lose a good deal of its potential vote. Yet the maintenance of local organizations in situations where there is no possibility of direct returns through control of local office is very difficult. As I pointed out earlier, a true nucleus will emerge only where there are short- or long-run expectations that organized effort will lead to winning office. As I also pointed out, the usefulness of local party activity may be of such importance to the larger nuclei that they will foster mock nuclei, those whose expectations of returns depend entirely on the success of the candidates for higher office.

The Disjoint Relationship
Most nuclear organizations have a disjoint relationship, that is, they share no voters. Neither, then, do they share the same ballot, although they can share the same electoral time. This relationship encourages the least cooperation between nuclei in the electoral phase. Geographically separate, they cannot help each other by sharing information about their constituents or technical services aimed at the same voters. On the other hand, they can benefit from the transfer of policies and money. The pressure to make these contributions between nuclei with a disjoint relationship comes primarily from the advantages, in the governmental phase, of electing as many fellow partisans as possible to office. The distribution of positions within government, whether it be by executive appointment or by legislative majorities, rests on having one's fellow partisans in control.

The Governmental Phase

The multinuclear party becomes most conspicuous because it is continuously active in the governmental phase. In this phase, the politically ambitious can enjoy the perquisites of the offices they have been seeking only if they have the cooperation of other successful nuclei. The office-seeking theory of parties in no way minimizes the importance of the party's activities in government. Quite the contrary. After all, the control of government is the continuous overriding goal of the office-seeking party. Parties are endemic to democratic government, particularly to legislatures that must regularly organize to allot positions, enact policies, and support or oppose executives. This is the reason all parties of any significance in democracies have had their origins within the legislature. Whereas one can imagine popular elections without political parties, it is less easy to perceive a legislature functioning without party organization.

As I pointed out in the discussion of the nominating and electoral phases, the pressure for multinuclear cooperation often comes from aspirations related to the governmental phase. Those with ambitions for places in government, the legislator who would gain a committee assignment or leadership post, or who would help secure an executive appointment, must cooperate with other officeholders and their nuclei. The competitive nature of officeholders' constituencies will certainly affect cooperation among nuclei in government. Yet even legislators who enjoy immunity from electoral tensions are under pressure from their own governmental ambitions to cooperate with their fellow partisans from competitive constituencies. Legislators in safe seats can enjoy the benefits of seniority only if the multinuclear party consists of enough successful legislative nuclei to control the legislature. To achieve this, officeholders from competitive constituencies need whatever record of accomplishment will make them attractive in subsequent electoral phases. It is during the governmental phase, therefore, that we expect to find the highest levels of multinuclear cooperation.

The Substance of the Multinuclear Party

The multinuclear party, then, is the revised Downsian team. Its various nuclei nominate candidates for office and pursue their election so that elective officeholders can govern in cooperation. The same party organization participates in the recurrent cycle of nominations, elections, and government. Each phase of the cycle of party activity is essential to its existence. Winning office is a continuous activity imposed on parties by the democratic principle of election and reelection. Yet the organized efforts made during the nominating and electoral phases make sense only as they relate to government. In turn, making a record that can lead to success in the next election is an overriding concern for those in government. Clusters of nuclei form and dissolve, therefore, as the reasons for their relationship change over the cycle of organized activity.

Ultimately, ambitions for office, channeled by the structures of political opportunities and electoral competition, determine the substance of the multinuclear party. Driven by ambitions for office, nuclear clusters emerge, fall apart, and re-form with the phases of the cycle. I argued earlier that multinuclear parties derive, in large part, from the differential behavior of the nuclear electorates. If all voters everywhere responded in identical terms, then all nuclei would perforce cooperate, for they would all stand or fall together, no matter what the ambitions of their office seekers. Differential electoral behavior for different offices, however, allows different types of ambitions, discrete, static, or progressive, to produce different and sometimes conflicting clusters of organization.

Discrete ambitions, ambition for a particular office for a specified term, will lead to clustering primarily in the electoral phase, in situations where cooperation has clear-cut advantages. The advantages are obvious for competitive nuclei with congruent constituencies and enclaved nuclei that are clearly affected by the fortunes of the larger nucleus. Discrete ambitions are least likely to produce cooperation between nuclei with disjoint constituencies. Of course, the level of discrete ambitions also affects electoral needs. Ambition for major offices such as governor, senator, or president, however discrete, may or may not be aided by contributions from enclaved nuclei. Presidents seeking reelection have, since the adoption of the Twenty-second Amendment, been limited to discrete ambitions. Richard Nixon's conduct of the 1972 reelection campaign stands as a classic example of a presidential nucleus with few ties to other nuclei of the same party.

Static ambitions, ambition for a long-term career in the same office, tend to produce cooperation between nuclei primarily in the governmental phase, insuring the conditions that can lead to reelection. Desirable offices that allow long-term service incite static ambitions. Given the favorable position allotted to the incumbents of these offices by the electorate, they will have little need to cooperate with other nuclei during the electoral phase, whether their constituencies are competitive or noncompetitive. During the governmental phase, however, they will need to cooperate to preserve the political conditions that will bring reelection. Thus, during the era of the one-party South, southern Democratic members of the House of Representatives could be counted on to form a solid bloc opposing civil rights legislation. As the South became more competitive, these Democrats were prepared to join with other Democrats to enact such legislation.

Only progressive ambitions, ambitions for higher office, produce complex nuclear clusters that exist during the complete cycle of party activity, at all levels of government. Only individuals with progressive ambitions will make use of those with discrete and static ambitions to create the multinuclear party essential to their needs. The state legislative leader who wants to become governor will emphasize the advantages of control of the state House for his fellow legislators' static ambitions. Presidential hopefuls will roam the country pointing out how their candidacy will help other candidates. Here Richard Nixon's behavior between 1964 and 1968 contrasts sharply with his subsequent behavior in 1972. In the earlier period, while he was seeking the Republican presidential nomination, he was the classic tireless campaigner for fellow Republicans, particularly in the midterm elections of 1966 (White 1970, 60–63). In this instance, progressive ambitions produced intense multinuclear activity, which discrete ambitions later suppressed (White 1973).

Progressive ambitions can even bring about cooperation between nuclei that have a disjoint relationship. Thus the effect of progressive ambition in one state, for example, a representative's defeat of an incumbent senator, has ramifications for office ambitions and nuclear cooperation within and without the state. The event is important to representatives from other states because the departure of the representative will cause the reshuffling of positions in the House, certainly a committee change, perhaps even the reallocation of a committee chairmanship. The same can be said for senators from other states. Where partisan division of the Senate is close, it may well mean a shift in party control with major ramifications for positions within the jurisdiction of the executive as well as the Senate. Within the state, the ramifications are particularly extensive: the movement of a representative to the Senate excites the ambitions of others in the promotional system established by the structure of political opportunities. City councilors, county prosecutors, state legislators, representatives, the governor, and the sitting senator all become concerned with what is happening in other nuclei. These concerns provide the rationale for the long-term multinuclear party. If the multinuclear party were dependent solely on static or discrete ambitions, it would exist only for the present. Momentary defeats, sudden discrepancies in electoral strength, would pull nuclear organizations apart. The survival of complex political organization requires long-term progressive expectations. It requires individuals who can and will project advancement during extensive public-office careers. For only they really stand in need of organizations that bind the nuclei of various offices together over time.

This is not to say that the multinuclear party held together by progressive ambitions will be free of conflict. Because the discordant potential of ambition is obvious, it is the cooperative potential that has rightly received our principal attention. Yet, among other things, the potential for conflict lies in the distinctive electoral conditions that nuclei can face. Certainty of victory in one or many nuclei may well produce conflict with the nucleus seeking higher office in a competitive situation. The classic situation is exemplified by the relationship between the Democratic legislative nuclei of the South and the Democratic presidential nucleus before the 1960s. Conflict can even arise within multinuclear parties whose several nuclei face competitive electoral situations. Here, conflict arises out of uncertainty about what will win elections. In competitive situations, nuclei must make strategic decisions about candidates and policy with considerably less than full knowledge of their electoral consequences. Multinuclear parties that operate in uncertainty may well suffer internal conflict over the best means of advancing the ambitions of multiple candidates. Such internal conflict is likely to exploit the conflict between the goals of office and benefits that I discussed in chapter 6.

We should, however, be aware that conflict serves an important function for the multinuclear party because it allows the party to adjust to changes in the political climate. Conflict allows the party to shed worn-out policies, and even worn-out candidates, without appearing excessively opportunistic. Although the primacy of office ambitions is central to the office-seeking theory of parties, I have also pointed out that parties must offer more than the ambitions of their office seekers to win votes. Indeed, the better the multinuclear party can mask these ambitions with attention to the voters' concerns, the better its chances of electoral success. Even more useful is the record of credibility the party establishes between electoral promises and their implementation in government. When current electoral promises and their likely implementation prove difficult for individual officeholders constrained by their past records, open conflict in the nominating phase gives the party flexibility to solve these difficulties with a minimum of opprobrium. Thus, the multinuclear party I have described is a chameleon. At the same time, its remarkable capacity to adapt translates into a remarkable capacity to survive.

REFERENCES

Berdahl, Clarence A. 1942. "Party Membership in the United States." *American Political Science Review* 36:16–50, 241–62.

Berelson, Bernard, Paul Lazarsfeld, and William McPhee. 1954. *Voting*. Chicago: University of Chicago Press.

Cutright, Philip, and P. H. Rossi. 1958. "Grassroots Politicians and the Vote." *American Sociological Review* 23:171–79.

Dallinger, Frederick W. 1897. *Nominations for Elective Office in the United States*. New York: Longmans.

David, Paul, Ralph Goldman, and Richard C. Bain. 1960. *The Politics of National Party Conventions*. Washington, D.C.: Brookings.

Ebel, Ronald H. 1960. "The Role of the Professional Staff in State Parties." Ph.D. diss., Michigan State University.

Eldersveld, Samuel J. 1956. "Experimental Propaganda Techniques and Voting Behavior." *American Political Science Review* 50:154–65.

Frost, Richard T. 1961. "Stability and Change in Local Party Politics." *Public Opinion Quarterly* 25:221–35.

Jacobson, Gary, and Samuel Kernell. 1981. *Strategy and Choice in Congressional Elections*. New Haven: Yale University Press.

Jewell, Malcolm E., and David M. Olson. 1982. *American State Political Parties and Elections*. Rev. ed. Homewood, Ill.: Dorsey Press.

Katz, Daniel, and Samuel J. Eldersveld. 1961. "The Impact of Local Activity upon the Electorate." *Public Opinion Quarterly* 25:1–24.

Keefe, William, and W. C. Seyler. 1960. "Precinct Politicians in Pittsburgh." *Social Science* 35:26–32.

Key, V. O., Jr. 1949. *Southern Politics*. New York: Knopf.

Key, V. O., Jr. 1956. *American State Politics*. New York: Knopf.

Key, V. O., Jr. 1958. *Politics, Parties, and Pressure Groups*. 4th ed. New York: Crowell.

Lane, Robert E. 1959. *Political Life*. Glencoe, Ill.: Free Press.

Lasswell, Harold. 1948. *Power and Personality*. New York: Norton.

Lasswell, Harold. 1954. "The Selective Effect of Personality on Political Participation." In *Studies in the Scope and Method of the "Authoritarian Personality,"* ed. R. Christie and M. Jahoda. Glencoe, Ill.: Free Press.

Merriam, Charles E., and Louise Overacker. 1928. *Primary Elections*. Chicago: University of Chicago Press.

Pool, Ithiel de Sola, and Robert Abelson. 1961. "The Simulmatics Project." *Public Opinion Quarterly* 25:167–83.

Rosenzweig, Robert M. 1957. "The Politician and the Career in Politics." *Midwest Journal of Political Science* 1:163–72.

Schlesinger, Arthur M., Jr. 1960. *The Politics of Upheaval*. Boston: Houghton Mifflin.

Schwartz, Mildred A. 1990. *The Party Network: The Robust Organization of Illinois Republicans*. Madison: University of Wisconsin Press.

Seligman, Lester. 1959. "A Prefatory Study of Leadership Selection in Oregon." *Western Political Quarterly* 12:153–67.

Seligman, Lester. 1961. "Political Recruitment and Party Structure: A Case Study." *American Political Science Review* 55:77–86.

Simon, Herbert. 1951. *Administrative Behavior*. Macmillan.

Standing, William H., and James A. Robinson. 1958. "Inter-Party Competition and Primary Contesting: The Case of Indiana." *American Political Science Review* 52:1066–77.

Turner, Julius. 1953. "Primary Elections as the Alternative to Party Competition in 'Safe' Districts." *Journal of Politics* 15:197–210.

Wahlke, John, Heinz Eulau, William Buchanan, and Leroy Ferguson. 1962. *The Legislative System*. New York: Wiley.

White, Theodore. 1970. *The Making of the President, 1968*. New York: Pocket Books.

White, Theodore. 1973. *The Making of the President, 1972*. New York: Bantam.

CHAPTER 8

The Changing Multinuclear Party: Twentieth-Century Parties in the United States

In the preceding chapter I characterized the multinuclear party as a changing organization. The multinuclear party emerged as an organization continuously responsive to the office seeker's ambitions, ambitions guided by the structures of political opportunities and electoral competition. In this chapter I shall more closely examine the multinuclear party as a changing organization by looking at parties in the United States over the course of the twentieth century. During the century, neither the structure of political opportunities nor the structure of electoral competition has been static. Rather, both structures have undergone two periods of major change. The first period, which ran from about 1900 through the 1950s, reflected the major changes imposed by the Progressive era. The result was the centrifugal multinuclear party. This was the party that the American Political Science Association's committee criticized in its report, *Toward a More Responsible Two-Party System* (1950). Ironically, at about that time, changes were beginning to take place in the opportunity and electoral structures that would result in the centripetal multinuclear party, a party closer to the model preferred by the committee.

The Centrifugal Party: The Structures of Opportunities and Competition in the Progressive Era

The changes in the two structures made during the Progressive era had the clear aim of reducing the presence of parties. The direct primary and ballot reforms altered the structure of electoral competition. The effect of the direct primary was to deprive the existing party apparatus of its most important function, the nomination of candidates for elective office. Ballot reforms deprived the parties of many of the mechanisms they had developed for controlling the vote in the general election. Meanwhile, reforms within the Congress altered the structure of political opportunities in such a way as to reduce the capacity of party leaders to direct the course of legislation.

The changes in electoral rules especially reduced the pressures for party nuclei to work together. In the nominating phase, nomination of several

177

offices by party activists in convention was increasingly replaced by the direct primary. The direct primary, by broadening participation in the nominating procedure, made it easier for candidates for one office to act independently of candidates for other offices. Changes introduced for the electoral phase had similar consequences. In the nineteenth century, the distribution of ballots by party required cooperation among nuclei. Ballots had to be printed and distributed in every precinct. A party that could not perform this task in every precinct was a party that would lose votes and offices all along the line. It was essential then that all nuclei establish ties in order to see that this basic task was carried out. At the same time, ballots printed and distributed by the party encouraged voting the straight party line. In contrast, after the Progressive reforms, ballots printed and distributed by the state in every precinct removed this need for multinuclear cooperation. Since all parties' nominees now appeared on the same ballot, it was also easier for voters to divide their votes between the parties. This, in turn, encouraged nominees who found advantages in distinguishing themselves from their fellow partisan candidates (Rusk 1970).

Links between party nuclei were also weakened by the Seventeenth Amendment (1913), which provided for the direct election of senators, another reform enacted during the Progressive era. Before the Seventeenth Amendment, state legislatures chose senators. Senatorial candidates and incumbents, therefore, had to be involved with every aspect of state legislative activity, from elections to internal organization (Rothman 1966). With the introduction of the direct election of senators, the two types of officeholders were freed from the ties that bound them. State legislators of the same party were also released from an important pressure to act together. One apparent consequence of the direct election of senators, as well as the direct primary, was the decline in state legislative experience for the offices of senator and governor (see chap. 4, table 4.3). This development also weakened multinuclear ties.

The reforms did not, however, eliminate parties, for parties remained essential to their principal clientele, candidates for elective office. On the other hand, the parties were required to change in order to meet the new conditions introduced for winning office. The principal effect of the changes was to make the office seeker's dominance, particularly the incumbent's dominance, of party organization clearer than ever. Thus, the introduction of the direct primary altered the method of nomination, as I pointed out in the preceding chapter, to one that greatly favored incumbents. A common practice in the nineteenth century was to rotate nominations among the counties or towns of an electoral district. Those who sought to replace nomination by convention with the direct primary were well aware that the change would benefit incumbents. Thus, Robert Luce, a state legislator and early student of legislative behavior, observed (1924, 365), "In helping to break down the system of party nomination by convention in Massachusetts and replacing it with direct nomination in 1902, one of the purposes I had in mind was to lessen the damage wrought by these rotation arrangements." These rotation arrangements could only damage one group, incumbents deprived of the opportunity for reelection.

The introduction of the Australian ballot also furthered the cause of the incumbent. Printed by the state with the names of all the candidates, the Australian ballot eliminated the possibility that an officeholder could be kept off the ballot in select precincts by intraparty competitors. It prevented the reoccurrence of the problem faced by the Democrat Grover Cleveland in his bid for reelection to the presidency in 1888. In the election of 1888, the former governor of New York failed to carry his home state by a little over 12,000 votes. At the same time, the incumbent Democratic Governor David Hill won reelection by over 17,000 votes. After the election, charges were made that, in select New York precincts, Cleveland's name had been kept off ballots distributed by Democrats interested in furthering Hill's presidential ambitions. Had Cleveland carried New York, one of the two instances in which the electoral college failed to choose the presidential candidate with the popular plurality would have been prevented (Fredman 1968, 28–29). Since both the direct primary and the Australian ballot had to be adopted state by state, the rapidity with which they were passed testified to incumbents' appreciation of their value.

The reforms in Congress that altered the structure of political opportunities also favored incumbents. Before the 1910 revolt against the Speaker of the House of Representatives, party leaders enjoyed great influence over the legislative agenda through the control of committees and procedures. After the revolt, seniority became the principal device for distributing positions of power (Fenno 1965). Seniority made patently clear, both to the party activist and the voter, the value of preserving incumbents. Seniority then reinforced the effect of the alterations in the electoral rules, so that, inside and outside government, the principal levers of control rested openly with incumbent officeholders and potential incumbents.

By 1920, with the adoption of women's suffrage, the alterations in the structures of political opportunities and of electoral competition inspired by the Progressive era were in place. Between 1920 and 1960, minor adjustments were made by the states in such matters as electoral timing and ballot forms. But, essentially, it was a stable period in which officeholders sought to reinforce their positions. Most significant were the changes that were not made. After 1920, for the first and only time, the Congress failed to follow the constitutional mandate to reapportion seats in the House of Representatives in accord with the new census. In state after state, legislatures reinforced and perpetuated the congressional failing by using a variety of devices to keep the districts of federal and state representatives from reflecting the population growth of the newer metropolitan areas (Jewell 1962). Firmly in control of the political machinery, officeholders were happy to use it to preserve their positions.

The officeholders whose importance the reforms of the Progressive era insured were those of the two existing dominant parties, the Republicans and Democrats. The irony is that reforms designed to control parties and even to inspire new organized political efforts resulted in making the two dominant parties semipublic institutions. By requiring that they make their nominations through a state-run primary election, the state abetted the already existing organizations by making, in effect, the contribution I singled out as the most crucial for parties in democracies, the nomination of a single legitimate candidate for each office. The new, state-distributed ballot, listing all of the candidates with their party labels, further facilitated the contribution by informing the voters of the party's candidates.

Greatly assisted by the state in carrying out their fundamental task, the two dominant parties could be more relaxed about their organizational activities. In sum, the reforms of the Progressive era helped alter both the opportunity and electoral structures in such a way as to make it easier for office seekers and officeholders and their nuclei, in both parties, to go their own way. Note how this was accomplished in each of the three phases of the organizational cycle I discussed in chapter 7. In the nominating phase, direct primaries gave candidates a mechanism for gaining the nomination independent of slate-makers. In the electoral phase, the Australian ballot, printed and distributed by the state, made it possible to run a campaign independent of other party nuclei. In the governmental phase, congressional reforms reduced the pressure for legislators within the same party to act in concert. Rules that rewarded longevity in office rather than cooperation or teamwork also encouraged the independence of officeholders and their party nuclei.

Independence was further encouraged by another alteration in the structure of electoral competition, the redistribution in support for the parties, following the electoral realignment of 1896 (Key 1955; Burnham 1970). I discussed the effects of the realignment in some detail in chapter 5. Here, let me recall a period in which the Democratic party came to dominate the states of the Deep South, as Republicans ceased even to field candidates. At the same time, large areas of the Midwest and the northeast became almost as strongly committed to the Republican party. Immediately the Republican party also gained dominance over the presidency and the Congress, a position threatened only in 1912, when internal divisions allowed the Democrat Woodrow Wilson to win the presidency. The general decline in competition can be seen by the increasing margins by which candidates won elections in this

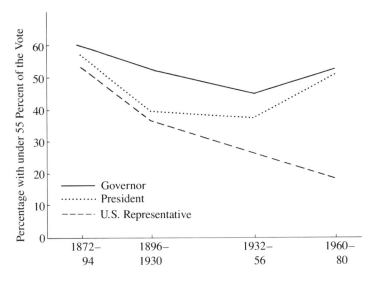

Fig. 8.1. Marginal elections. (From Schlesinger 1985, 1157.)

period. In the latter half of the nineteenth century, more than half the contests for the offices of U.S. representative, governor, and president were won by less than 55 percent of the vote (see fig. 8.1). After 1896, these marginal wins declined substantially.

The most significant aspect of the new competitive conditions was the unevenness of competition among offices. Using party turnover as the measure of competition, I found that the offices with broader constituencies such as the presidency and the governorship were more competitive and, in some instances, became increasingly competitive over time. In contrast, offices with smaller constituencies, such as the office of representative, became increasingly dominated by one party. Figures 8.2 and 8.3 demonstrate this difference for successive twenty-year periods. During the latter part of the nineteenth century, competition for the presidency took place within a few states; a majority of the states never shifted their vote from one party to the other. During the twentieth century, the proportion of one-party states for the presidency dropped in each successive twenty-year period. In contrast, at the end of the nineteenth century, only one-third of the House districts were noncompetitive; by the later part of the twentieth century, over half the House districts were noncompetitive. Similarly, I found that the proportion of volatile constituencies, that is, those with a turnover rate of three or more in a twenty-year period, rose for the presidency and the governorship, while it declined steadily for the lower house of Congress (see fig. 8.3).

The consequence of uneven competition was the further weakening of

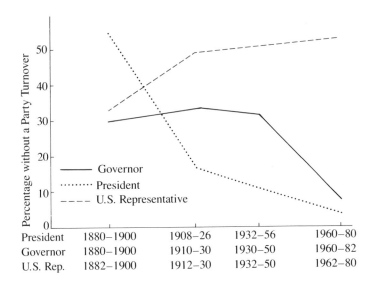

Fig. 8.2. **Percentage of one-party constituencies. (From Schlesinger 1985, 1157.)**

the ties between offices. It was, of course, part of the Founding Fathers' plan that the Congress and the president should respond to different constituencies (Hamilton, Madison, and Jay 1961; Burns 1963). The uneven competition in the twentieth century for the two offices strengthened the difference in response. On the one hand, the mechanics of the electoral college weakened the position of one-party states in the presidential nucleus, as the parties vied for the competitive states. Thus, the one-party southern states did not have much influence within the presidential nuclei of either party. At the same time, given the seniority rule, the one-party southern states increased the influence of southern Democrats within the Congress. Much the same thing happened in the states, weakening the ties between governors and the state legislatures (Key 1956). Malapportionment insured that legislative control rested with representatives of constituencies distinct from the more competitive constituencies, which usually elected governors.

The alterations in the structures of political opportunities and of electoral competition contributed to uneven competition because they amplified the voting discrepancies between large and small constituencies. The larger presidential and gubernatorial nuclei had always been incapable of varying their appeal among the congressional and state legislative districts that comprised

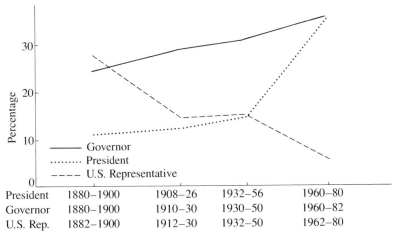

President	1880–1900	1908–26	1932–56	1960–80
Governor	1880–1900	1910–30	1930–50	1960–82
U.S. Rep.	1882–1900	1912–30	1932–50	1962–80

(In the above, President refers to the vote in individual states.)

Fig. 8.3. Percentage of volatile constituencies. (From Schlesinger 1985, 1158.)

their constituencies. In contrast, the smaller nuclei had to tailor their appeal to their districts. Furthermore, the smaller and therefore the more homogeneous House and state legislative constituencies were bound to be less volatile in their partisan responses. The earlier structures had nevertheless provided links between the offices. By eliminating the links, the alterations merely released the tendencies toward centrifugal multinuclear organization that the U.S. structure of electoral competition had always encouraged.

At the same time, the alterations in both structures more directly abetted the decline in competition between the parties. Thus, the introduction of the seniority rule in Congress made it profitable for House districts to keep sending back the same representatives. The introduction of the primary deprived the minority party in a constituency of its most precious resource, its monopoly of electoral opposition. As a result of the primary, competitors were able to fight it out, at least electorally, within the dominant party.

The decline in overall competition for office, as well as the unevenness of competition characteristic of the first six decades of the twentieth century, were also due, in large part, to the growing rigidity of the electorate's behavior. We know little about the strength of partisan identification before the development of systematic voter surveys. We do know that, in the early 1950s, approximately 75 percent of the electorate expressed some degree of party identification; half of these voters expressed strong identification

(Abramson 1983, chap. 7). We may, therefore, infer that the predominance of party identifiers contributed substantially to the decline in the level of competition in individual constituencies. Indeed, I would argue that the key to the competitive conditions of the period was the strength of partisan identification in the electorate. Once the parties made their nominations, the results of most elections became quite predictable.

As I noted in the preceding chapter on party organization, the level of competition critically affects the multinuclear party. Upon the level of competition, to a large extent, depends the distribution of party nuclei, the amount of nuclear activity, and the ties of nuclei to each other. We can clearly observe this effect upon the development of parties in the United States between 1900 and 1960. The simplest test of the distribution of party nuclei is whether or not a party fields candidates for elective office. For the two major U.S. parties, getting a candidate's name on the ballot during these years was a relatively simple task. More of a problem was finding candidates willing to run with the party's label for every office. Certainly, over a large part of the country for many lesser offices, only one party's candidate ran in the general election. It is true that for more significant offices such as the office of U.S. representative, the two major parties fielded candidates in most constituencies. All the same, when we examine the first six decades of the twentieth century, we see a steady increase in the number of House districts where one party failed to run a candidate (see fig. 8.4).

In 1900, only 22 districts did not have candidates from both parties; by 1918, the proportion had risen to 30 percent, or 128 districts. For the rest of the period, the proportion remained high, ranging around 20 percent of all districts. The bulk of the noncompetitive districts, of course, were in the South, where the Republicans failed to run candidates. Yet as we can see from the time-series, a significant number of Democratic nuclei failed to compete in the pre–New Deal era.

In effect, as the office-seeking theory leads us to expect, in the areas where parties were unable to compete, their organizational presence disappeared. Moreover, as the theory also indicates, the less competitive the constituency, the less the organizational effort put forth by either party. By effort, I mean simply getting candidates to run and then conducting a campaign. Since no good general data exist to measure effort over time, we must rely on regional and specialized studies. These studies leave the impression that, during the period of decreased competition, partisan organizational effort was also on the decline. V. O. Key's classic study of the southern states describes minimal partisan effort, consisting almost entirely of individual attempts to capture the Democratic nomination (1949, chap. 18); the nomination captured, nothing more was needed and nothing more was done. In his later work on the nonsouthern states, Key used the word *atrophy* to describe the condi-

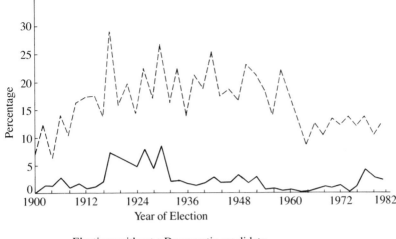

- —— Elections without a Democratic candidate
- ----- Total elections without one of the major party's candidates

Fig. 8.4. Congressional elections lacking one major party candidate, House of Representatives. (From Schlesinger 1985, 1159.)

tion of partisan organization (1956, chap. 6). In a systematic survey of Detroit's voters in the 1950s, Eldersveld (1964, 442) found that as many as 44 percent had never been approached in any way by a party; they had not even received campaign literature. In the study of four state legislatures of the same era, Wahlke et al. (1962, 98) found that only in New Jersey did a majority of the legislators mention their party as having sponsored their careers in any way. In Ohio, California, and Tennessee only about one in four saw the party in the role of sponsor. In a survey of all state party organizations as of the 1960s, Mayhew (1986) classified only six states as having strong, hierarchic party organizations. This was, then, hardly an era of highly visible coordinated partisan effort.

During this period the widely recognized decay of the urban political machine also took place. Its decline has usually been attributed to the decline in immigration that deprived the machine of its ready supply of dependent voters, as well as to the emergence of the welfare state that deprived it of the need to do favors for the poor. To these explanations I would add the general decline in electoral competition during the first half of the twentieth century. After 1932, the urban population became increasingly attached to the Democratic party. But this was clearly an attachment based on the appeal of the national presidential nucleus, with which the local machines of both parties had nothing to do. As a result, the Democratic label became more useful to candidates and officeholders than the machines. Once this was apparent, candidates and officeholders were prepared to abandon the machines. Given the lack of competition, however, it was the label, not cooperation between the presidential nucleus and other party nuclei, that replaced the machine.

Ultimately, electoral competition stimulates cooperation among the nuclei of parties. As I pointed out in chapter 7, according to the office-seeking theory, cooperation should be strongest among the nuclei of competitive constituencies. We should, therefore, expect less cooperation among the parties' nuclei during the first six decades of the twentieth century. Once again there is little systematic evidence by which to test the hypothesis. Little direct evidence exists of cross-nuclear recruitment of candidates or joint campaigns. We do know something about monetary transfers between candidates, but we also know that reporting of campaign finances was spotty (Heard 1960). Caro (1981, 608) describes how the inventive Lyndon Johnson, in an effort foreshadowing PACs, gathered and distributed Texas oil money among Democratic candidates for the House in 1940. But this was certainly an exceptional effort, if only because it was an era in which campaign expenditures were relatively small and probably less important in deciding elections than they became with the advent of television.

The best and most important indicator of cooperation among party nuclei occurs in the governmental phase. It is the degree to which legislators of the same party vote together in legislatures and the extent to which these legislators support their party's executive officeholders. We have systematic evidence of this behavior. In accordance with the office-seeking theory, as competition for the relevant offices declines, so should cooperation in government among officeholders of the same party. Figure 8.5 demonstrates support for this hypothesis. The graph consists of the cohesion scores for each party in the House of Representatives in each Congress between 1900 and 1980. In the Congresses elected between 1900 and 1908, before all the alterations in both structures were in place, the graph shows that cohesive voting for both parties was above 75 percent. After the alterations and the decline in competition, cohesion declined in both parties, but most sharply among the Democrats. The decline in cohesion for the Democratic party calls our attention again to the party's inclusion of the larger number of officeholders elected in one-party districts. The party also represented more demographically and economically diverse metropolitan constituencies. After 1920, the cohesion scores for both parties remained below 75 percent with the exception of 1946. In that year, the Republicans, invigorated by their midterm electoral victory, stood together in opposition to the Democratic president, Harry Truman, who had acceded to the presidency upon Roosevelt's death in 1945. Note that after 1932, during the period of Democratic dominance of both the presidency and the Congress, cohesion among House Democrats normally fell below an average of 65 percent. In the 1950s, the period of maturity for the centrifugal

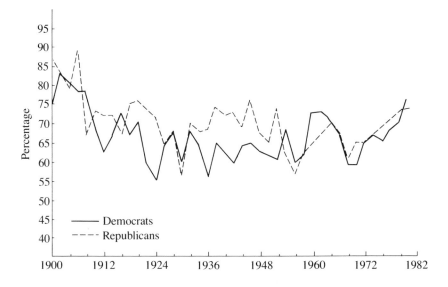

Fig. 8.5. Average cohesion scores, House of Representatives. (From Schlesinger 1985, 1161.)

party, the cohesion rate for both Democrats and Republicans fell below 60 percent.

The period, then, between 1932 and 1960 was one in which presidents had great difficulties gaining the support of their parties in Congress. Roosevelt's sizable victory in 1932 did, indeed, bring in many new members of Congress from competitive districts in need of support from the presidential nucleus. These new members of Congress provided the cohesive behavior that passed the president's initial programs. But as the new members of Congress became more secure, their automatic support for the president weakened. Indeed, after the mid-1930s, the Congress was controlled by a coalition of southern Democrats and northern Republicans for the most part (Patterson 1974). This arrangement emerged from the ever-growing number of noncompetitive districts for house seats.

Toward the Centripetal Multinuclear Party

After the 1950s a different multinuclear party began to emerge in the United States, different from its predecessor in that it appeared less centrifugal. More nuclei and more cooperation among nuclei made the party appear more national in scope and more active at all levels. This was true for both the Democratic and Republican parties. New alterations were made in both the structures of political opportunities and of electoral competition during the 1960s. But the purpose of most of these alterations, opening up, in some fashion, the political process, did not differ markedly from that of the alterations made during the Progressive era. The difference between the two periods lay mostly in the increased volatility of the electorate that resulted in increased levels of competition for all offices in all areas. As a consequence, in accordance with the office-seeking theory, office seekers found organizational effort increasingly necessary not only within their own constituencies but all along the line. Thus, even representatives from safe districts had to worry about electing enough partisans to comprise the majorities required to secure them positions of leadership within the House. To clarify the origins of the new centripetal party, we must examine each of the structures for its impact.

The Structure of Political Opportunities after 1960

The principal alterations in the structure of political opportunities after 1960 were once again reforms within the Congress. In fact, foreshadowings of these reforms, directed at reducing the power concentrated in the hands of a few senior members, occurred in the 1950s. In 1953, Lyndon Johnson, as Senate majority leader, adopted the rule that assured freshman senators of a choice committee assignment. He thus weakened the monopoly that senior Senators had on these positions (Ripley 1969, 134). In the House, the major changes occurred during the 1970s. Seniority became a less-than-absolute principle in the selection of committee chairmen. Critical reforms deprived the committee chairmen of their broad powers over agendas and procedures. In addition, the number of subcommittees was expanded, thus enabling junior members to gain positions of power (Ornstein and Rohde 1978).

These changes within the Congress were perceived as making members more independent of the party leadership. I would assert the new rules were simply permissive. In this respect, the relaxation of the seniority rule made it easier, if anything, for members of the same party to act in concert, rather than the reverse. As the device for allocating power, seniority more often than not frustrated the creation of party majorities. With the decline in the power of leaders chosen by seniority, the way was open for the exertion of greater influence by the leaders chosen by legislators acting as partisans, the party whips and caucus chairmen. Whatever the reason, party cohesion scores in the 1970s rose perceptibly, not only for the House as a whole but especially for committee chairmen (Brandes and Hibbing 1984).

This, of course, did not mean that the new rules barred independent action on the part of members of Congress. Much depended, as the office-seeking theory posits, on which form of behavior they believed would be most likely to win them reelection. For this reason, we must pay special attention to the changes that took place in the structure of electoral competition.

The Structure of Electoral Competition after 1960

The most striking change in the electoral rules after 1960 was the adoption of the peculiar sequence of direct primaries for the selection of presidential candidates. The great increase in the number of states choosing their delegates to the presidential nominating conventions by a direct primary followed upon the Democrats' adoption of the multifaceted reforms recommended by the McGovern-Fraser commission for the 1972 presidential nomination. The commission did not apparently set out to increase the number of primaries. Nevertheless, its directives to state parties to open up the procedures for selecting delegates proved to be most easily implemented by adopting the primary (Ranney 1975, 206). Because the implementation of a presidential primary required a state law in most states, reforms enacted by the Democratic party affected the Republican party as well. The adoption of the primary also raised the controversial issue of how primary votes were to be translated into numbers of convention delegates (Crotty 1983). This, along with the issue of delegates' characteristics, became subjects for quadrennial revisions. States that did not adopt the primary were under pressure to broaden participation in their caucuses and conventions. The fundamental change, however, was the transfer of the de facto presidential nomination from the convention to the primary, albeit primaries that operated differently from those used by the states for other offices.

The overt effect of the presidential primary was much the same as that of the reforms within Congress. On the one hand, as for other offices, the primary made it possible for candidates to seek the presidency with a greater degree of independence from other party nuclei. Thus, Jimmy Carter, a former governor with few links to Democratic officeholders, could win his party's presidential nomination by means of the primary. The primary also made plausible Ronald Reagan's efforts in 1976 and Edward Kennedy's in 1980 to unseat incumbent presidents. At the same time, the primary did not reduce the need for organizational effort. If anything, by extending the nominating process and making it more complex, it increased the need for organizational effort by the presidential nucleus. In so doing it provided a powerful incentive for presidential hopefuls to get all the help they could, including the invaluable help of their fellow partisans in state and local offices. Of course even before the introduction of the presidential primary, most presidential hopefuls had to contest for the honor and, in so doing, had to make an organized effort to round up convention delegates. This was true of Franklin

Roosevelt before 1932 and Thomas Dewey before 1944 and 1948. The introduction of the primary merely made the task of rounding up delegates more
arduous. As with congressional reforms, the extent to which multinuclear
cooperation took place depended upon whether or not officeholders saw it to
their advantage in winning reelection. Much depended on whether or not they
perceived a potential presidential candidate as helpful to the ticket in the
general election.

The another alteration in the structure of electoral competition that had its
impact on party organization after 1960 was the expansion of the potential
electorate. Again, the alteration did not, in and of itself, dictate a new type of
multinuclear party. Significant expansion of the potential electorate came
about by lowering the voting age. Even more important was the assurance
guaranteed by federal law that black citizens in the South could exercise the
right to vote. This alteration did facilitate greater competition in the South's
one-party states, where Democratic dominance had rested upon the exclusion
of the black voter. The introduction of competition in one-party states laid the
groundwork for greater organizational effort and multinuclear cooperation on
the part of office seekers in both parties.

Also affecting party organization after 1960 were the Warren Court's
rulings requiring that legislative districts be equal in population. In general,
the effect of this change in the structure of electoral competition was the
encouragement of multinuclear cooperation. It is true that the strict application of the equal population requirement served to weaken some of the links
between local officials and legislators by abolishing legislative districts constructed out of existing political units, counties and towns. More important,
however, was the effect the "one person, one vote" rulings had in bringing
into closer alignment the constituencies of numerous offices. Thus, the constituencies of U.S. representatives were brought more into line with that of the
state as a whole and, therefore, with the offices of governor, senator, and even
of president. In turn, the constituencies of state legislators resembled more
closely those of representatives, governors, and senators. Since the state
legislatures now were responsible for redrawing legislative districts with each
census, ties among these officeholders were further strengthened. Representatives now found their futures tied not only to state legislators who bore the
prime responsibility for redistricting but also to governors who could veto
legislative redistricting plans. In turn, state legislators found themselves dependent upon each other as well as the governor.

The inference about multinuclear cooperation is strengthened by the
increase in office movement between the offices affected by redistricting.
During the 1970s, the importance of the office of representative as the manifest
office for the Senate increased. There was also an increase in the proportion of
representatives going on to the governorship after the steady decline from 1850

through 1959, when the proportion reached a low of 9.8 percent. In turn, state legislative office rebounded as an important position for advancement to the three higher elective offices of representative, governor, and senator, after suffering a decline between 1900 and 1960 (see chap. 4, table 4.3).

Alterations in the rules for campaign financing also affected the multinuclear party. Until the 1970s, efforts to regulate campaign financing had little significance because there were no effective means of enforcement. Since the 1970s, federal and state laws and court rulings have changed the ways the parties gather and spend money. In the 1970s, a Federal Election Commission was established to oversee campaign financing at the national level and to provide a central public place for reporting sources of funds and their expenditure. The states followed suit in requiring public reporting of campaign finances. Government regulations also limited the amounts any single contributor could make, as well as the amount spent on any given campaign. Government intervened directly in the party's money-raising activities by providing for public financing of some campaigns, notably those for the presidency and some governorships.

With some exceptions, the state and federal regulations of campaign financing introduced in the 1970s reinforced the need for the centripetal multinuclear party. The very regulations that required detailed accounting procedures placed a spotlight on monetary transfers between nuclei, thereby regularizing and reinforcing the practice. Limits on the size of campaign contributions also encouraged nuclear cooperation. Candidates, officeholders, and party agencies, as well as interest groups and corporations, created political action committees (PACs) that could put together small amounts of money and distribute the larger sums for common political purposes.[1] Even public financing, dependent as it was upon legislators to determine who got what, when, and with what restrictions, worked in favor of multinuclear cooperation.

It is true that the new regulations also raised some problems for nuclear cooperation. By requiring a strict accounting of how money was collected and spent, nuclear cooperation foundered on questions about which nucleus was to be credited with the funds raised and expenditures made. To which candidate's account was to be allotted the money raised by a joint fundraising dinner? Which candidate's account would record the expenditures for a joint rally? The most convenient course of action was to keep all campaigns separate. Furthermore, the emergence of special interest group and corporate PACs strengthened the independence of the incumbent. It institutionalized the

---

1. The new regulations on campaign financing led to a voluminous literature; the growth of PACs, especially, attracted much attention. PACs varied greatly, as did their tactics. Useful studies may be found in Malbin 1984, especially Adamany's chapter (1984, 70–121).

financial link between incumbents, particularly legislative incumbents, and these groups, each of which had to develop its own PAC.

On the other hand, subsequent court rulings and interpretations of the laws on campaign financing worked in favor of nuclear cooperation. This was particularly true for the limits on campaign expenditures that the courts vitiated. Thus, court rulings allowed "independent" expenditures, that is, those not attributable to a particular candidate's campaign organization and therefore not legally chargeable to the candidate's campaign. Loose interpretations of the laws regulating campaign financing left expenditures for such activities as "voter education" and voter registration drives free of legal controls. Interpretations allowing for independent expenditures and expenditures for civic activities made it plausible for nuclei to engage in mutually rewarding activities.

In addition, the increasingly high costs of campaigning provided powerful incentives for the centripetal multinuclear party that the new regulations did not deter. The regulations by no means deterred the increasingly more conspicuous and substantial efforts of members of the House and Senate to raise funds for their fellow partisans who were up for reelection. Nor did they deter the presidential nucleus, as represented by the national committee, from engaging in more conspicuous and extensive efforts to raise funds for other nuclei. Thus, faced with the importance of redistricting after the 1990 census for Democratic legislators the Democratic National Committee designed Project 500 to raise $2.25 million to help Democrats running for state legislative seats. The money was targeted for such expenditures as polling, campaign ads, voting research, and other campaign tools.

While all the factors I have just discussed played their part, ultimately, I would argue, the electorate's increasingly volatile behavior was the critical factor in producing multinuclear parties less centrifugal than those in the period from 1900 to 1960. On the surface, the electorate's post-1960s behavior would seem to reinforce the centrifugal party. Split-ticket voting, steadily on the rise since 1920, reached great heights during the 1970s (see fig. 8.6). One consequence was the Republican party's control of the presidency, the Democrats' control of the federal legislature. This situation was duplicated at the state level, where voters were prepared to elect governors and state legislative majorities of different parties. Similarly, far more than in the past, voters were willing to vote for a president of one party and a governor of the other party (see fig. 8.7). Their willingness to do so was aided by the transfer of most gubernatorial elections to presidential midterm years. Such behavior on the part of the electorate might well have encouraged the successful nuclei of both parties to go their own ways. Indeed, it was this possibility that led students of voting behavior, looking at how constituencies were voting after 1960, to conclude that U.S. parties were on the decline

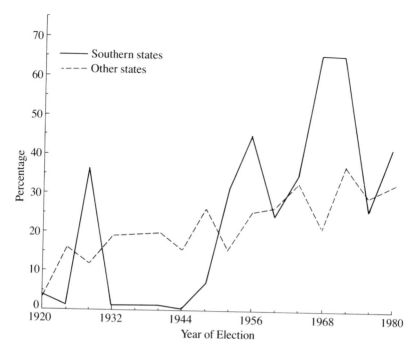

Fig. 8.6. Percentage of split-ticket congressional districts. (From Schlesinger 1985, 1164.)

(Fiorina 1980). Arguing that straight-ticket voting unified parties, they concluded that split-ticket voting had forced them into disarray.

They failed to recognize, however, that the most striking consequence of the electorate's behavior was to make every election unsure and, therefore, every office seeker a candidate in need of assistance from fellow partisans. There was no longer any state in which either party was incapable of winning any office. This meant that candidates could count on fewer constituencies in which devotion to one party sufficed for election than was the case before 1960. Whatever the incentive, then, for separatism, the incentive for the spread of party nuclei and for cross-nuclear cooperation was even greater. The impact of increased competition on the spread of party nuclei is evidenced by the large drop in the number of uncontested seats for the House of Representatives in the 1960s (see fig. 8.4). Figure 8.4 also shows that there were usually, though not always, fewer uncontested seats for the House in presidential election years. We should expect the higher turnout and more intense competition encouraged by presidential elections to stimulate efforts for lesser offices. In turn, we should also expect that presidential candidates might find it useful

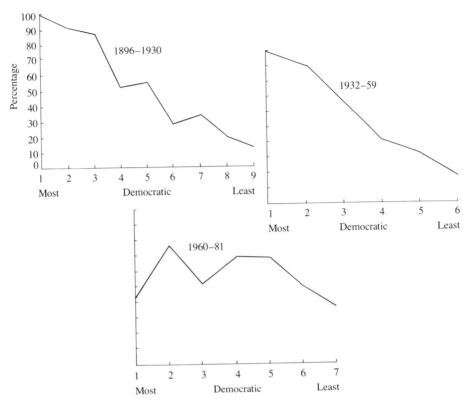

Fig. 8.7. Percentage of electoral wins for Democratic candidates for governor related to scale positions of states in voting for president. The scale positions of states in voting for the president are presented in chapter 5. (From Schlesinger 1985, 1165.)

to stimulate turnout by having fellow partisans compete for office at the lower level. On the other hand, presidential candidates might also find it disadvantageous to have fellow partisans run for lesser office if it meant stirring up the opposition. In either case, in highly competitive situations, the nucleus of the one office could no longer be indifferent to the nucleus of the other.

Students of voting behavior after 1960 also failed to recognize that straight- or split-ticket voting could arise for different reasons with vastly different consequences for party organization. To understand these reasons and their consequences, we need to distinguish between rigid and flexible voter attitudes. Rigid attitudes limit variations in voting behavior and permit long-run projections about voting trends. Flexible attitudes have the opposite effect. They mean voters are willing to ponder short-run considerations, such as the candidates and the candidates' program. Such attitudes, therefore, leave the results of every election in doubt. The point we must recognize is that both rigid and flexible attitudes can result in straight- and split-ticket voting. What makes the difference to party organizations is whether rigid or flexible voter attitudes are the cause.

As far as straight- or split-ticket voting is concerned, flexible voting attitudes are neutral. A constituency totally devoid of voters with fixed partisan attachments can, nevertheless, produce elections in which straight party-voting prevails, if all the candidates of one party appeal to voters more than those of the opposing party. On the other hand, some split-ticket voting is inevitable in the United States, as I pointed out earlier, given the variations in constituencies for office. As I pointed out, candidates for president or governor must appeal to national or statewide constituencies. They are, therefore, greatly limited in the extent to which they can vary their appeal within their constituencies. In contrast, the nuclei of smaller office constituencies must tailor their appeal to their localities. Thus, even if voter attitudes were always flexible, we should expect both straight- and split-ticket voting.

Rigid voter attitudes, on the other hand, appear at first to lead only to straight-ticket voting. This is certainly the case if strong party-identification appears ingrained in the electorate. On the other hand, there is nothing to prevent rigid voting attitudes from producing split-ticket voting. Nothing better demonstrates this possibility than changes in the southern states' voting behavior after 1950. The electorates of the southern states, as we know, had been the most rigid in voting straight party tickets. As figure 8.6 shows, in the period between 1920 and 1948, with the exception of the Smith-Hoover presidential contest of 1928, only a few southern constituencies divided their vote. In contrast, the electorates of the nonsouthern states divided their votes in about 20 percent of the constituencies. Once southern voters relaxed their loyalty toward Democratic candidates for the presidency, the proportion of divided constituencies in the South soared, reaching 65 percent or more in the elections of 1968 and 1972. Split-ticket voting rose in the nonsouthern states as well, but only by about 10 percent. In the years before 1950, rigid voting attitudes in the South depressed the national figures on split-ticket voting; after 1950, the weakening of southern voters' loyalty to the Democratic presidential nucleus elevated the figures.[2] These alterations in southern voting behavior

---

2. The information on split-ticket voting in fig. 8.6 probably understates its prevalence in the period before 1950. The presidential election of 1952 was the first in which presidential election results were broken down by House districts. Approximately 100 House districts, therefore, are missing from the calculations for the pre-1950 period. Since the earlier calculations had to rely on districts consisting of whole counties, the missing districts were nonsouthern and metropolitan districts where we would expect split-ticket voting to be higher than in the southern and more rural areas for which the data were available. If this inference is correct, then practically all of the increase in split-ticket voting was a product of the changes in southern voting attitudes.

did not mean that voting attitudes were any less rigid. Rather, it meant that southern voters had divided their loyalties. They were now prepared to identify with the Republican party for the presidency and with the Democratic party for the House of Representatives.

For party organization, the consequence of a rigid electorate is that it frees the party nuclei to go their own way. This is true whether the electorate's rigidity results in straight- or split-ticket voting. Where the voters' behavior can always be counted on, straight party voting provides no pressure for multinuclear cooperation that arises out of immediate electoral needs. Straight party voting based on long-run attachments weakens the multinuclear party in terms of the distribution of organization, the level of organizational effort, and the transfer of organizational effort between nuclei. Much the same effect can be inferred from voters who can be counted on to divide their loyalties between the two parties.

In contrast, the more flexible the electorate's attitudes, the more organized activity becomes a matter of mutual concern among party nuclei. The more flexible the electorate, the less secure any and all candidates for office. With a flexible electorate, there are none of the safe offices made possible by rigid electorates. The more rigid the electorate, the more likely all offices are taken by safe margins. The more flexible the electorate, the more likely all margins are unsafe. On the one hand, this compels each party nucleus to tailor its appeal to its own constituency. It can take nothing for granted. Since candidates cannot rely upon partisan identification to win election, they must constantly evaluate their campaigns and the issues they address to attract support, as well as their behavior in office if they are incumbents. But candidates in this situation also need as much organized help as they can get. The very volatility of the electorate in their own constituency, therefore, leads them to turn to other party nuclei, faced with the same type of flexible or competitive conditions, for possible mutual assistance. Flexible electorates responsible for high levels of competition stimulate then not only high levels of partisan organizational effort but also multinuclear cooperation. In effect, flexibility on the part of the voters and the competition between candidates for office it produces return the voters to the rightful role the office-seeking theory assigns them, that of choosers. It removes the ambiguities created by strong partisan identification that tempt observers to see voters as party members and to equate strong party-identification with strong parties.

The impetus of the voter as chooser for party organization becomes clearer if we exaggerate, for the sake of argument, the effect of strong partisan identification. By the 1950s, the electorate in the United States had emerged as one strongly identified with one or the other party, an electorate that consistently voted straight party tickets. Ironically, this strong partisan identification undermined the reasons for candidates for elective office to organize. With the outcome of elections assured, what need was there for the partisan candidate favored or disfavored by the electorate to expend effort? After the 1950s, partisan identification eroded. This is not to say that it did not remain a force in politics in the United States. Nevertheless, there was enough erosion to demonstrate that the electorates of most constituencies were capable of voting Republican or Democratic. This fact was not lost on politicians. If a Democrat could become governor of Utah, there was no longer any need for Democratic presidential candidates to write off the state. If Republican candidates for president could win in House districts in South Carolina, Republicans could aspire to win both House and state legislative seats in these same districts. To realize these aspirations, however, required organizational effort. Certainly, most helpful was assistance from the office nucleus that paved the way. In turn, that nucleus benefited from any additional effort to attract uncommitted voters. Thus, the very weakness of partisan identification among voters acted as the stimulus for the growth of party organization. By fostering hope in situations that previously had appeared hopeless, a fickle electorate justified the expenditure of effort.

The fickle electorate even affected congressional office, which had increasingly emerged, especially for representatives, as a career office, with incumbents seemingly assured of lifetime tenure. After the 1950s, incumbent representatives certainly continued to win reelection by margins that would be considered safe by any historical standard. The difference was that such margins no longer gave representatives a sense of security. Fenno's (1978) close observations of representatives in the 1970s revealed a high level of insecurity. Insecurity was based upon the new reality. Before the 1950s, when the party label was enough to assure victory, a representative could certainly feel secure with an electoral margin of 60 or even 55 percent. After the 1950s, even incumbent representatives were aware that such margins could evaporate, votes could be transferred. To hold votes, organization was essential (Garand and Gross 1984). It does not appear accidental that the growth of congressional staffs, the increased concentration on constituency services, and the near continuous campaigning that most members of Congress engaged in coincided with the decline in partisan identification among the electorate.

Certainly the reshaping of the internal power structure of the Congress appeared to be related to the increased need of members to achieve prestige that could be used back home. The old system of waiting one's turn to achieve power by seniority was a weak weapon with which to fend off electoral attacks. Thus, electoral insecurity reinforced ambition in the push for the reforms of the 1970s that spread power among more subcommittees and reduced the domination of committee chairmen, as well as such once all-powerful committees as Ways and Means. At the same time, electoral insecurity made mutual assistance as a means for electing the numbers required to gain internal positions of power more desirable than ever.

As the office-seeking theory leads us to expect, electoral competition, by making all office seekers and officeholders in the United States insecure after the 1950s, provided the greatest impetus for party organization. As a consequence, both parties, unlike their predecessors, were more national in the sense that they had more nuclei in every region and state. Certainly the level of organizational activity increased substantially after 1960. This is true whether one takes a circumscribed view of organization to encompass only the formal apparatus laid out by the state or my broader view that includes all efforts to win office under a party label. We are indebted to the wide-ranging studies of the formal party apparatus by Gibson and his colleagues (1983 and 1985; Cotter et al. 1984) for firm evidence of the growth of state and local organization during this period. Undoubtedly more organizational effort contributed to sustaining competition, which in turn made organizational effort ever more necessary.

Parties in the United States also became more national in the sense that multinuclear cooperation increased. Again, we have no exact measure of the extent to which cross-nuclear efforts to recruit candidates and provide resources took place. At the same time, mailings by the national committees, state chairs, and press reports of such activities leave the strong impression that such efforts increased considerably after 1960. Such efforts were greatly aided by computer technology, which facilitated targeting and keeping track of widely dispersed electorates for a variety of offices. It is true that, given the way Congress acts, many PACs, the organizational devices for raising campaign funds that appeared after 1960, directed much of their attention toward congressional incumbents of both parties. This was especially true of PACs interested in the implementation of a single policy. At the same time, the need to work within a competitive electoral structure meant that even those PACs could by no means ignore nonincumbents. As for PACs with broader concerns, businesses, special interest groups, not to mention ideological groups, they often saw their needs best served by concerted partisan action. Such PACs were capable of providing sophisticated professional services linking candidates of the same party.

As I pointed out earlier, the ultimate test of multinuclear cooperation is the behavior of partisan officeholders in government. From this point of view, there is striking proof of increased partisan cooperation, as evidenced by party line voting, in the House of Representatives after the 1950s (see fig. 8.5). Between 1920 and 1960, the era of the centrifugal multinuclear party, Democratic voting cohesion rarely rose above 65 percent, while Republican cohesion was somewhat higher. In the 1960s, cohesion in both parties fluctuated, undoubtedly because of the trauma of the Vietnam War. After 1968, however, voting cohesion rose in both parties. Indeed, in terms of voting cohesion, both parties looked more like each other than ever before. In 1983, voting cohesion for the Democrats reached the rate of 76 percent; congressional Democrats had not been so united since 1908. This was especially remarkable since the earlier mechanisms for enforcing party discipline no longer existed. Greater cooperation among partisans in the governmental phase is exactly what the office-seeking theory leads us to expect when the structure of electoral competition is highly competitive.

Thanks largely to increased electoral competition for all offices after 1960, then, political parties in the United States became more conspicuous multinuclear organizations than ever before. Far from the party being over, both parties appeared more national and more active. Not only did the two parties have more nuclei in more office constituencies throughout the United States; there was more cooperation among nuclei outside and inside government. In 1984, Senator Richard Lugar, appealing for funds for Republican lawmakers in the name of the national Republican senatorial committee, observed: "There is no such thing as a 'safe' seat any more." That being the case, candidates needed all the help they could get. They were finding that the best place to get it was from their fellow partisans.

REFERENCES

Abramson, Paul R. 1983. *Political Attitudes in America*. San Francisco: Freeman.
Adamany, David. 1984. "Political Parties in the 1980s." In *Money and Politics in the United States: Financing Elections in the 1980s*, ed. Michael J. Malbin. Chatham, N.J.: Chatham House.
APSA 1950. *Toward a More Responsible Two-Party System*.
Brandes, S., and John R. Hibbing. 1984. "Congressional Reform and Party Discipline: The Effects of Changes in the Seniority System on Party Loyalty in the U.S. House of Representatives." Paper presented at the annual meeting of the American Political Science Association, Washington, D.C.
Burnham, Walter D. 1970. *Critical Elections and the Mainsprings of American Politics*. New York: Norton.
Burns, James M. 1963. *The Deadlock of Democracy: Four-Party Politics in America*. Englewood Cliffs, N.J.: Prentice-Hall.
Caro, Robert A. 1981. *The Path to Power*. New York: Random House.
Cotter, Cornelius P., James L. Gibson, John E. Bibby, and Robert J. Huckshorn. 1984. *Party Organization in American Politics*. New York: Praeger.
Crotty, William. 1983. *Party Reform*. New York: Longman.
Eldersveld, Samuel. 1964. *Political Parties: A Behavioral Analysis*. Chicago: Rand McNally.

Fenno, Richard R., Jr. 1965. "The Internal Distribution of Influence: The House." In *The Congress and America's Future*, ed. David Truman. Englewood Cliffs, N.J.: Prentice-Hall.

Fenno, Richard R., Jr. 1978. *Home Style: House Members in their Districts*. Boston: Little, Brown.

Fiorina, Morris. 1980. "The Decline of Collective Responsibility in American Politics." *Daedalus* 109(3):25–45.

Fredman, L. E. 1968. *The Australian Ballot*. East Lansing: Michigan State University Press.

Garand, James C., and Donald A. Gross. 1984. "Changes in Vote Margins for Congressional Candidates: A Specification of Historical Trends." *American Political Science Review* 78:17–30.

Gibson, James L., Cornelius P. Cotter, and John F. Bibby. 1983. "Assessing Party Organizational Strength." *American Journal of Political Science* 27:193–222.

Gibson, James L., Cornelius P. Cotter, John F. Bibby, and Robert J. Huckshorn. 1985. "Whither the Local Parties? A Cross-Sectional and Longitudinal Analysis of the Strength of Party Organizations." *American Journal of Political Science* 29:139–60.

Hamilton, Alexander, James Madison, and John Jay. 1961. *Federalist Papers*. New York: New American Library.

Heard, Alexander. 1960. *The Costs of Democracy*. Chapel Hill: University of North Carolina Press.

Jewell, Malcolm E., ed. 1962. *The Politics of Reapportionment*. New York: Atherton.

Key, V. O., Jr. 1949. *Southern Politics*. New York: Knopf.

Key, V. O., Jr. 1955. "A Theory of Critical Elections." *Journal of Politics* 17:3–18.

Key, V. O., Jr. 1956. *American State Politics*. New York: Knopf.

Luce, Robert. 1924. *Legislative Assemblies*. Boston: Houghton Mifflin.

Malbin, Michael J., ed. 1984. *Money and Politics in the United States: Financing Elections in the 1980s*. Chatham, N.J.: Chatham House.

Mayhew, David R. 1986. *Placing Parties in American Politics*. Princeton: Princeton University Press.

Ornstein, Norman J., and David Rohde. 1978. "Political Parties and Congressional Reform." In *Parties and Elections in an Anti-Party Age*, ed. Jeff Fishel. Bloomington: Indiana University Press.

Patterson, James T. 1974. "A Conservative Coalition Forms in Congress, 1933–1939." In *Political Parties in American History, 1890–Present*, ed. Paul L. Murphy. New York: Putnam.

Ranney, Austin. 1975. *Curing the Mischiefs of Faction: Party Reform in America*. Berkeley: University of California Press.

Ripley, Randall B. 1969. *Power in the Senate*. New York: St. Martin's Press.

Rothman, David J. 1966. *Politics and Power: The United States Senate 1869–1901*. Cambridge, Mass.: Harvard University Press.

Rusk, Jerrold G. 1970. "The Effect of the Australian Ballot Reform on Split Ticket Voting." *American Political Science Review* 64:1220–38.

Wahlke, John C., Heinz Eulau, William Buchanan, and Leroy C. Ferguson. 1962. *The Legislative System*. New York: Wiley.

CHAPTER 9

A Comparative Theory of Parties

In the preceding chapters I developed a theory of parties that I considered useful for the study of parties in all democracies. I demonstrated its usefulness, however, by applying it to parties in the United States. There was some virtue in doing this. Among democracies, the United States has arguably the most complex structures of political opportunities and of electoral competition. Moreover, the domination of its two major parties by office seekers and officeholders has never been challenged, although it has often been lamented.

In the present chapter my objective is to demonstrate how the theory can be used for the comparative study of parties. This is not the same thing as saying it is applicable for the study of parties within other democracies, although that is certainly true. The present objective is more ambitious. It seeks to show how the theory can help us find similarities and differences in party organizations within and between democratic political systems. It is, of course, not the only theory that attempts to do so. Of the other theoretical efforts, the most influential have been those that derive from Marxist precepts. This is so despite the vicissitudes that Marxism has experienced since World War II. Many who readily acknowledge the office orientation of parties in the United States are nevertheless convinced that parties "really" represent class or group interests and, therefore, are really issue oriented rather than office oriented. The most widely accepted variation of the Marxist theme was developed by the French political scientist, Maurice Duverger (1951). Duverger's comprehensive theory of parties followed from the assumption that all the important characteristics of party organization derive from group and class interests. Also, in accordance with Marxist doctrine, parties do not change and adapt, they come and go, as one class replaces another as the ruling class. Thus, in the final stage, the Socialist and Communist mass-based parties of the workers replace the elitist cadre parties of the bourgeoisie. Writing in 1950, Duverger found that contemporary European democracies resembled geological formations where the more primitive bourgeois organizations existed alongside the more advanced, working-class parties. Meanwhile, the two major parties in the United States had stagnated for the moment at the bourgeois stage. If they appeared preoccupied with the winning of office, it was only because both major parties represented middle-class inter-

ests and could mask their class base and dispense with ideological distinctions.

It is doubtful if any amount of investigation will determine the correct
view of parties. To me, at least, from the vantage point of the last decade of
the twentieth century, the weight of historical evidence indicates that parties in
democracies that have any chance of capturing public office are dominated by
office drives. Duverger saw the mass-based party and its elaborate organization of nonofficeholders whose purpose was to subsume office seeking to
doctrinal goals as the inevitable product of universal suffrage. Yet in all
representative democracies, major political parties have inevitably drawn criticism, not for the pursuit of principle at the cost of office, but for their
stubborn pursuit of office even at the cost of program. In 1914, the French
political journalist Robert de Jouvenel (1914, 17) observed, "there is less
difference between two deputies, one of whom is a revolutionary and the other
who is not than between two revolutionaries, one of whom is a deputy and the
other who is not." At about the same time, Robert Michels ([1915] 1949) was
publishing his famous critique of the German Social Democratic party, whose
appetite for office had been whetted by the limited representative institutions
of Kaiser Germany. More than sixty years later, observers watched the Socialist parties of France, Spain, and Italy abandon one doctrinal commitment after
another in the pursuit of office.

By 1990, the Western democracies were watching in amazement as one
Eastern European country after another called for the dissolution of their all-
powerful Communist parties, the embodiment of Marxist-Leninist doctrine.
They sought to replace them, instead, with parties capable of contesting in
competitive elections. Tired of the prospect of being or envying party members, the people of Eastern Europe clamored in the streets to become voters,
the choosers between or among parties. Far from being the doomed political
organization of a doomed class, the office-seeking party, along with the political democracy that fostered it, appeared to have reached an unprecedented
degree of acceptance and admiration.

I would certainly assert, therefore, that history has proved the office-
seeking view of parties to be as valid as any for the purposes of comparative
analysis. Indeed, there is much to recommend its preferment. The comparative study of parties has been hampered by the great variety of organizations,
including pressure groups and totalitarian governing agencies, to which the
term *party* has been applied. The office-seeking view, by focusing on the goal
of elective office, restricts the term to organizations that compete according to
an accepted set of political rules for political control, which is clearly de-
limited by an established set of institutions. I recognize that, for those concerned with such questions as party program and party members, not to

mention the broader questions of the sociological origins of party leaders and party followers or their motives, the restrictive nature of the office-seeking definition destroys its usefulness. At the same time, it is not impossible that the eagerness of the populations of Eastern Europe to abandon the more inclusive party model they had lived with for simple electoral parties, to exchange the role of party member for voter and chooser, might perhaps lead to a less critical view of the office-seeking definition. In any event, I would argue that the compulsion to seek an all-inclusive definition of parties blinds us to the great varieties and types of political organizations that the restricted view allows us to identify in democracies and, therefore, the crucial distinctions that should be made between them. Modern political parties, after all, developed within the framework of representative institutions as office-seeking organizations. Within that framework, and with interesting variations that I shall discuss later, these office-seeking organizations persist and function.

Political Parties and Political Opportunities

Once we accept the office-seeking view of parties for comparative study, we must devise techniques for analyzing our three major variables, the structure of political opportunities, the structure of electoral competition, and party organization in different democratic settings.[1] Since a country's opportunity and electoral structures are very much the result of its own peculiar history and customs, the focus on office and office careers as the key to party organization appears to pose difficulties. A U.S. member of Congress is not a replica of the British M.P., and membership in the British House of Lords is not equivalent to membership in the French Senate. Admittedly, the structures that allow us to plot the careers of officeholders in the United States differ from those we would use to plot the careers of officeholders in Great Britain or France. If parties are organized to capture offices, are we not limited to analyzing the relationship between the parties and institutions of particular democracies?

---

1. Party organization, which is determined largely by the structures of political opportunities and of electoral competition, can affect both structures. Certainly the developments that took place in British party organization at the end of the nineteenth century transformed the process of becoming prime minister. Similarly, in the United States, parties early captured the electoral college, which had been designed to choose the president. At the same time, the differences between U.S. and British parties reflect the different methods by which the two countries choose their chief executives.

The Structure of Political Opportunities

Size

I would suggest that we can compare and contrast party organizations across democracies as long as we focus our attention on the universal characteristics of opportunity and electoral structures and of public office careers. We can, for example, compare the number of political opportunities in various democracies. The number of political opportunities, as I pointed out in chapter 3, is critical to both the generation and satisfaction of political ambition. For the politically ambitious in all democracies, the number of offices of significance and the frequency with which they become available to new individuals define the chances for advancement. In all democracies, then, the opportunity and electoral structures must hold out the promise of adequate and orderly means of advancement for the politically ambitious.

The number of individuals who attain significant elective positions, as well as the pace of change critical to the sense of expectations, are measurable quantities, comparable from democracy to democracy. The measure I propose to use for comparative purposes is the opportunity rate that I presented in chapter 3, a measure of the size of the structure of political opportunities in the United States. The universe of significant offices is not clearly defined. Thus we need a flexible measure that can tell us, on the one hand, the opportunities for elective office at the national, state, or local level in the United States and can also provide us with totals that can be compared across national boundaries.

Recall that the opportunity rate is the calculation of the frequency with which new personnel are elected for a given set of offices, in a given number of elections, over a significantly long time span. The time span should be long enough to encompass more than spurts of high turnover produced by atypical competitive elections. I have again chosen twelve years, which is also a common multiple of most formal office terms, as the standard time span. With the opportunity rate, we can calculate the typical number of chances to hold office in any elective institution in any democracy.

Thus we can compare the typical number of chances of becoming a British M.P. with the chances of becoming a U.S. representative over a twelve-year period or political generation. Table 9.1 compares the opportunity rates for the House of Representatives in the United States with the British House of Commons. Since the House of Representatives has a fixed term of two years, the number of elections in a twelve-year period is a product of the six regular elections times the number of seats (column D). Since the term of office in the British House is variable, the number of seats was multiplied by the average number of elections held in a twelve-year period. The results show that, for comparable generations from 1914 through 1964, there were 611 chances of being one of 435 representatives and 558 chances of being one of 620 members of parliament. While the turnover rates for the two legislatures were not substantially different, the opportunity rate for the British House of Commons was reduced because of the typically longer time between elections. On the other hand, the per capita chances of becoming an M.P. were considerably higher in Great Britain because of its smaller population. Of course, calculating the chances for the lower houses of the two legislatures hardly exhausted the total number of political opportunities in either country. As we saw in chapter 3, chances for other offices could be easily added to those already calculated to give us the broader national picture.

In assessing the total number of opportunities in a democracy, some account must be taken of multiple officeholding. Obviously, when one individual holds several offices, other individuals' chances are reduced. In this respect, wide differences exist among democracies. In the United States there is little, if any, multiple officeholding. In part this is because the federal constitution bars an individual from holding congressional and executive office. On the other hand, no federal law prevents a federal elective official from holding state or local elective office at the same time. It simply is not done. In contrast, the ethos of parliamentary democracies has been more conducive to multiple officeholding. Almost all allow cabinet members to retain their legislative positions, although de Gaulle's Fifth Republic forbids such dual officeholding. At the same time, it retains the custom widely practiced in the two previous Republics of multiple national and local officeholding, a practice rarely followed in Great Britain.

Indeed, joint officeholding has been a fundamental aspect of the French structure of political opportunities in the Third, Fourth, and Fifth Republics

TABLE 9.1. Opportunities for the U.S. House of Representatives and the British House of Commons

	A	B	C	D	E
	Average No. of Offices	No. of General Elections	No. of Personnel Changes	Personnel Turnover Rate (B/A)	Average No. of General Elections in a 12-year Period	Opportunity Rate (C × D)
U.S. House (1914–58)	435.0	9509	2228	0.234	2610.00	610.74
British House (1919–64)	621.3	7455	2142	0.287	1944.67	558.12

Source: Schlesinger 1967.

(Dogan 1961, 79–80; Masclet 1979, 176–87). Table 9.2 demonstrates this point by analyzing the last National Assembly elected in the Fourth Republic. One-third of the deputies elected in 1956 retained a local office that they had held before entering the National Assembly for the first time. One out of four deputies added a local office after becoming deputies. The posts that both groups of deputies held were not minor: 177 were mayors and 25 were presidents of the departmental General Councils. Thus, almost 30 percent of all the presidents of the governing bodies of the departments were also de-puties. Most took on the position after winning election to the National Assembly.

Although joint officeholding in France and elsewhere on the continent can be seen as providing a measure of local influence in centralized unitary states, it also can restrict political opportunity (W. J. M. Mackenzie 1959, 272–80). In France, the restrictions can be of some significance, because deputies not only retain local offices that would otherwise be available to others but also gain additional, more important local positions. This modifies the orderly advancement encouraged when one individual's promotion opens up his or her position for others. Undoubtedly, this consideration contributed to the controversy over multiple officeholding or *cumuls des mandats* in the Fifth Republic. In 1985, a law was passed limiting the number of additional elective positions parliamentary members could hold. But Maus (1987, 7) found the law had little immediate effect on multiple officeholding by mem-bers of the National Assembly. Thus, in 1981, 46 percent of the deputies were also mayors, in 1986, 45.9 percent; in 1981, 47.4 percent were general councillors, in 1986, 47.3 percent. Note that these figures were much higher than those for the Fourth Republic. Maus also found that in 1981, 4.0 percent of the deputies were presidents of the departmental general councils, in 1986, 4.1 percent. This was about the same as in 1956. On the other hand, it should

TABLE 9.2.   Joint Officeholding in France,
Based on the National Assembly Elected in 1956

	Prior Office Held Concurrently[a]	Office Added After Election to Assembly[b]
Municipal Council	25.6%	5.7%
Mayor	16.3	13.4
General Council	21.2	10.9
President	0.8	3.4

Source: Schlesinger 1967.
Note: Total Deputies = 595.
[a]Total prior officeholders = 33.8%.
[b]Total winning election after election to Assembly = 25.7%.

be pointed out that France, unlike Great Britain, has had numerous intermediary, as well as local elective positions, in the form of the departmental general councils, to which the Fifth Republic added elected regional councils. The number of elective positions has gone a long way toward offsetting the restrictions imposed by multiple officeholding.

Shape

The comparative analysis of the size of opportunity structures across boundaries provides the basis for comparing the relative shares of political opportunities that parties claim. In effect, these shares, or the public office careers of the parties' personnel, reveal the shape of the structure of political opportunities. By examining these shares, we have a measure of comparison across borders that allows us to compare and contrast party organizations. For this purpose, I examined the careers of selected public officials in five developed representative democracies during the first six decades of the twentieth century. All five countries, the United States, Great Britain, Canada, Australia, and France, have institutional similarities and differences that are well known. The United States, Canada, and Australia are federal governments; they have provinces or states that provide a significant intermediate and independent career outlet for office seekers. All but the United States have parliamentary systems that assume that the leading members of the executive branch will also be members of the legislature. The United States is a presidential system in which members of the executive branch are explicitly excluded from membership in the legislature. Great Britain and her Commonwealth partners, Canada and Australia, are parliamentary systems in which the cabinet dominates. In contrast, the French Fourth Republic was a parliamentary system, in which parliament, or at least the popularly elected National Assembly, predominated. All four English-speaking democracies elect the members of the lower houses of their national legislatures in single-member districts by the plurality rule. The French Fourth Republic elected its national legislature in multimember districts according to a variant of proportional representation.

The public officials whose careers I examined were roughly comparable across the five countries. They included the members of the lower house of each country's national legislature elected at some point during the 1950s. They also included the members of each country's cabinets during the first six decades of the twentieth century. While it is true that neither the lower houses nor the cabinets under consideration enjoyed exactly the same status in one country as in another, I shall not attempt to evaluate the differences arising from constitutional prescriptions. Rather, I am concerned with the differences in status revealed by differences in public office careers.

I used the first arrival in the lower house and in the cabinet as the points

from which to analyze the public office careers that reveal distinctive characteristics of political parties.[2] As in my analysis of political opportunities in the
United States, I focused on two aspects of office careers: the ages at which
individuals were first elected to the selected posts and their office careers prior
to election to these posts. For the legislators, I recorded the age at which they
first won election to the legislature, not their age during the particular legislature under consideration. The former age better reveals how parties manage
and control political careers.

The analysis of public office careers immediately revealed significant
differences and similarities in the number of parties that could aspire to office
in each country.[3] In the four English-speaking democracies, whose structures
of electoral competition use single-member districts and plurality rules for
election, career analysis revealed that only two parties had a good chance for
national office.[4] In the United States, individuals pursued national careers
primarily as Republicans or Democrats; in Great Britain, as Conservatives or
Labourites; in Canada, as Liberals or Conservatives; and in Australia, as
Labourites or Liberals. In contrast, in the French Fourth Republic, whose
structure of electoral competition used multimember districts and proportional
rules, five parties dominated national office: the Socialists (SFIO), Radicals,
Communists, the Catholic, the Movement Républicain Populaire, and the Independents.[5]

As I pointed out in chapter 4, the age of arrival in a select office points up
two important traits of a political career. It calls our attention, first, to the
potential length of a prior office career for an individual entering the selected
office. Second, it leads us to consider how long a public office career the
individual can expect to have. From the point of view of political parties, such
collective information is vital because it allows them to plot the strategy of the

---

2. Several notable statistical studies deal with the backgrounds of the members of the
legislatures and cabinets under study here. For Australia, see Encel 1961 and 1962. For Canada,
see Meisel 1962; Banks 1965; Kornberg and Thomas 1965–66; Kunz 1965. For France, see
Dogan 1961, 1967, and 1979. For Great Britain, see Richards 1958; Wilson 1959; Buck 1963;
Guttsman 1963; Ranney 1965.

3. For another simple but highly suggestive scheme for classifying party systems, see Dahl
1966, 335–38.

4. For the relationship between electoral rules and the number of parties in democracies,
see Schlesinger and Schlesinger 1990.

5. In all five countries, other parties could elect legislators. A small number of Liberals sat
in the British parliament. In Australia, the Country Party could usually gain some seats. An
occasional Independent won election to the Congress in the United States. In Canada, the
Cooperative Commonwealth Federation (CCF) and its successor in 1961, the New Democratic
party (NDP), could send some members to the national legislature. In France, small political
groups came and went. The parties I mentioned, however, emerged in the career analysis of the
legislatures of the 1950s as the dominant parties.

multiple office careers that are their prime responsibility. Among the thirteen parties that the career analysis led me to examine, there were sharp differences in the ages at which legislators were first elected to the lower house (see table 9.3). At one extreme were the British Conservatives, 75 percent of whom were first elected before middle age (forty-five years). At the other extreme were the Canadian Conservatives, 51 percent of whom were first elected after they were forty-five years old. Given these differences, we could begin to make inferences about the differences in each party's promotional structures.

These inferences are strengthened when we consider the other major aspect of office careers I selected for analysis, prior officeholding. Since all democracies have public positions in which individuals can serve before they attain national office, the use or nonuse of these positions can tell us much about parties' promotional structures. I have assumed the officeholders' control of parties as promotional structures. Prior officeholding or the role played by public office in political advancement is a simple but valuable indicator of the depth of such control within and across national boundaries. It is true that the precise nature of prior officeholding, as distinct from the mere holding of prior office, is less readily comparable among democracies. Nevertheless, all five democracies whose national officeholders I studied had comparable local offices. Only Great Britain lacked some form of intermediate office. Because the levels of British government are less neatly arranged, I considered all the offices below the national level to be local elective offices (see tables 9.4 and 9.5).

As with age, there was a great range of difference among the thirteen parties with respect to prior officeholding (see table 9.4). British Conservatives had held office the least, 29.8 percent. Since they were also the youngest legislators, it seems reasonable to conclude that their lack of office experience was related to their youth. On the other hand, the U.S. Democrats, who had the greatest amount of prior office experience (75.4 percent), were also among the youngest legislators; 67 percent arrived before the age of 45. Thus, age and prior officeholding appeared to be independent indicators of the parties' promotional patterns.

A Comparative Model of Parties

We need both indicators, age and prior office experience, to construct a comparative model of parties. The indicators point up two basic characteristics of parties as organizations whose principal function is to provide governing personnel. Since I view all parties capable of winning office in democracies as more or less dominated by their officeholders, one characteristic that age and prior officeholding are useful in pointing up is the extent to which professional or careerist officeholders dominate the parties. The other is the

TABLE 9.3.   Age at First Election to Lower House of the National Legislature, in Percentage

Age	United States (elected 1956)			Canada (elected 1957)			Australia (elected 1954)			Great Britain (elected 1959)			France (elected 1956)					
	Rep.	Dem.	Total	Cons.	Lib.	Total[a]	Lib.	Lab.	Total[b]	Cons.	Lab.	Total[c]	C.P.	SFIO	Rad.	MRP	Ind.	Total[d]
65+	1.6	1.4	1.5	0.0	1.0	0.8	2.2	2.0	2.7	0.0	0.0	0.0	2.0	1.0	1.8	1.3	1.0	1.8
60–64	3.6	1.4	2.4	7.4	8.6	7.4	0.0	2.0	0.9	0.0	1.6	0.8	1.4	1.0	3.5	2.7	3.0	2.0
55–59	6.6	5.9	6.3	7.4	6.8	7.0	10.8	2.0	7.1	3.1	7.9	4.9	3.9	2.0	7.0	2.7	8.0	4.5
50–54	14.4	11.5	13.1	20.1	13.4	14.4	6.5	14.0	10.7	8.9	12.2	10.1	4.6	14.2	10.5	5.3	16.8	10.0
45–49	20.6	13.2	16.4	16.5	12.5	15.2	15.2	24.0	21.4	12.8	23.2	17.4	13.9	21.3	8.8	14.9	15.8	16.3
40–44	20.6	22.3	21.8	13.8	20.2	18.3	28.3	20.0	22.4	19.6	18.5	18.7	17.1	24.6	24.6	17.6	28.7	21.7
35–39	18.6	26.5	22.5	19.2	14.4	17.1	21.7	20.0	20.5	25.8	17.7	22.3	22.2	24.6	22.8	36.5	9.9	22.0
30–34	12.4	15.5	14.1	11.9	20.2	16.7	10.9	14.0	11.6	19.6	10.6	16.3	30.3	8.2	14.0	14.9	15.8	18.0
25–29	1.6	2.3	1.9	3.7	2.9	2.7	4.4	2.0	2.7	8.8	7.9	8.5	4.6	3.1	7.0	4.1	1.0	3.7
20–24	0.0	0.0	0.0	0.0	0.0	0.4	0.0	0.0	0.0	1.4	0.4	1.0	0.0	0.0	0.0	0.0	0.0	0.0
N	194	219	413	109	104	257	46	50	112	352	254	625	152	98	57	74	101	595

Source: Schlesinger 1967.

[a] Includes 44 members of other parties.
[b] Includes 16 members of other parties.
[c] Includes 19 members of other parties.
[d] Includes 113 members of other parties.

TABLE 9.4. Prior Office Experience of Legislators, in Percentage

Office	United States (elected 1956)			Canada (elected 1957)			Australia (elected 1954)			Great Britain (elected 1959)			France (elected 1956)					
	Rep.	Dem.	Total	Cons.	Lib.	Total	Lib.	Lab.	Total	Cons.	Lab.	Total	C.P.	SFIO	Rad.	MRP	Ind.	Total
Local elective	13.1	11.7	12.3	31.3	26.7	27.0	14.9	20.0	17.7	22.3	36.8	27.8	19.7	45.9	31.6	32.4	37.6	28.9
Provincial legislature[a]	33.8	38.5	36.5	9.8	8.6	10.6	17.0	25.0	21.0				13.2	34.7	35.1	14.9	41.6	23.8
Provincial executive[b]	2.0	1.3	1.6	1.8	2.9	2.3	6.4	6.7	6.4				1.3	4.1	0.0	0.0	1.9	0.7
Law Enforcement	28.2	35.3	31.2	8.9	5.7	6.1	0.0	5.0	3.0									
Administrative																		
National	5.6	7.4	6.5	0.9	4.8	2.3	4.3	11.7	7.3	5.1	2.7	4.6	1.3	13.3	26.3	9.5	7.9	9.6
Provincial	6.6	4.8	5.6	3.6	3.8	3.4	8.5	6.7	6.4									
Local	4.0	3.0	3.5	8.0	2.9	4.9	2.1	6.7	4.8									
No office experience	31.3	24.6	27.8	49.2	51.3	52.2	59.6	40.0	50.7	70.2	58.5	65.5	68.4	38.8	31.6	47.3	34.7	50.9
N	198	231	429	112	105	263	47	60	124	352	258	630	152	98	57	74	101	595

Source: Schlesinger 1967.

Note: The columns in this table do not add to 100 percent because each legislator could have more than one experience.

[a]For France this is the General Council; for Great Britain, all offices below the national level.

[b]For United States, statewide elective executive positions. For Canada and Australia, provincial or state cabinet membership. For France, president of the General Council.

TABLE 9.5. Last Office Held before Election to Lower House of the National Legislature, in Percentage

Office	United States (elected 1956)			Canada (elected 1957)			Australia (elected 1954)			Great Britain (elected 1959)			France (elected 1956)					
	Rep.	Dem.	Total	Cons.	Lib.	Total	Lib.	Lab.	Total	Cons.	Lab.	Total	C.P.	SFIO	Rad.	MRP	Ind.	Total
Provincial legislature	26.2	25.2	25.6	7.1	4.8	6.8	8.4	13.4	11.2				15.1	27.6	31.6	16.1	36.7	21.7
Provincial executive	1.1	0.9	1.0	0.9	1.9	1.5	6.4	6.7	6.3				0.0	3.1	0.0	0.0	1.9	1.0
Local elective	7.6	6.5	7.0	23.3	23.8	22.2	8.5	13.3	12.0	21.3	33.7	25.8	13.2	18.4	10.5	18.9	18.8	14.1
Law enforcement	18.2	28.6	23.8	2.7	3.8	2.8	0.0	5.0	3.1	0.7	0.0	0.6						
Administrative	11.1	11.6	11.4	10.7	9.5	9.2	10.7	20.0	13.4	2.3	1.6	2.2	0.0	8.2	14.0	6.8	3.0	5.4
Upper house national legislature		0.4	0.2										1.3	1.0	5.3	1.4	3.0	2.7
No recent office	35.8	26.8	31.0	55.3	56.2	57.5	66.0	41.6	54.0	75.7	64.7	71.4	70.4	41.7	38.6	56.8	36.6	55.1
N	198	231	429	112	106	263	47	60	124	352	258	630	152	98	57	74	101	595

Source: Schlesinger 1967.

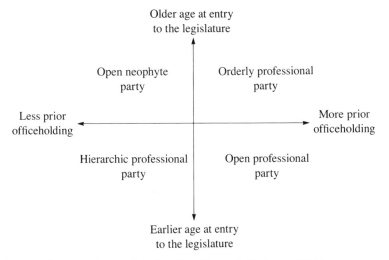

Fig. 9.1. Comparative model of parties. (From Schlesinger 1967.)

extent to which the parties' promotional structures are orderly or open. Thus, the more office experience and the younger the experienced advanced officeholders, the stronger the indication that professional officeholders dominate the organization in a free and open fashion. The more office experience and the older the experienced advanced officeholders, the stronger the indication that professional officeholders dominate the organization in an orderly fashion.

Combining the two characteristics of parties, age and prior officeholding, I constructed a four-way typology of parties for comparative analysis (see fig. 9.1).[6] I infer from early entry into advanced office with prior office experience the open professional party. From later entry into advanced office with prior office experience, I infer the orderly professional party. Early entry into advanced office without much office experience indicates the hierarchical professional party. Late entry into office without prior office experience indicates the open neophyte party.

The open professional or careerist party, inferred from early entry into office with prior office experience, is the haven of professional officeholders. It is a party dominated by individuals who arrive at advanced office early, not as novices but as experienced officeholders. Thus, not only have they devoted their past to public office, they have the time to devote their futures to public office also. This is a party where the holding of public office is the key to

---

6. For a typology of parties useful for comparative analysis based on the ways parties win in elections, see Schlesinger and Schlesinger 1990.

advancement. But it is also a party of equals, where peers are subject to few constraints. When a party's officeholders consist mostly of individuals with prior office experience who have mostly advanced in office before middle age, we must infer an organization incapable of confining individuals if they wish to advance, regardless of who may be there before them in age. In this organization, the individuals themselves make the crucial decisions about promotions.

The orderly professional or careerist party that I infer from later entry into office with prior office experience is also a party where public office careerists play the central, dominant role. This, too, is an organization composed of individuals who have devoted their pasts to public officeholding and an organization where public officeholding brings advancement. But there is a significant difference. Later arrival in advanced office indicates an organization in which those seeking advancement are prepared to wait their turn. When a party's officeholders consist mostly of individuals with prior office experience who mostly advance in office after middle age, we infer an organization whose personnel have agreed to keep order, individuals in agreement on waiting for advancement until others have had their chance.

The hierarchical professional party that I infer from early entry into advanced office with little prior office experience indicates a party whose officeholders have a commitment both to professionalism and to authority. Early entry into advanced office indicates an interest in, as well as the possibility of, long-term public officeholding. On the other hand, early advancement without experience indicates a more tightly controlled promotional system than in the other two parties. Young, inexperienced individuals are being coopted into higher office; they are then far more likely to be beholden to those within the organization who have coopted them than is the case in the two other types of organizations I have described. In any event, decisions about promotion have been made by others than themselves.

Finally the open neophyte party that I infer from late entry into advanced office without prior office experience indicates a party where the officeholders' commitment both to professionalism and order is minimal. Late entry into advanced office without prior office experience indicates an organization dominated by officeholders less interested in public office as a profession. Indeed, such individuals achieve advanced public office by having made their professional mark elsewhere. Given their late arrival, their opportunities for making public office a second career are reduced. Their ability to arrive late on the basis of accomplishments achieved elsewhere indicates their domination of an organization that is open and receptive to outsiders. Receptivity makes it difficult to institute orderly, not to mention hierarchical, patterns of promotion.

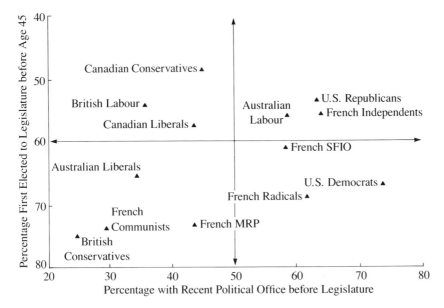

Fig. 9.2. Positions of parties of five democracies in the comparative model in the 1950s. (From Schlesinger 1967.)

National Legislative Office and the Comparative Model

Assigning our thirteen assorted national parties to one of the four models allows us to see similarities and differences in parties across national boundaries, as well as similarities and differences within nations, that would otherwise go unnoticed (see fig. 9.2). Thus, my typology reveals that, among the thirteen parties, only the Democrats in the United States and the Radicals and the Socialists (SFIO) in France were open professional parties. Of the thirteen parties, it was only these in which more than 60 percent of the members arrived in the national legislature before age forty-five and more than 55 percent arrived with prior office experience. In all three parties, a relatively high proportion of these young national legislators advanced directly from intermediate public offices. One in four Democratic representatives came directly from the state legislature. Some 30 percent of the Radicals and Socialists came directly from a departmental council (see table 9.5). Although Radicals and Socialists both had extensive local office experience also, like the Democrats, they used intermediate office as their stepping stone to the national legislature. Thus, all three parties emerge as the principal vehicles of political careerists, organizations used by the politically ambitious to advance at will. Others have recognized the resemblance between the French Radical party and the two major parties in the United States, due to a similar voracious appetite for office (see, for example, Duverger 1951, 85). My typology limits the resemblance to the Democratic party, while at the same time associating the French Socialist party with this model. It therefore confirms that Georges Dupeux's (1959, 129) observation about the radicalizing of the Socialist party in the Third Republic was also pertinent in the Fourth.

Among the thirteen parties, the typology reveals the Republican party in the United States, the French Independent party, and the Australian Labour party as orderly professional parties. Only in these three parties did more than 50 percent of the membership reach advanced office after age forty-five and more than 50 percent arrive with prior office experience. Of all thirteen parties, the French Independents and the U.S. Republicans advanced the fewest younger individuals to the national legislature: among the Independents only 27 percent of their new legislators were under forty, among the Republicans only 32 percent (see table 9.3).[7] At the same time, promotion in both parties came very much in the same way as for legislators in the preceding parties, from intermediate office. This was also true of the Australian Labour party, where some 20 percent of the new legislators came from state parliaments, a higher figure than for any other party in Australia or Canada.

Again the typology reveals a link between parties in the United States and France, this time between the dominant conservative parties of both countries. In these parties, the combination of professionalism and order seems appropriate. On the other hand, the similarities that the typology reveals between these parties and the Australian Labour party indicates the unexpected relationships the typology can expose. Certainly the relationship we would be more likely to expect would be between the Australian Labour party and the Australian Liberal party or the two parties of the other Commonwealth federal parliamentary state, Canada. While the validity of the unexpected relationship requires empirical research far beyond the confines of this study, the typology leads us to test for a relationship that would otherwise be far from apparent.

Much the same thing can be said of the relationships that the typology reveals among the parties identified as hierarchical, officeholding parties. These included the British Conservative party at one extreme and the French Communist party at the other. In between were the Australian Liberal party

---

7. During the period of increased electoral competition after 1960 in the United States, the age of entry for members of both parties to the House of Representatives declined. The entry age of the Republicans declined more precipitously, making them appear much like the Democrats (Schlesinger and Schlesinger 1981, 225–26).

and the French Catholic party, the MRP. Without the typology we would hardly expect any of these parties to have much in common. Yet the British Conservatives and the French Communists were at the extremes for both youth and inexperience; only a very small proportion of their new legislators (slightly more than 10 percent) were age fifty or older. Once placed in conjunction by the typology, it was not unreasonable to think of both parties as oligarchic organizations with tight promotional systems.[8] Nor was it inconceivable to think of the Australian Liberal party as having tendencies in this direction. As for the MRP, as the new party among the four, it might well be expected to rely on young, inexperienced personnel.[9]

Finally, three parties emerged as open neophyte parties, the two Canadian parties and the British Labour party. Among the four English-speaking democracies, only the two Canadian parties emerged as the same type of organization. Their placement leads us to look for an aspect of the Canadian structure of political opportunities that might account for the similarity. One aspect is a federal structure that, unlike that of the United States, makes possible long-run careers at the intermediate or provincial level of government. Such a structure might well foster national parties more open and receptive to neophytes who had made their mark outside of politics. This possibility was reinforced by the extent to which local, rather than provincial, office accounted for whatever office experience both parties' legislators had. Advancement came most often for those with no prior office experience; barring that, it came by advancing directly from the lowest rung of the ladder of offices. Moreover, both parties have been conspicuous in Western parliamentary democracies for their willingness to promote to positions of national legislative leadership individuals with little or no prior parliamentary experience. In the 1980s, Conservative Brian Mulroney and the Liberal contender, Paul Martin, Jr., were examples.[10]

The placement of the British Labour party is more provocative. Based on other schemes of party organization, one might well have expected the party to emerge along with the British Conservatives, as well as the French Communists, as a more structured, promotional organization. Indeed, it does share with the Conservative party the trait of relative inexperience, reflecting the

8. For a good discussion of how the British Conservative party selected its young, inexperienced candidates for parliament, see Hugo Young's (1989) excellent biography of Margaret Thatcher, who began her elective office career in 1959.

9. Table 9.4 gives the office experience of these parties' legislators. None of these parties were completely cut off from lesser office experience, although such experience was largely local office. Approximately 25 percent of their national legislators had held a local office.

10. The Canadian structure of political opportunities also helps account for the ability of minor parties to succeed in a way in which they cannot in the United States. See, for example, Meisel 1963.

relative paucity of office, other than parliamentary office, in the British structure of political opportunities. How can we, however, account for differences in the age patterns, for the youth of the Conservatives, which supports inferences of a hierarchical promotional organization, for the elderliness of the Labourites, which implies a more open party? The Labour party's seeming openness undoubtedly derives from its receptivity to a single external source of personnel, the trade unions. Given the party's special relationship with the unions since its founding, union officials have found few barriers within the party to their advancement to high public office after a trade union career.

National Executive or Cabinet Office and the Comparative Model

Having established a typology of parties on the basis of age and prior officeholding for the national legislators of five Western democracies, I wished to test whether the typology would be sustained if we looked at the age and office experience of those who went from national legislative office to national executive or cabinet positions. There were, of course, differences, relevant for further analysis, in the relations between the cabinet and the legislature in the five democracies. The relationships ran the gamut from the well-defined path between legislative and cabinet office that characterized the British parliamentary system to the presidential system in the United States, where no relationship existed. The intermediary legislative positions that lead to the cabinet were most finely worked out in the British parliament. Here, the host of positions as whips, parliamentary secretaries, undersecretaries, junior ministers, and ministers provided the parliamentary stepping stones to the cabinet. The picture of the House of Commons, then, as hosting a relatively small group of about twenty cabinet ministers and a mob of back benchers is hardly accurate. According to one estimate (Buck 1963, 47), 25 percent of the members of parliament from 1918 to 1955 had held some legislative leadership post. Indeed, if one views the British parliament from the perspective of ambition, it becomes evident that the widespread orderly outlets for the hopes and expectations of the politically ambitious foster the discipline that tightly links the legislature to the cabinet. Such arrangements have not been as completely worked out in the Canadian parliament. Only in 1943 did the cabinet make provision for parliamentary assistants. As for the French assembly system with its powerful network of legislative committees, no such clear path existed, although the chairmen and *rapporteurs* of important committees (such as finance and foreign affairs) were often seen as having an edge for advancement to the cabinet. In the United States, of course, there is little, if any, relationship between being a member of the House of Representatives and becoming a member of the president's cabinet.

Nevertheless, the analysis of career data should provide us with a more refined picture of the relation between legislative and cabinet office. Analyzed by parties, it can add to the inferences about party organization that were derived from the analysis of legislative officeholding. To relate the two analyses, I devised an index of differentiation between cabinet and legislative careers that applied to all thirteen parties. The index measures the difference between the total distributions of age at entrance to the legislature and age at entrance to the cabinet ($[a - a'] + [b - b'] + [c - c'] + \ldots$) (see fig. 9.3). If the two distributions are the same, the result is zero; if the two never overlap the total difference is 200. Therefore, it takes into account the effect of both the indicators, age at entry and prior office experience, on party organization, for built into the result is the possible time spent in legislative office before accession to the cabinet.

Using the typology of parties depicted in figure 9.1, I projected the index of differentiation for each type of party. I projected the highest index for the officeholding hierarchical party, which combined youth with a highly defined promotional system. In a party where legislators arrived early under some sort of control, they might well be expected to serve a longer legislative apprenticeship before advancing to the cabinet. I projected the lowest index for the open neophyte party, which combined a late start in the legislature with relatively open access to advanced office. In such an organization it was less likely that there would be a distinction between legislators and cabinet members or that late starters in the legislature would be willing or able to spend a long apprenticeship in the legislature before advancing to the cabinet. For the other two types of parties, the expectations were mixed. On the one hand, the youth of the open professional party allowed for a longer legislative apprenticeship. On the other, the openness of the party implied that its members would be no more willing to wait their turn for advancement to the cabinet than they had been willing to wait to advance to the legislature. As for the orderly professional party, while the advanced age of its legislators argued in favor of rapid promotion, the willingness of the party's members to wait their turn for advancement to the legislature might well also apply to advancement to the cabinet.

When I applied the index to the thirteen parties, I found that it advanced our understanding of parties as office-seeking organizations. Both the British Conservative and the Australian Liberal parties had the high indices of differentiation we projected for hierarchical professional parties (see table 9.6). The MRP did not have a high index, but again its status as the new party could well account for the lower index. The Communist party is not included because none of its members held cabinet positions. Similarly, the two Canadian parties had the relatively low indices I projected for the open neophyte party. The British Labour party did not. Indeed, its index was almost identical

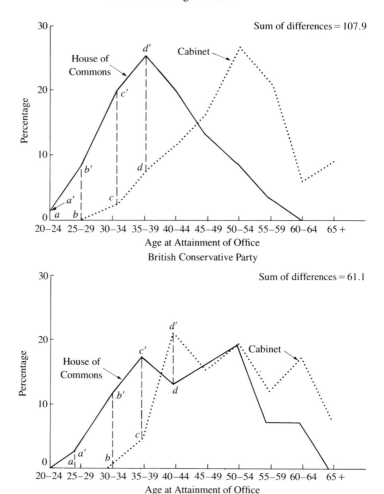

Fig. 9.3. Index of age differentiation between attainment of legislative office and cabinet status, British and Canadian Conservative parties. (From Schlesinger 1967.)

to that of the British Conservative party. Here recall that the party had a single external source for its older legislative personnel, a factor that may well modify its appearance as an open organization.

The findings, however, most likely reflect the impact of the structure of political opportunities and the structure of electoral competition on party organization. In the case of the British Labour party, this influence was continuously at work, bringing the Labour party closer to the Conservative organizational model. Certainly the observation has been made elsewhere that, as the Labour party emerged as Britain's major second party, it came to emulate more closely the office-seeking model and, therefore, the Conservative party (see, for example, McKenzie 1963). Thus, the high index of differentiation for both British parties confirms the British democracy as the classic example of the cabinet system. More than half of the cabinet members in both British parties spent ten years or more in the Commons (see table 9.7). One in four Conservative cabinet members came from the House of Lords, but half of these had served also in the Commons. Fewer than 10 percent of the ministers of both parties had less than five years in the Commons. In both parties, then, full parliamentary apprenticeship before advancement to the cabinet was the rule, forging the strong link between parliament and the cabinet that the classic view of the cabinet system leads us to expect.

I have already made a similar observation about the impact of the truncated office structure upon the organization of the two Canadian parties. Their position as open neophyte parties, supported by the low index of differentiation, was confirmed by the translation of the index into a conspicuously low level of parliamentary apprenticeship for the members of both parties. Thus

TABLE 9.6. Index of Age Differentiation between Attainment of Legislative Office and Cabinet Status, by Country and Party

	Party Index	National Index
Great Britain		102.1
Conservative	107.9	
Labour	109.2	
Australia		62.8
Liberal	76.8	
Labour	68.8	
United States		98.3
Republican	79.4	
Democrat	117.6	
Canada		63.3
Conservative	61.1	
Liberal	63.6	
France[a]		68.9
Independent	94.2	
Radical	91.4	
MRP	59.0	
SFIO	51.8	

Source: Schlesinger 1967.
[a]French Communist party had never gained a cabinet position.

TABLE 9.7. Years in Lower House before Attaining Cabinet Post, in Percentage

No. of Years	Canada (1921–57)			Australia (1946–57)			Great Britain (1922–60)			France (1947–58)				
	Cons.	Lib.	Total	Lib.	Lab.	Total	Cons.	Lab.	Total	SFIO	Rad.	MRP	Ind.	Total
20+	5.2	0.0	2.0	0.0	0.0	0.0	11.9	11.5	11.7	4.6	0.0	5.0	0.0	1.7
15–19	5.2	5.9	5.5	0.0	0.0	0.0	15.6	16.4	15.9	9.1	4.0	0.0	8.3	4.9
10–14	15.5	15.4	15.4	4.2	10.5	8.0	23.9	27.9	25.3	13.6	20.0	5.0	4.2	9.9
5–9	36.2	18.8	25.9	29.2	15.7	20.0	12.8	22.9	16.5	9.1	32.0	15.0	62.5	32.3
1–4	19.0	18.8	18.9	33.3	21.0	30.0	4.6	6.6	5.3	31.8	20.0	45.0	8.3	28.9
0–1	17.2	36.4	28.7	4.2	10.5	6.0	5.5	1.6	4.1	31.8	8.0	30.0	4.2	15.7
Upper house	1.7	4.7	3.5	29.1	42.3	36.0	25.7	13.1	21.2	0.0	16.0	0.0	12.5	6.6
N	58	85	143	24	19	50	109	61	170	22	25	20	24	121

Source: Schlesinger 1967.

the Canadian Liberals, a party that governed Canada for twenty-two consecutive years, promoted over 35 percent of their cabinet members after less than
one year in the House of Commons. When a significant proportion of a party's
cabinet has spent less than five years, and some even less than one year, in the
legislature, it is hard to accept the legislature as the base for advancement. As
with the promotion of this type of party's members to the national legislature,
promotion to the cabinet is based on accomplishment outside the public office
hierarchy.

As for the parties of the remaining types, the results were mixed. Among
the open professional parties, both the French Radicals and U.S. Democrats
had high indices of differentiation, a real possibility for those who get an early
start in the legislature. Indeed, the index for Democrats was the highest of any
of the thirteen parties. In contrast, the Socialists (SFIO) had the lowest index
of differentiation. This might well indicate that the Socialist party's taste of
executive power, acquired in the last legislature of the Third Republic, had
intensified in the Fourth, making its young legislators as unwilling to wait to
achieve cabinet office as they had been to advance to the legislature from the
intermediate office of departmental council. Among the orderly professional
parties, the U.S. Republican and Australian Labour parties had relatively low
indices in comparison with their competitors, a likely result since both their
competitors sponsored young legislators. In contrast, the index of differentiation for the French Independents was as high as that for the French Radicals.
In the Independents' organization, then, order continued to prevail for promotion to the cabinet.

Again, the index of differentiation directs our attention to the opportunity
and electoral structures that fostered the parties. The largest difference in the
index was between the French Independents on the one hand and the French
Socialists on the other. This meant that, while most of the cabinet members of
the Independent party had spent between five and nine years in the National
Assembly, 32 percent of the Socialists had spent less than one year in the
Assembly (see table 9.7). These differences reflected both the Assembly and
electoral systems that fostered multiple parties and multiple routes to the
cabinet.

Certainly we must look to the presidential system and the separation of
powers in the United States for the extreme differences in the index between
the two major parties there, differences almost as large as those between the
French parties. This meant that very different paths could be taken to cabinet
office. It also meant that, for both parties, the legislative path was relatively
inconsequential, although it was more important for the Democrats than the
Republicans. While there were important differences among the parties in the
four parliamentary democracies as far as the legislative apprenticeships served
by their cabinet members, in all, except the new French MRP and the Aus-

tralian Labour party, more than a third of the cabinet members had at least five years' legislative experience. Even in these two parties, one-fourth of the cabinet members had at least five years' legislative experience. This stands in sharp contrast with the cabinet in the United States, where less than 20 percent of the members had any national legislative experience and less than 10 percent came directly from the Congress. There was, however, some difference between the two parties. Whereas 13.0 percent of the Democrats had had national legislative office as their last public office experience before becoming cabinet members, this was true of only 5.5 percent of the Republicans who went on to hold cabinet positions (see chap. 3, table 3.5). This confirms our picture of the Democrats as the open professional party and the Republicans as the orderly professional party.

Conclusions

In this chapter I have shown how the office-seeking theory of parties can be used for comparative purposes. I demonstrated that it can enhance our understanding of party organization across, as well as within, national boundaries. Despite differences in national structures of political opportunities and electoral competition, I have arrived at common ways of comparing these structures and their impact on party organization. I focused on the size of the structure of political opportunities and the shares held by the parties of five major democracies. I arrived at the shares by examining, by party, two universal indicators of public office careers, age at first achievement of advanced office and prior office experience, for two advanced offices common to all democracies, national legislative and national executive office. In this way, we were able to see similarities and differences between and among the parties in the five democracies that would otherwise go unnoticed. Thus, our attention was called to the similarities between the French Communist party and the British Conservative party, on the one hand, and between the Democratic party in the United States and the Socialist party in France, on the other. At the same time, we were also made aware of differences between the Democratic and Republican parties in the United States and the Liberal and Labour parties in Australia. Certainly a scheme that makes possible such findings has some utility.

The theory of party organization I have set forth throughout this book should make possible other comparative analyses of political parties in democracies (see, for example, Schlesinger and Schlesinger 1990). There is no reason why the assumptions I made about parties as organizations in chapter 1 should not be applicable to the parties of Western Europe or, for that matter, to the nascent parties of Eastern Europe. Certainly the central role I assigned to political ambition in a theory of parties in chapter 2 has applicability beyond the United States. It is of course true, as I implied in the subsequent chapters and as I demonstrated in this chapter, that the structures of political opportunity and electoral competition greatly affect the direction of ambitions and, therefore, the character of party organization. To the extent that opportunity and electoral structures vary from democracy to democracy, so also do parties. Moreover, just as parties in the United States have altered over time in accordance with changes in these structures, so too, the theory suggests, have parties in other democracies. Only further empirical investigation, of course, can test the validity of these propositions. Nevertheless, parties in all democracies should share many of the organizational traits I discussed in chapter 7. In all democracies, parties need to balance the ambitions of different office seekers and officeholders through the ever recurring cycle of nomination, elections, and government that is common to democratic polities.

REFERENCES

Banks, Margaret A. 1965. "Privy Council, Cabinet and Ministry in Britain and Canada." *Canadian Journal of Economics and Political Science* 31:193–205.
Buck, Philip W. 1963. *Amateurs and Professionals in British Politics, 1918–1959.* Chicago: University of Chicago Press.
Encel, S. 1961. "The Political Elite in Australia." *Political Studies* 9:16–36.
Encel, S. 1962. *Cabinet Government in Australia.* Melbourne: Melbourne University Press.
Dahl, Robert A. 1966. *Political Oppositions in Western Democracies.* New Haven: Yale University Press.
de Jouvenel, Robert. 1914. *La république des camarades.* Paris: Bernard Grasset.
Dogan, Mattei. 1961. "Political Ascent in a Class Society: French Deputies 1870–1958." In *Political Decision Makers,* ed. Dwaine Marvick. Glencoe, Ill.: Free Press.
Dogan, Mattei. 1967. "Les filières de la carrière politique en France." *Revue française sociologique* 8:468–92.
Dogan, Mattei. 1979. "How to Become a Cabinet Minister in France." *Comparative Politics* 12:1–25.
Dupeux, Georges. 1959. *Le front populaire et les élections de 1936.* Paris: Armand Colin.
Duverger, Maurice. 1951. *Les partis politiques.* Paris: Armand Colin.
Guttsman, W. L. 1963. *The British Political Elite.* London: Macgibbon and Kee.
Kornberg, Allan, and Norman Thomas. 1965–66. "Representative Democracy and Political Elites in Canada and the United States." *Parliamentary Affairs* 19:91–102.
Kunz, F. A. 1965. *The Modern Senate of Canada, 1925–1963.* Toronto: University of Toronto Press.
McKenzie, Robert. 1963. *British Political Parties.* 2d ed. London: Mercury Books.

Mackenzie, W. J. M. 1959. "Local Government Experience of Legislators." In *Legislative Behavior*, ed. John Wahlke and Heinz Eulau. New York: Free Press.

Masclet, Jean-Claude. 1979. *Le rôle du deputé*. Paris: Librairie générale de droit et jurisprudence.

Maus, Didier. 1987. "Le parlement français de l'alternance à cohabitation, 1981–1987." Maison Française d'Oxford. Typescript.

Meisel, John. 1962. *The Canadian General Election of 1957*. Toronto: University of Toronto Press.

Meisel, John. 1963. "The Stalled Omnibus: Canadian Parties in the 1960s." *Social Research* 30:367–90.

Michels, Robert. [1914] 1949. *Political Parties*. New York: Free Press.

Ranney, Austin. 1965. *Pathways to Parliament*. Madison: University of Wisconsin Press.

Richards, Peter G. 1958. *Honourable Members: A Study of the British Backbencher*. London: Faber and Faber.

Schlesinger, Joseph A. 1967. "Political Careers and Party Leadership." In *Political Leadership in Industrialized Societies*, ed. Lewis Edinger. New York: Wiley.

Schlesinger, Joseph A., and Mildred Schlesinger. 1981. "Aging and the Opportunities for Elective Office." In *Aging, Social Change*, ed. James G. March. New York: Academic Press.

Schlesinger, Joseph A., and Mildred Schlesinger. 1990. "The Reaffirmation of a Multiparty System in France." *American Political Science Review* 84:1077–1101.

Wilson, F. M. G. 1959. "Routes of Entry of New Members of the British Cabinet, 1868–1958." *Political Studies* 7:222–32.

Young, Hugo. 1989. *The Iron Lady*. New York: Farrar Straus Giroux.

Index